Christian Scholz | Joachim Zentes [Eds.]

Beyond Sustainability

 Nomos

Die Deutsche Nationalbibliothek lists this publication in the
Deutsche Nationalbibliografie; detailed bibliographic data
is available in the Internet at http://dnb.d-nb.de.

ISBN 978-3-8487-0680-8

1st edition 2014
© Nomos Verlagsgesellschaft, Baden-Baden 2014. Printed in Germany.

Introduction

Since 1990, the year the MBA School in Saarbrücken was founded, questions dealing specifically with corporate ethics and with corporate responsibility in general have constituted a cross-disciplinary dimension and conceptual framework of the school's teaching programme, which reflects the programmatic guiding principle "people, markets and morals".

In the light of this the Directors of the Section Management and Economics of the Europa-Institut regularly publish works that examine current issues which will be covered by lecturers from Germany and abroad in the courses offered in the Europa-Institut's MBA programme:

- "Strategisches Euro-Management" (Vol. 1, 1995) dealt with an initial positioning of European management issues and particularly with a review of the start of our work as the first MBA programme offered by a German university.
- In 1998 "Strategisches Euro-Management" (Vol. 2) had taken on very clear contours as a form of management that was not only based on US American ideas, but deliberately took into account German and European considerations on corporate management.
- In 2002 these ideas were consolidated in "Strategic Management – A European Approach" into an independent European school of thought, which now shapes our institute's claim of "Managing with(in) Europe".
- 2006 focused on political considerations and Europe's position in terms of competitive strategy, which, based on a well-known quote at that time, led to the book title "Strategic Management – New Rules for Old Europe".

The contributions have all been penned by German and foreign lecturers at the Europa-Institut, so that not only the conceptual depth but also the broad content of our programme can be deduced from the publications.

Many of the current topics revolve around the term "sustainability". The collected edition now being presented is thus dedicated to this group of subjects, which are extremely relevant from an empirical point of view. A total of 13 contributions go into the question of what is really behind the concept of sustainability and also what is to follow.

Part 1 involves conceptual ideas and begins with the contribution by Dermot Breslin ("Towards a Generalised Darwinist View of Sustainability"), who argues from a systems theory and evolutionary perspective and thus clearly pursues the research tradition of our institute. This is followed by two central aspects of the entrepreneurial management of sustainability, namely externally in an intercultural context as in the contribution by Volker Stein ("Sustainable Intercultural Management") and internally in an organisational-conceptual context as in the contribution by Christian Scholz/Stefanie Müller ("The HR-Department as Driver for Sustainability").

The contributions of Part 2 take a macroeconomic and above all monetary policy approach. Heinz-Jürgen Axt ("The Rule of 'No-Bail-Out' in the European Monetary Union: Why it Failed to be Sustainable") and Ansgar Belke/Florian Verheyen ("Sustainability of Currency Unions: What Went Wrong in the EMU and How to Fix it?") focus on the sustainability of the European Monetary Union. These contributions clearly show the relevance of economic deliberations and our institute's competence in this sphere.

The interests, impacts and courses of action of selected stakeholders form the subject matter of Part 3. The contributions by Andrea Gröppel-Klein ("The Problem of Consumer Sovereignty and the Concept of Consumer Democracy") and Hanna Schramm-Klein/Sascha Steinmann ("How Sustainable is Sustainability? The Impact of Corporate Social Irresponsibility on Consumer Behaviour in Retailing") focus on the consumer. The cooperation of NGOs with businesses, which is an important yet equally controversial subject of discussion for matters of sustainability, is dealt with in the contribution by Stefan Kolb/Joachim Zentes ("Firm-NGO Alliances as a Proactive Approach to Credible Corporate Social Responsibility").

Sustainability issues are discussed in Part 4 from an economically functional and process-oriented viewpoint by Dirk Morschett/Valentin Wepfer ("Sustainability in Collaborative Supply Chains"), Christian Berg/Stefan Hack/Constantin Blome ("How IT Can Enable Sustainability Throughout Supply Chains"), Christopher Hossfeld/Alain Mikol ("Financial Reporting and Sustainability") and Stefan Strohmeier ("Sustainable Electronic Human Resources Management: Why Information Technology Matters in Sustainable Human Resources Management"). Martin Dietrich/Nadine Molter/Matti Znotka extend the considerations to include the health management sector ("Sustainable Business Models in Health Care").

In examining the four parts of our book and the diversity of the subjects taken into account it becomes immediately obvious that sustainability is much more than just a political and ecological catchphrase: behind it lies a variety of aspects ranging from globally strategic considerations and monetary policy models to quite definite economic management challenges. The task of a modern business school is thus to provide concrete basics just as much as a perspective focus. The collected edition on hand, which is part of a 25-year-old tradition, shows how we in Saarbrücken are trying to master this task with our Europa-Institut's MBA programme.

We take this opportunity to offer our warm thanks to all the authors who have contributed to the success of this work and also to Ms Tatjana Freer, M.Sc., for her dedicated editorial support and subsequent layout work.

Saarbrücken, October 2013

Christian Scholz   Joachim Zentes

Contents

Part 1:
Conceptual Frameworks and Management Perspectives

Towards a Generalised Darwinist View of Sustainability

Dermot Breslin

Overview

1. Introduction

1.1 Overview

The issue of sustainability has been tackled from a wide range of perspectives within the social sciences and beyond. Sustainability might be interpreted as the capacity to endure over time, involving the reconciliation of environmental, social and economic demands. In this sense, sustainable development should both foster adaptive capabilities and maintain prosperous social, economic and ecological systems (Holling 2001; Folke et al. 2002). Given its multi-dimensional nature, with a dynamic inter-relationship between environmental, social and economic spheres of influence, one might wonder whether the issue might be examined through a co-evolutionary lens. With a view towards shedding new light on this phenomenon, this chapter explores evolutionary foundations of sustainability, putting forward a Generalised Darwinist view on the field of study. The chapter therefore begins with a review of the Generalised Darwinist approach, and its use in sustainability research. In brief, this approach examines the co-evolution of cultural practices across groups, communities and societies through the evolutionary mechanisms of variation-selection-retention. Drawing on Breslin (2011a), it is argued that three tensions underpin co-evolutionary change in socio-cultural systems, which rest at the core of the sustainability question. These tensions reflect communities in which cultural practices become path-dependant over time, with local- and group-level behaviors tending to dominate the evolutionary process and constrain deviations from this path.

To explore these tensions and how they might impact upon sustainability, a historical re-examination of the Norse settlements in Greenland between the 10th and 15th centuries is presented. It was seen that Euro-Centric practices dominated the behaviors of the settling Norse, despite the maladaptive nature of these practices for the marginal environment in Greenland. These dominant cultural practices continued to reflect the past, and failed to adapt to changing challenges faced in the local environment tying the fate of the Norse community to a past world that was no longer relevant. The community thus became trapped by the interpretation of the past (first tension), by the collective interpretation of the wider group (second tension) and the dominance of local evolutionary pressures (third tension). The net effect of these tensions resulted in the suppression of the mechanism of variation, as the interpretation of the need for change and/or the ability to then enact this change was reduced. The chapter concludes with a discussion on co-evolutionary implications for sustainability, and implications for individuals at all levels of society. It is argued that:

- community members need to develop anticipatory systems based on the co-evolutionary account presented, and so consider the broader multi-level and community-wide implications of choices made at a local behavior. In this way, individuals can also use a co-evolutionary approach as an anticipatory system to interpret future events, and in so doing create new interpretations, worldviews and futures.

- community leaders need to manage the higher level process through which local knowledge evolves through the management of people and processes (without becoming directly involved in the evolutionary process itself), in much the same manner as Darwin's pigeon fanciers selected and pruned key desired characteristics in their prize pigeons (Darwin 1859).
- community elders finally need to focus on the management of the wider co-evolutionary process through the interaction of levels within society. In this sense community elders need to consider the competitive selection environment at each level of the community hierarchy. Managing this broader process and the competing needs for exploitation and exploration, thus involves balancing the interaction between the evolutionary systems of the different hierarchical levels within the community, from individual to group and community.

1.2 What is Generalised Darwinism

Since the publication of Darwin's Origin of the Species (Darwin 1859) 150 years ago, scholars have explored the possibility of developing an evolutionary approach beyond the domain of biology to fields of study as diverse as language, psychology, economics, behaviour and culture (Breslin 2010; Breslin 2011b). As with the publication of Darwin's original work, these moves have been met with much criticism within these respective scientific communities (Breslin 2011b), and a misunderstanding that generalising Darwinism to study society, culture and economics implies a commitment to genetic determinism. Whilst some have clearly taken this approach viewing socio-cultural change as a product of biological and genetic evolution, others have treated cultural evolution as a distinct and separate, yet parallel process of information inheritance (Durham 1991). These cultural evolutionists maintain that once humans had evolved brains big enough to generate collective knowledge, then this knowledge itself began to evolve over time largely independent of any underlying inherited instructional processes (Blackmore 1999; Dawkins 1982; Dennett 1995; Durham 1991; Plotkin 1994; Richerson/Boyd 2005). Plotkin (1994) argues that if humans had not evolved this capability to generate knowledge and if behaviour were purely the result of inherited instincts, then the resultant behaviour might be "explained entirely by a reductionist genetical account" (Plotkin 1994, p. 176). At a broader cultural level, Richerson/Boyd (2005, p. 45) argue that whilst an individual's innate psychology shapes culture, culture itself evolves through gradual, cumulative adaptations over many generations that "no single individual could evoke on his or her own". As a result they conclude that cultural evolution "cannot be based directly or in detail, on innate, genetically encoded information" (Richerson/Boyd 2005, p. 45). Whilst these authors believe that the leash between socio-cultural and biological evolution is weak, they still argue that socio-cultural change can therefore be described in evolutionary terms (Breslin 2010).

In sum, these researchers seek to abstract from the domain-specific details of genetic evolution to a higher-level set of Darwinian principles which might apply to other "evolving systems". Indeed, the question relating to whether these systems evolve separately, and whether more abstract Darwinian principles might have relevance for developing theory in these different domains, dates back to Darwin himself (1871), who argued that the spread of languages parallels the evolution of species, for example in terms of its variability, its crossing or blending together and its extinction. Darwin (1871, p. 139) remarked that "the survival or preservation of certain favoured words in the struggle for existence is natural selection". In this way, he tries to conceptualise the development of languages in evolutionary terms without spelling out the details of the mechanisms involved. Dennett (1995, p. 345) argues that "cultural evolution recapitulates all the features of genetic evolution", as "the whole edifice of biological theory is perfectly mirrored in the medium of culture". Drawing on this stance, Generalised Darwinists maintain that Darwinian concepts can be broadened from the domain of biology (Lewontin 1970) and applied to all forms and levels of life (Hodgson 2002). In the biological world evolution occurs over time through the key Darwinian mechanisms of variation (of genotypes), selection (of the consequent phenotype) and retention (of the underlying genotype), where the genotype is defined as the material inherited by an individual from its parents (i.e. genes), which has the potential to be transmitted to future generations. The phenotype on the other hand represents the manifestation of the genotype in the physical characteristics of the organism. Generalised Darwinists argue that at a sufficiently general level of abstraction this core set of general Darwinian principles of variation, selection and retention can be used to describe evolution within a variety of domains (Campbell 1965; Hodgson/Knudsen 2004; Hodgson 2003), including biology, psychology, culture and economics. In this manner, whilst the details of socio-cultural evolution may be different from biological evolution, the concept of Generalised Darwinism can nonetheless be used as a starting point for the development of theory in both (Breslin 2010; Breslin 2011b).

In addition to the evolutionary concepts of variation-selection-retention, the question of what evolves, or the unit of evolution remains a thorny one. In biology the mechanisms of variation-selection-retention act on the genotype-phenotype as outlined above. In socio-cultural evolution, however the concepts of the "replicator" and "interactor" are put forward (Dawkins 1976; Hull 1988), where the replicator is defined as anything in the universe of which copies are made such as genes in the biological world. The interactor on the other hand is the development expression of the replicator in a particular environment. A number of different definitions of the replicator and interactor have been put forward to describe socio-cultural evolution. Cloak (1975) differentiated between the concept of the i-culture which represents the cultural instructions individuals carry in their heads, and the m-culture which includes features of an individual's behaviour, technology and social organisation. Whilst elements of i-culture are "tiny, unrelated snippets, acquired and stored in a rather helter-skelter fashion like a genotype, the behavioural outcomes of those elements, the features of m-culture, often exhibit a high level of orderliness, pattern, functional integration etc like a phenotype" (Cloak 1975, p. 168). A number of researchers identify the meme as the replicator (Blackmore 1999; Dawkins 1976; Dennett 1995; Distin 2011) in socio-cultural evolution, where a meme is defined as a self-replicating element of culture, passed on by imitation, such as behaviors or skills (Dawkins 1976). The corresponding interactor is the "outward and visible" manifestations of the meme in the outside world through words, music, visual images, gestures and skills (Dawkins 1982), or the behaviours (Blackmore 1999; Dennett 1995). Durham (1991) differentiated between cultural units of information such as ideas, values and beliefs, and the associated behaviour which results from enacting this information, as he stressed these units of information were distinct from the resultant actions themselves. He argued that if research focused on traits or artefacts as units of analysis, it would be unclear whether that trait represented a cultural unit of analysis or was the phenotypic expressions of underlying genetic units of analysis (Durham 1991).

1.3 Generalised Darwinism and Sustainability

Developing this Generalised Darwinist approach, recently a number of scholars have put forward a co-evolutionary framework for studying sustainability, by analysing the mutual interrelationship between ecological and socio-economic systems (Foxon 2011; Hodgson 2010; Kallis/Norgaard 2010; Norgaard 1984; Gowdy 1994; van den Bergh/Gowdy 2003). Foxon (2011) for instance examines the multi-level co-evolution of institutional frameworks, technologies and user practices. Similarly Simmie/Martin (2010) put forward a Generalised Darwinist approach to study the related phenomena of resilience, in which economic organisations *vary* behaviors which are subsequently *selectively retained* within the wider system. The notion of sustainability has been related to that of resilience (Levin 1993), where the latter refers to a systems ability to recover from a severe shock or stress. In addition to absorbing shocks resilience also deals with the capacity for renewal and development, which is key to the sustainability discourse (Folke 2006). Adapting a co-evolutionary framework these evolutionary economic geographers conceptualise how socio-cultural rules might emerge and become institutionalised within regions (Martin/Sunley 2007). In this way the structures and features of an economic landscape would be viewed as the manifestations of systems of rules or knowledge (Boschma/Martin 2007). In this sense social rules are seen as the units that evolve in the complex system. "The economic landscape is the product of knowledge, and the evolution of that landscape is shaped by changes in knowledge" (Boschma/Martin 2007, p. 544). Likewise Simmie/Martin (2010) explore the adaptive ability of resilient systems, as regions adapt to socio-economic and political shocks and changes. They argue against the notion that resilient systems respond to shocks by returning to or retaining some previous equilibrium points. *Selection* however is a mechanism which occurs at multiple levels spanning local, regional, national and global spaces (Essletzbichler/Rigby 2005). Clearly, the more *variations* put forward, the more opportunities exist in finding solutions to unexpected shocks from the wider environment.

In sum, what is emerging within this community of scholars is an evolutionary narrative in which cultural units are seen to co-evolve through the Generalised Darwinist mechanisms of variation-selection-retention. However, as noted above, what remains to be resolved is the question of what is evolving, and how the mechanisms of variation-selection-retention operate on these phenomena (Waring 2010). Addressing this question,

Foxon (2011) identifies these cultural entities as institutional frameworks, technologies and user practices. Others have pointed to socio-cultural rules, as noted above (Martin/Sunley 2007), systems of rules or knowledge (Boschma/Martin 2007), and simple rules and heuristics (Waring 2010). Drawing on these works and the wider literature on cultural evolution summarised above, it is argued here that cultural practices, norms and routines evolve over time at multiple levels within a society. These practices are represented by a duality of tacit, cognitive knowledge and expressed, situated behaviors (Bourdieu 1990; Orlikowski 2002). In the account that follows these cultural practices are put forward as the units that evolve over time through the mechanisms of variation-selection-retention. It is argued below that understanding the dynamics of evolutionary change at multiple levels can thus shed light on the competing tensions which lie at the core of the sustainability question.

1.4 Co-Evolutionary Tensions

Breslin (2011a) outlined three core tensions which define multi-level co-evolutionary social systems. These include:

- temporal tension: where the past is reflected in the present through the practices of individuals and how this impacts on the anticipation of futures;
- tension between levels: where the more established a collective cultural practice becomes then the more they "police" individual variations, and;
- tension with localism: where the more local the interpretations made by the group, the more these may diverge from wider communal and societal considerations.

Using an evolutionary approach, Breslin (2011a) develops a co-evolutionary conceptualisation of a changing social system. In this manner, units of culture are seen to evolve at multiple levels, through the mechanisms of variation-selection-retention. So at the level of the individual, each person use and participates in a series of cultural practices. Some of these practices might be shared with others within the person's peer group or community, whereas others might be more idiosyncratic and unique to their own past or life path. So for instance, the individual might drive a gas-fueled car, and regularly fill up the tank of the vehicle with gas. This practice is clearly shared within the wider community of car drivers. However, the same individual may choose to adopt practices on their own, which they believe make a contribution towards lowering their carbon footprint. For instance, individual may "free-wheel" down hills (a practice I observed my uncle continue throughout his life to save on fuel costs). So while the former practice is collective, the latter is more individual. Taking an evolutionary perspective, these practices change over time through the mechanisms of variation-selection-retention. So the individual might experiment and *vary* the free-wheeling practice by for instance varying the start point at which he releases his foot on the accelerator, or by even deciding to turn off the car engine during downhill runs. These experimental variations are first *pre-selected* in thought based on the individual's anticipation of expected benefits (Dewey 1922). However, ultimately *selection* involves enacting the behaviors and interpreting feedback based on resultant performances (Breslin 2011a). So our free-wheeler turns off the car engine on approaching the descent of a steep hill, and assesses the performance based on the resultant maneuverability of the vehicle without power. If the result is interpreted as positive, then the individual *retains* that variant practice for future use (i.e. he switches off the engine every time, until future performances give evidence to the contrary). In this manner the *selection* and *retention* of practices becomes path-dependant, as individuals choose to enact behaviors which they believe are suited to the task in hand, based on past experience.

However in addition to this path-dependency individuals are also forward-looking as they anticipate reactions from the external world, based on expected responses following the enactment of a practice (Dewey 1922). In this way individuals anticipate future events based on cognitive representations they hold of those "expected futures". Such anticipatory systems incorporate models of themselves and their environment, allowing individuals to anticipate future events and adapt their behavior in response (Rosen 1985). So the individual might anticipate positive feedback on expected performances of switching the car engine off. This expectation might be based on previous experiences in using the same free-wheeling practice. In this sense, the associated interpretative system acts as a vicarious selector, anticipating higher-level selection from the external world, and providing guidance to the localised selection and emergence of practices over time. The worldviews represented by these interpretations are then used to interpret and make sense of actual feedback received following the enactment of these behaviors. In this way, if unexpected feedback is received based on the use of the practice, the individual might dismiss this if it does not fit with the worldview built up over time. So if our free-wheeler has one negative experience after months of fuel savings, he may dismiss this event as a one-off. Established practices thus have a strong influence on choices made, both through the anticipation of the future and through the interpretation of the present and past. This represents the *temporal tension* in the anticipation and interpretation of futures outlined by Breslin (2011a).

A fuller understanding of the evolutionary process at the level of the individual can be gained by examining the process at the level of the collective. As noted above, some cultural practices used by individuals are shared within peer-groups, organisations, communities and wider societies. For instance communities might share practices regarding the filling of car tanks. Recently in the UK, industrial action resulted in fuel supply being limited, with long queues forming at gas stations. As a result a collective practice emerged in which drivers chose to keep tanks full, as opposed to empty, topping up each time they passed a gas station. Both the behaviors and the reasoning behind them emerged as a shared cultural practice amongst a large group of drivers. Examining the evolutionary process behind this emergence, drivers first *vary* their previous practice of filling up tanks. This variant is *pre-selected* first in thought, so the individuals concerned might perceive the expected benefits of having a full tank in the event of industrial action. Drivers then carry out the practice, and *select* behaviors based on actual performances. This feedback is received from others within the group and beyond. Some might react positively and endorse the risk-reducing nature of this behavior. Others however might react negatively to such "selfish" practices, which they might argue lead to panic buying and long un-necessary queues forming at gas stations. Given the complexity of this feedback, and the possibility of different interpretations of the same being made by other individuals, the process will inevitably involve interaction between individuals through communication, dialogue and negotiation, as individual choices are reconciled within a *collective selection* mechanism. For instance, our individual might interpret the "full tank" practice positively. However this interpretation may not be shared by others. In this way, competing interpretations are resolved through dialogue, interaction and even negotiation as collective practices emerge. With this emergence, individuals even develop expectations of the behavior and understandings of others (Mead 1934). As a result the development of collective practices includes a socio-political dimension, as competing interpretations of futures are resolved through dialogue, communication and negotiation. The resultant truce can act to constrain future interpretations within the group, and indeed police "variations" as it reinforces the collective status quo. This represents the second *tension between levels* outlined by Breslin (2011a).

Finally in addition to different interpretations being made by individuals, the "importance" or strength of the various feedback signals received by the group from the "external world" might differ, and over time some signals may be given more "importance" than others. For instance, more importance may be given to local actors and neighbors, as opposed to more distance thought leaders. In this way, our tank-filling individual might be swayed to abandon such behaviors if local residents continually disapprove of such actions. On the other hand, our same individual might travel to a more distant gas station outside the local community to continue the practice, given that local opinions are less significant there. As a result, interpretative systems can become increasingly focused on localised issues over time as behavioral and socio-political factors act to strengthen local feedback signals (i.e. those local to the group) as opposed to wider external factors. Rosen (1975) argued that this can result in "inappropriate" behaviors which ultimately might detrimentally affect the longer term survival of the community. Depending on the strength of feedback signals received by the individual or group from the outside world, practices can tend towards reflecting the future of a local world, and local actors within that world. So whilst individuals and groups make local choices which they believe offer local improvement, the resultant behavior may detrimentally affect the wider community's longer term evolution and survival. These local world views can act to downplay signals from outside the local environment, and as a result can result in resistance to change and evolutionary drift. This trend represents the third and final *tension with localism* put forward by Breslin (2011a).

In sum, the tensions put forward by Breslin (2011a) reflect a socio-cultural system in which practices become path-dependant over time, with local- and group-level behaviors tending to dominate the evolutionary process and constrain deviations from this path.

2. The Multi-Level Co-Evolution of Cultural Practices Among the Greenland Norse

2.1 Overview

Breslin (2011a) argued that these tensions might develop within any co-evolving, socio-cultural system. In this way, they might be further developed to shed light on the issue of sustainability, given the complex co-evolutionary nature of the phenomenon. Reexamining the case of the Greenland Norse, who established settlements in that remote part of Europe between the 10th and 15th centuries, one can draw out how these tensions underpinned the key challenges facing this community during that period. These following accounts are drawn from Jared Diamond's (2005) seminal work "Collapse: How Societies Choose to Fail or Survive". The case of the Greenland Norse is an interesting one, as the community clung on to survival for several centuries. Given the marginal nature of the settlement, even the smallest variation, such as a change in the summer temperature, or failure of migratory harp and hooded seal, might have spelt disaster for the community. This marginal, knife-edge existence was exacerbated over the centuries, as Greenland's climate changed from mild to cold, with the *Little Ice Age* beginning around 1300.

2.2 Temporal Tension

Diamond (2005) argued that Viking Greenland was very conservative and Euro-centric in its outlook, despite the very different sets of challenges facing them in their new home and the hundreds of years of occupation of this land. As a result, they tended to continue to adopt the same cultural practices used by the first settlers in the 10th century. Indeed, they used the same tools, produced the same carvings, and crucially failed to learn new practices needed for survival in Greenland's harsh climate (such as the Inuit (Eskimos) practices of hunting for ringed seal or whale). The Norse survived on a combination of pastoralism and hunting wild animals. In the European tradition they kept goats, sheep and cows, with the latter being kept in barns during the winter. Milk produced in the summer months was turned into dairy products which they ate during the winter, such as cheese, butter and a yoghurt-like product known as *skyr*. Wool was also taken from the sheep and goats. To support the feeding of livestock during the winter months, hay was produced on the narrow pasture-lands bordering the fjords. So despite the very different climate and geographic challenges facing them, the Norse adopted practices better adapted to life in Norway. To supplement their marginal existence, the Greenland Norse also hunted. Caribou were hunted in the fall, and common, harp and hooded seal were hunted in the spring, when food reserves would be running low. Occasionally trips might be carried out towards the North of the country during the summer to hunt for walrus and polar bears. Despite an abundance of fish in the lakes and rives, the Greenland Norse did not eat fish. Diamond (2005) posits the idea that perhaps a taboo against fish-eating emerged during the early stages of the Norse settlements in Greenland, perhaps as a result of food poisoning. This taboo became so ingrained that latter inhabitants continued to avoid fish.

The Euro-centric and Christian nature of the Greenland Norse further resulted in other maladaptive practices becoming established. For example they followed European fashions despite the much colder climate. And while imports from Norway were rare, and confined to essentials such as iron, lumber, tar, luxury items for high-status individuals and the church were highly sought after. These high-value goods were exchanged for animal skins, wool and rarities such as walrus tusks and polar bears. However to obtain these latter items, resources had to be diverted from the important summer hay harvest to risky hunting expeditions to the north. So while their Christian identity may have helped maintain a functioning, integrated society (see below), it also resulted in key maladaptive practices which may have threatened the Norse's ultimate survival in Greenland (Diamond 2005). Such maladaptive practices including "stubbornly maintaining cows in Greenland's climate, diverting manpower from the summer hay harvest to the Nordrseta hunt, refusing to adopt useful features of Inuit technology and starving to death as a result" (Diamond 2005, p. 247). However, as Greenland's climate began to got cooler around 1300, the marginal existence of the community was doomed given the ill suited nature of the cultural practices being used. "The values to which people cling most stubbornly under inappropriate conditions are those values that were previously the source of their greatest triumphs over adversity" (Diamond 2005, p. 275). In summary, what emerges is a story in which dominant cultural practices continued to reflect the past, and failed to adapt to changing challenges faced in the local environment. This temporal tension tied the fate of the Norse community to a past world that was no longer relevant.

2.3 Tension Between Levels

Breslin (2011a) argued that the more established a collective practice becomes, then the more they "police" individual interpretations, representing a tension between levels which rests at the core of social systems. A total of 5000 Norse lived in Greenland, with 4000 of these living in the more southerly (and therefore milder) fjord. These inhabitants were settled into 250 farms, of about 20 people per farm. Farms were further organised around churches, with about 20 farms per church. The local economy was tightly integrated and controlled, with the rearing of livestock, production of hay and hunting for seals and caribou tightly coordinated within the community. As a result of this, and as a consequence of the Euro-centric Norse culture noted above, the society was sharply stratified and hierarchical, with most of the power resting in the hands of a few rich farms. Therefore, cultural practices were designed to fit within the tightly integrated system, with little opportunity for variation. In addition, maintaining the system and the practices that went with that, acted to maintain the status quo and power relations between different farms and communities. So while some innovations may have improved the survival chances of the settlements, "those innovations could have threatened the power, prestige and narrow interests of the chiefs. In the tightly controlled, interdependent society of Norse Greenland, the chiefs were in a position to prevent others from trying out such innovations. Thus the Norse society's structure created a conflict between short-term interests of those in power, and the long-term interests of the society as a whole" (Diamond 2005, p. 276). Those socio-political factors thus acted to suppress variations from individuals or sub-groups of settlers. Say for instance one farmer decides to divert hay production and try a new crop one year. As a result, less hay is produced within the local collective, with fewer heads of cattle being fed over the winter, less dairy products being produced, and so less food to see the community through the lean winter months. Or say a small group of farmers decide to go on a hunt to Nordrseta for Walrus tusks, in the hope of exchanging these with Norwegian traders for jewellery. By diverting resources to the hunt, less time would be devoted to hay production, resulted in less hay, livestock and so forth. In this manner, the wider community acts to restrain these individual and sub-group decisions to deviate from collective practices. As a result collective practices acted to constrain and indeed police the practices of individuals over time, leading to a tension between levels.

2.4 Tension With Localism

Finally, the tension with localism outlined by Breslin (2011a) refers to the divergence of practices between local groups from those of the wider community and environment. It was noted above, that the Greenland Norse were characterised by an inwardly-focused, past-orientated, Eurocentric culture, which was organised in a rigidly, hierarchical and integrated community. Despite the "cultural baggage", surely this community was aware of the challenges facing it in Greenland and able to adapt to them? After all the Norse had shown incredible resilience and adaptability as they moved to conquer and settle lands across the North Atlantic, from Britain and Ireland to Iceland and Newfoundland. However Diamond (2005) points to a number of irreversible actions taken by the Greenland Norse on the local habitat, including destroying the natural vegetation, causing soil erosion and cutting turf. On arrival the Norse cleared woodlands for pasture. These trees were later prevented from regrowing by grazing animals. As a result of this deforestation, the Norse had a very limited supply of lumber. Furthermore, the Norse needed wood to extract iron from local bog iron. Despite the scarcity they also continue to use willow and alder wood for heating, unlike the Inuit who used animal blubber. They further resorted to using turf to make walls for buildings and heating. As a result of this deforestation, the Norse were short of lumber, fuel and iron. Finally, the loss of plant cover resulted in topsoil erosion due to wind and rain.

Most of these actions were taken as a result of using maladaptive practices adapted to a very different environment in Europe. For example, while the clearing of forests and digging of turf might have been suited in areas of Britain and Ireland, with greater resources and milder climates, it was clearly ill-suited in the much more marginal and resource-limited fjords of Greenland. As a result, the settlers adopted established practices to meet the local and immediate needs of the local community (e.g. to clear land, make hay, or produce heat). The tension towards localism resulted in the community failing to adapt to wider environmental changes (both as a result of their own actions and wider climate change). Furthermore, they failed to learn from the Inuit, who also inhabited Greenland during the same period. Unlike the Norse, the Inuit predominantly relied on hunting for survival. However they had developed a number of practices uniquely suited to the environment of Greenland. First they did not rely of lumber, using ice to build homes, animal skins to make canoes and blubber for heating. Second, in addition to caribou, they had learned how to hunt whale, and ringed seal, using harpoons from canoes and blow holes respectively. These practices allowed them to take advantage of food resources available throughout the year. Despite these innovations, the Norse failed to learn from the Inuit, either in terms of making and heating their homes and hunting. As a result when the climate got cooler, and hay production was severely reduced, the Norse could no longer rely on their livestock to provide food.

3. Co-Evolutionary Implications for Sustainability

3.1 Overview

The above co-evolutionary narrative might have some interesting implications for the issue of sustainability. While cultural practices are altered based on the interpretation of past events through a post hoc sense-making process (Daft/Weick 1984), they influence the anticipation of futures, resulting in the selection and retention of practices in anticipation of feedback from others within the group and beyond. Crucially this process is played out within the socio-political dynamics of the group, community and wider society, with an ecology of cultural practices competing for dominance. As these practices become more collective in nature, the resultant socio-political truces and coalitions (Cyert/March 1963) established within groups can act to constrain deviations from this accepted view of the world. This biased interpretation and anticipation of futures is further compounded when the strength of local feedback signals overpowers those received from other sources, including the wider environment. As noted above, in some cases these practices can tend to reflect the world and actors local to them (Breslin 2011a; Rosen 1975), and not that which is representative of the selection environment external to the community as a whole. Indeed, Sober/Wilson (1999) argue that humans have evolved altruistic and cooperative behaviors towards other members of their group, where "group selection favors within group niceness and between group nastiness". However, this between group competition can hinder wider, even global-level cooperation needed for sustainability. Therefore, whilst individuals make local choices which they believe offer local improvement, the resultant behavior may detrimentally affect the group and community's longer term evolution and survival, as seen with the Greenland Norse. The net effect of these tensions might result in the suppression of the mechanism of variation, as the interpretation of the need for change and/or the ability to then enact this change is reduced. As a result variation and with it the continued evolution of the system can be either encouraged or suppressed.

Some authors have commented on how the establishment of collective practices over time can result in taken-for-granted ways of viewing the external world, and indeed interpreting feedback from that world (Aldrich 1999). Given that collective interpretive systems are used to anticipate responses from the external world following the enactment of practices, it is importance that these can also adapt to reflect changing worlds. However, clearly the "accuracy" of these "anticipatory vicarious selectors" is based on the interpretation of prior feedback from the external world, and following previous success it can be seen how this could lead to the entrenchment of established practices, resulting in competency traps (Miller 1999). As Diamond (2005, p. 275) noted "the values to which people cling most stubbornly under inappropriate conditions are those values that were previously the source of their greatest triumphs over adversity". In this way, feedback might be interpreted in a manner which is consistent with the view of the world held by the existing interpretive system. This might result in the anticipation of futures becoming trapped by the interpretation of the past (first tension), by the collective interpretation of the wider group (second tension) or the dominance of local evolutionary pressures (third tension). In this extreme account it might even be argued that the community becomes tied to historical, collective and localised cultural practices as exploration, and indeed continuing evolution through variation is suppressed. As a result, a mismatch can exist between cultural practices which were evolved for a different world, than the wider ecological challenges faced by societies today (Waring 2010). However, communities can and do overcome inertia, break with past interpretations, un-tap variations from individuals and broaden their understandings of the external challenges they face. In this manner, communities can explore new futures through variation. This involves un-tapping the sources of variation from individuals within the community itself or introducing it through new arrivals (Breslin 2011a). Exploration of new practices can also be initiated from higher levels within the community including political, and community leaders. In this way, communities are not inextricably linked to the past through certain cultural practices.

One might argue that by sitting together and working through future scenarios, community leaders can identify and thereby overcome some of the constraining effects of these tensions. For example, new narratives that challenge past worldviews could be put forward. Or different "voices" from across levels or sections of the community could be encouraged in open brainstorming sessions. However many of these approaches do not specifically explore the multi-level complexity of changing practices within communities, and how choices made at the level of the individual and collective can over time influence the survival of the wider community. In addition while these approaches challenge the constraining effects of the past and the collective on anticipatory frameworks, the potential of such approaches are themselves constrained to a certain degree by focusing on a limited number of possible futures or scenarios. The problem we are dealing with is multi-level and complex, and it is argued here that it requires a multi-level, complex and co-evolving solution. In essence, the net effect of the tensions outlined above is to constrain variation and innovation emerging from within levels of the community. Variations are the fuel of any evolutionary system, and novelty must be nurtured in order to guarantee the longer term survival of the system. Examining the evolutionary process at different levels in the community, a number of evolutionary solutions might be put forward.

3.2 *"Learning to Evolve"*

Each member of the Greenland Norse community was at the "frontline" living on the very edge of survival. As noted above, they relied on practices which were inherited from the past, and maintained by local and collective pressures. However, these same practices became increasingly maladaptive for the challenges they faced. One might argue that had individuals within those communities developed anticipatory systems based on the evolutionary account given above, broader multi-level and community-wide implications of evolving local behavior would have been considered in the choices that they made. For instance, they would have seen that the continuation of local practices was preventing the community for innovating and learning from the Inuit. Or they would have become more aware of the detrimental affects of continuing to use practices adapted for milder climates in Europe. In effect, by understanding how our cultural practices evolve over time, we can better learn to evolve (Breslin/Jones 2012). This involves members of the community asking themselves a number of questions. Is *variation* and innovation encouraged within the community? After all this is the fuel of further evolution. How are choices made regarding the *selection* of practices? Are these adversely affected by socio-political differences, or are choices made based on a clear and accurate understanding of the wider challenges facing the community? Finally, are systems in places to ensure the *retention* of good practices, and the discontinuation of maladaptive ones? In this manner individuals might interpret their behavior and those of others in terms of the broader hierarchy of evolutionary systems which ultimately influence the survival of the community. In this way, individuals can also use an evolutionary approach as an anticipatory system to interpret future events, and in so doing create new interpretations, worldviews and futures. Such anticipatory systems or "mind tools" (Dennett 1995, p. 378) allow individuals to learn how to "think better about what they should think about next".

Community Members "Learning to Evolve"	
Variation	Nurturing novelty through variation and innovation.
Selection	Clear and accurate understanding of wider challenges faced. Overcoming historical and socio-political resistance.
Retention	Retaining practices through new competences and skills.

Table 1: Community Members "Learning to Evolve"

Following this argument it is seen that practices evolve through the mechanisms of *variation*, *selection* and *retention*, however this process occurs through the behaviors of individuals and groups. Therefore one cannot separate the process from the individual. For instance, how do individuals in frontline groups facilitate or hinder the process of *variation, selection* and *retention*? Are the right individuals put together in the right way to facilitate or constrain the resulting evolution of knowledge? While existing practices can provide stability, they can also act to resist change, and in this sense the exploration of new practices might be resisted by the experiences and socio-political status quo directly associated with key individuals within the community. In this sense, while the focus of our evolutionary story shifts towards evolving knowledge, individuals and groups also matter and cannot be divorced from the evolutionary processes which define the development of that knowledge over time. It then becomes the job of community leaders to manage the higher level process through which local knowledge evolves (without becoming directly involved in the evolutionary process itself), in much the same manner as Darwin's pigeon fanciers selected and pruned key desired characteristics in their prize pigeons (Darwin 1859). In the case of the Greenland Norse, these community leaders might include the most powerful farms around whom other families were organised, as noted above. It then becomes the job of these separate settlement leaders to manage the process of evolution through the management of the broader process and people involved, in a sense acting as "artificial breeders" controlling the means through which knowledge evolves within groups.

Community Leaders as "Artificial Breeders"	
Process	Managing the processes through which knowledge evolves.
People	Identifying people who enable/constrain this process.

Table 2: Community Leaders as "Artificial Breeders"

3.3 Managing the Co-Evolutionary System

While one might argue that individuals can "learn to evolve" (Breslin/ Jones 2012), by considering the wider implications of their decisions in terms of the broader co-evolutionary process, clearly a coordination of the resultant multitude of voices might be needed. This might involve a number of measures in which the co-evolutionary system is managed at a higher level.

The wider co-evolutionary process can also be managed through the interaction of levels. In this sense community elders need to consider the competitive *selection* environment at each level of the community hierarchy. The greater the number of levels within this hierarchy, then the greater the complexity involved in managing this process. Balancing the need for both the exploitation and exploration of knowledge, involves on the one hand communities breaking down the invisible barriers within the hierarchy of evolving systems and unlocking creativity and *variations* from all levels, and on the other hand allowing enough stability to become established within the various levels to ensure this knowledge is then *retained* and exploited within these same groups. When the community's behavior is dominated by the exploitation of existing practices (as in the case of the Greenland Norse), the resultant socio-political situation can lead to *variations* coming from lower levels within the community being suppressed. So for example, lower level *variations* introduced by individuals or other groups are inhibited because they disagree with the established practices and/or because they challenge the existing status quo. Whilst exploitation involves bringing individuals into the collective fold and modifying their individual behavior to that of the group, exploration involves unlocking the sources of *variation* from lower levels through individual creativity and learning. In particular this involves un-tapping sources of *variation* from individuals within the group, and as well as exploring different practices used by other groups and individuals both within the community and beyond.

Community Elders Managing the Co-Evolutionary Process	
Systems	Managing the hierarchy of co-evolving systems.
Multi-Level	Managing the interaction and competitive selection environments at different hierarchical levels.
Culture	Cultivating a Co-Evolutionary Language within the community.

Table 3: Community Elders Managing the Co-Evolutionary Process

From the community elders' perspective, managing this broader process and the competing needs for exploitation and exploration, thus involves balancing the interaction between the evolutionary systems of the different hierarchical levels within the community, from individual to group and community. This involves taken a wider perspective on the co-evolution of separate local communities and examining the interaction between them. For instance, increasing the interaction can be achieved by increasing the competitive *selection* pressures at lower levels within communities, as community elders act to encourage diversity and competition amongst individuals and groups (Breslin 2011a). This might involve the strengthening of key feedback signals from sources external to the group, with a view towards increasing the influence of key sources at different levels on choices made within the group (Waring 2010). Crucially the separation of roles and responsibilities between community leaders and elders, allows the former to focus on managing the evolution of specific communities, while the latter direct their attention towards the interaction and co-evolution of these separate processes to ensure competing short-term and long-term needs are balanced.

4. Conclusion

The world around us shows evidence of nature's survivors who have adapted to changing environments, whilst other species have become extinct. Whilst clearly the detailed mechanisms between biological and cultural evolution differ, we can nonetheless learn from these broader principles of evolution. Reinterpreting the challenges faced by communities in this manner shifts the focus of attention onto co-evolving cultural practices. Examining this multi-level process, it is argued in this chapter than three key tensions can develop within such communities, in which practices become backward-looked, collective and increasingly local in focus. In the case of the Greenland Norse the development of these tensions had disastrous consequences for the sustainability of the community in that marginal environment. However, it is further argued that communities can break free from this cycle, and each member of the community has a role to play in managing and leading this evolution. By developing an evolutionary language in this way, broader multi-level and community-wide implications of evolving local behavior can be considered in the development of sustainable communities and societies. In this manner community members, leaders and elders might interpret their behavior and those of others in terms of the broader hierarchy of evolutionary systems which ultimately influence the survival of the community, and longer-term sustainability of cultural practices.

References

ALDRICH, H.E. (1999): Organizations Evolving, London.

BLACKMORE, S. (1999): The Meme Machine, Oxford.

BOSCHMA, R.; MARTIN, R. (2007): Constructing an Evolutionary Economic Geography, in: Journal of Economic Geography, Vol. 7, No. 5, pp. 537-548.

BOURDIEU, P. (1990): The Logic of Practice, Cambridge.

BRESLIN, D. (2010): Generalising Darwinism to Study Socio-Cultural Change, in: International Journal of Sociology and Social Policy, Vol. 30, No. 7/8, pp. 427-439.

BRESLIN, D. (2011a): Interpreting Futures through the Multi-Level Co-Evolution of Organizational Practices, in: Futures, Vol. 43, No. 9, pp. 1020-1028.

BRESLIN, D. (2011b): Reviewing a Generalized Darwinist Approach to Studying Socio-Economic Change, in: International Journal of Management Reviews, Vol. 13, No. 2, pp. 218-235.

BRESLIN, D.; JONES, C. (2012): The Evolution of Entrepreneurial Learning, in: International Journal of Organizational Analysis, Vol. 20, No. 3, pp. 294-308.

CAMPBELL, D. (1965): Variation, Selection and Retention in Sociocultural Evolution, in: BARRINGER, H.R.; BLANKSTEN, G.I.; MACK, R.W. (Eds.): Social Change in Developing Areas: A Reinterpretation of Evolutionary Theory, Cambridge, pp. 19-49.

CAVALLI-SFORZA, L.L. (2001): Genes, Peoples and Languages, London.

CLOAK, F.T. (1975): Is a Cultural Ethology Possible?, in: Human Ecology, Vol. 3, No. 3, pp. 161-182.

CYERT, R.M.; MARCH, J.G. (1963): A Behavioral View of the Firm, London.

DAFT, R.L.; WEICK, K. (1984): Toward a Model of Organizations as Interpretation Systems, in: Academy of Management Review, Vol. 9, No. 2, pp. 284-295.

DARWIN, C.R. (1859): On the Origin of Species by Means of Natural Selection or the Preservation of Favoured Races in the Struggle for Life, London.

DARWIN, C.R. (1871): The Descent of Man, and Selection in Relation to Sex, London.

DAWKINS, R. (1976): The Selfish Gene, New York.

DAWKINS, R. (1982): The Extended Phenotype, New York.

DENNETT, D. (1995): Darwin's Dangerous Idea, New York.

DEWEY, J. (1922): Human Nature and Conduct, New York.

DIAMOND, J. (2005): Collapse: How Societies Choose to Fail or Survive, London.

DISTIN, K. (2011): Cultural Evolution, Cambridge.

DURHAM, W.H. (1991): Coevolution: Genes, Culture and Human Diversity, Stanford.

ESSLETZBICHLER, J.; RIGBY, D. (2005): Competition, Variety and the Geography of Technology Evolution, in: Tijdschrift voor Economische en Sociale Geografie, Vol. 96, No. 1, pp. 48-62.

FOLKE, C. (2006): Resilience: The Emergence of a Perspective for Social Ecological Systems Analyses, in: Global Environmental Change, Vol. 16, No. 3, pp. 253-267.

FOLKE, C.; CARPENTER, S.; ELMQVIST, T.; GUNDERSON, L.; HOLLING, C. S.; WALKER, B. (2002): Resilience and Sustainable Development: Building Adaptive Capacity in a World of Transformations, in: Ambio: A Journal of the Human Environment, Vol. 31, No. 5, pp. 437-440.

FOXON, T.J. (2011): A Co-Evolutionary Framework for Analysing a Transition to a Sustainable Low Carbon Economy, in: Ecological Economics, Vol. 70, No. 12, pp. 2258-2267.

GOWDY, J.M. (1994): Coevolutionary Economics: the Economy, Society, and the Environment, Boston et al.

HODGSON, G. (2002): Darwinism in Economics: From Analogy to Ontology, in: Journal of Evolutionary Economics, Vol. 12, No. 3, pp. 259-281.

HODGSON, G. (2003): The Mystery of the Routine: The Darwinian Destiny of an Evolutionary Theory or Economic Change, in: Revue Economique, Vol. 54, No. 2, pp. 335-384.

HODGSON, G.; KNUDSEN, T. (2004): The Firm as an Interactor: Firms as Vehicles for Habits and Routines, in: Journal of Evolutionary Economics, Vol. 14, No. 3, pp. 281-307.

HODGSON, G. (2010): Darwinian Coevolution of Organisations and the Environment, in: Ecological Economics, Vol. 69, No. 4, pp. 700-706.

HOLLING, C. S. (2001): Understanding the Complexity of Economic, Ecological, and Social Systems, in: Ecosystems, Vol. 4, No. 5, pp. 390-405.

HULL, D.L. (1988): Science as a Process, Chicago.

KALLIS, G.; NORGAARD, R. (2010): Coevolutionary Ecological Economics, in: Ecological Economics, Vol. 69, No. 4, pp. 690-699.

LEVIN, S. (1993): Forum: Science and Sustainability, in: Ecological Applications, Vol. 3, No. 4, pp. 545-546.

LEWONTIN, R. (1970): The Units of Selection, in: Annual Review of Ecology and Systematics, Vol. 1, pp. 1-18.

MARTIN, R.; SUNLEY, P. (2007): Complexity Thinking and Evolutionary Economic Geography, in: Journal of Economic Geography, Vol. 7, No. 5, pp. 573-601.

MEAD, G.H. (1934): Mind, Self and Society: From the Standpoint of a Social Behaviorist, Chicago.

MILLER, D. (1999): Selection Processes Inside Organizations: The Self-Reinforcing Consequences of Success, in: BAUM, J.C.; MCKELVEY, B. (Eds.): Variations in Organization Science, In Honor of Donald T. Campbell, New York, pp. 93-109.

NORGAARD, R.B. (1984): Coevolutionary Agricultural Development, in: Economic Development and Cultural Change, Vol. 32, No. 3, pp. 525-546.

ORLIKOWSKI, W.J. (2002): Knowing in Practice: Enacting a Collective Capability in Distributed Organizing, in: Organization Science, Vol. 13, No. 3, pp. 249-273.

PLOTKIN, H. (1994): Darwin Machines and the Nature of Knowledge, Cambridge.

RICHERSON, P.J.; BOYD, R. (2005): Not by Genes Alone: How Culture Transformed Human Evolution, Chicago.

ROSEN, R. (1975): Complexity and Error in Social Dynamics, in: International Journal of General Systems, Vol. 2, No. 3, pp. 145-148.

ROSEN, R. (1985): Anticipatory Systems: Philosophical, Mathematical and Methodological Foundations, Oxford.

SIMMIE, J.; MARTIN, R. (2010). The Economic Resilience of Regions: Towards an Evolutionary Approach, in: Cambridge Journal of Regions, Economy and Society, Vol. 3, No. 1, pp. 27-35.

SOBER, E.; WILSON, D.S. (1999): Unto Others: The Evolution and Psychology of Unselfish Behavior, Cambridge.

VAN DEN BERGH, J.; GOWDY, J. (2003): The Microfoundations of Macroeconomics: An Evolutionary Perspective, in: Cambridge Journal of Economics, Vol. 27, No. 1, pp. 65-84.

WARING, T.M. (2010): New Evolutionary Foundations: Theoretical Requirements for a Science of Sustainability, in: Ecological Economics, Vol. 69, No. 4, pp. 718-730.

Sustainable Intercultural Management

Volker Stein

Overview

1. Intellectual Challenge: What Is Sustainable Intercultural Management?

This article aims to go beyond the basic knowledge on intercultural management as well as on sustainability, raising the question "What is Sustainable Intercultural Management (SIM)?". Up to the author's knowledge, this term is not yet coined in academic literature.

Since sustainability is an omnipresent buzzword (e.g., Palmer/ Cooper/van der Forst 1997; de Lange/Busch/Delgado-Ceballos 2012, p. 151) with everybody seemingly knowing what is meant, the spontaneous answer to this question appears easy: SIM means "stay involved in intercultural management, but somehow broader, more supportive, and with more enduring effects". However, what should be changed, if corporate intercultural management has already been broadly oriented to cultural differences, if it has already considered the interests of foreign business partners, and if it has already aimed at long-term profits in international affairs?

The starting point of the argumentation is the systems approach (going back, among others, to the General System Theory of von Bertalanffy, e.g. 1968). According to systems theory, a system is defined as a set of interdependent elements and the relationships between these elements (e.g., Vester 1980, pp. 27-29). Moreover, systems can be characterised by four aspects, i.e. structure, behaviour, strategy, and effectiveness. Specifying them for SIM leads to four objects of more detailed study:

- the *structural* aspect is highly influenced by the international environment, forming the situational background for SIM.
- the *behavioural* aspect focuses on the systemic approach to sustainability creation, in particular referring to system complexity.
- the *strategic* aspect organises the interactive processes of SIM, by the use of a new, meaningful way of thinking.
- the *effectiveness-related* aspect is intended to control the progress made in moving towards SIM.
- These four aspects will each be addressed with regard to *system elements* which are representing the static facets as well as *system relationships* which are representing the dynamic issues.

2. International Environment as Situational Sustainability Background

2.1 Overview

Intercultural management stands for a specific "augmented management challenge". In addition to the common and already complex set of managerial issues in strategic management, intercultural management is faced with the even more complex challenges of international collaboration where economic agents who are originated in different national cultures interact across cultural systems, attitudes, and identities and create something new, something common (e.g., Barmeyer 2011, pp. 37-38).

Before enlarging upon sustainability of and in intercultural management itself, it will, therefore, be necessary to approach the following basic question related to the structural context of action: What is the function of the *international environment*, in particular in respect to SIM?

2.2 System Elements Perspective: Contextual

The environment of a system is its exterior, separated from the system by the system boundary. The environment effects organisations by being a source of uncertainty (e.g., Downey/Hellriegel/Slocum 1975; Leblebici/Salancik 1981), by providing resources (e.g., Pfeffer/Salancik 1978), and by serving as a frame of reference for variation and selection in the sense of the population ecology theory (e.g., Aldrich/Pfeffer 1976). Organisational environments are potentially complex, dynamic, and restricting (e.g., Child 1972, pp. 3-5; Tung 1979, pp. 673-675).

Typically in economic-oriented business science, the organisational system is in the focus of interest, while the environment, seen as the remaining surrounding, fades into the background or is even widely ignored. Nevertheless, the environment contains potential system elements as well as information needed for the system behaviour. Especially in international business, the environment brings along cultural similarities and cultural contrast which have to be taken into account and interpreted within the task of contextualisation (e.g., Barmeyer 2012, pp. 92-93).

In intercultural management, the distinction between system and environment remains fuzzy. On the one hand, if the system is defined as a corporation which intends to work on the international level, the foreign countries make the international environment. On the other hand, if the system is defined as a corporation that is already working on the international level, the collaboration partners have become part of the system and only the not-involved parts of the surroundings make the international environment. The structures, processes, and people which are involved in intercultural work are moving from external to internal environment (in the sense of Duncan 1972, pp. 314-315, who defines environment "as the totality of physical and social factors that are taken directly into consideration in the decision-making behaviour of individuals in the organization" (p. 314) and differentiates between internal and external environment).

In this article, the second connotation of "international environment" is chosen. Consequently, in international corporations, local employees of subsidiaries in other countries as carriers of a foreign national culture can be integrated into the system, but not the foreign national culture itself. The foreign national culture remains part of the external environment. Therefore, a corporation can already interact with people as part of the own system (employees, business partners) in foreign countries and at the same time the international environment still provides "context". This context then describes the situation, in particular the cultural situation. It is made of the respective country's collectively shared set of underlying assumptions, of prevalent values, and of visible behavioural patterns and artificial cultural symbols (e.g., Schein 1992; Hatch 1997, p. 363; Hofstede 2001, p. 11). This cultural environment is characterised by pluralism since the people of a country differ in their cultural preferences, and it is characterised by dynamics since cultural patterns change over time. Dealing with such an external environment and its inherent cultural differences in relation to the own system is a relevant matter of corporate strategy.

2.3 System Relationships Perspective: Legitimate

Exceeding the function of providing the situational context, the international environment becomes important for the relationships among the system elements, in particular with newly integrated employees in foreign locations. The environment exerts influence across the permeable boundary between inner system and outer environment. The outer environment provides external restrictions as well as external facilitations.

The logic of this environment-system-influence follows the basic idea of the resource dependence theory (Pfeffer/Salancik 1978), pointing out that external resources are important for an organisation's behavioural options. When resource dependence theory was developed, material resources had conceptual priority. In the course of time, resource dependence was extended to immaterial resources. A new organisational theory, new institutionalism (e.g., Powell/DiMaggio 1991; Walgenbach 2002), was developed, stressing societal and cultural influences on organisations. As a theory with strong sociological references, new institutionalism explains that organisations depend among others on environmental response to their activities. Institutional peer pressure of the external environment, i.e., institutionalised assumptions, rules, and expectations (e.g., Zucker 1977; Scott 1991) results in the need for legitimacy which is seen as a decisive precondition for organisational survival. The international environment is no longer pure context but provider of legitimacy.

Consequently, not alone the corporation as the agent, but also the international environment determine the interpretation of the outcomes of SIM. Therefore, intercultural management is a relational dynamics which means that there is an intersectional relationship between the "self" of a corporation and the "foreign" of the international environment (e.g., Thomas 2003, p. 46), being in a continuous exchange. Dealing with intercultural issues within corporations, i.e., among the system elements, and between corporation and environment, can no longer be mentally separated.

3. Systemic Behaviour as Basic Requirement for Sustainability

3.1 Overview

Further approximating the definition of SIM, a crucial question is what the particularities of a *sustainable* behaviour are. Corporations and their employees "behave" – they act according to the objectives of the corporation and according to individual objectives. However, the "how to" and, therefore, the specific quality of a sustainable behaviour is difficult to grasp.

In general, there are various definitions of sustainability in theory, mostly based on corporate social responsibility (e.g., Carroll 1999; McWilliams/Siegel 2001), as well as multiple guidelines for sustainability in practice such as ISO 26000 as the guideline for social responsibility of the International Organisation for Standardisation. They have in common that corporations should admit their corporate responsibility and that stakeholders' interests should be incorporated in economic behaviour. However, the addressed behavioural principles such as accountability, transparency, ethical behaviour, respect of the rule of law, or respect of human rights, are predominantly content-related or objective-related.

Looking for behavioural principles which are more *process*-related raises the questions how the system elements deal with the complexity of the contextual situation and how they manage to create external legitimacy.

3.2 System Elements Perspective: Cybernetic

In order to underline that the process-oriented approach is an appropriate anchor for the discussion of sustainable behaviour from the system elements perspective, it can be shown that the alternative sustainability anchors are insufficient in regard to behavioural dynamics:

- taking the *necessity* for sustainability would only lead to the widely undisputed insight that sustainability is an absolutely essential objective for up-to-date corporations (e.g., Agyeman/Warner 2002), resulting in the demand to foster sustainability out of conviction or at least for image reasons.
- taking the *object* of sustainability would only lead to concepts such as the well-known "triple bottom line" model (Elkington 1997) referring to three fields of sustainable behaviour – economy, ecology, social –, but such models usually do not go beyond agenda setting.
- taking the *formal responsibility* for sustainability – and there is a broad discussion on who should take the lead and why, for example top management, organisation department, human resource management, marketing (e.g., Scholz et al. 2011) – would mainly lead to thematic priorities and the decision who can in the end be held accountable and who can exculpate himself if something goes wrong.

By contrast, a *process*-oriented approach has to deal with the behavioural options which system elements have to ascertain that the substance of the system elements such as resources, people, and environmental linkages can be preserved. This is part of the basic cybernetic idea to make regulatory systems more efficient and effective (e.g., Ashby 1956). On the overall system level, therefore, ways to proactively deal with system complexity have to be addressed. As long as "sustainable" means the complex task of "preserving the substance of a system", the elements of a system – here: the employees who are involved in in intercultural management – have at least to avoid the typical pitfalls of complex systems in order to behave sustainably. Dörner (1976; 1989, pp. 288-295) points out the most charac-teristic pitfalls:

- acting without preceding analysis of the situation which leads to a "re-pair service" pattern without systematic recognition of objectives;
- ignoring side effects and long-distance effects as well as the non-linear process logic;
- exaggerating method-orientation only because negative effects of ap-plying a method did not yet become visible;
- tending to oversteer if hesitant system intervention does not lead to im-mediate system response;
- compensating helplessness by authoritative leadership or cynicism.

In order to avoid these mechanistic pitfalls, the suggestion is to proceed in a cybernetic way, to take the turbulent cycles of cause and effect into con-sideration (e.g., Morgan 1983, pp. 349-350), and to strive after pattern recognition (e.g., Vester 1980, pp. 35-42). The more blurred the details, the more the relationships between the system elements become apparent and allow comprehending the system as a whole (e.g., Vester 1980, p. 36).

Therefore, there is a need for a systemic meta-strategy for SIM which incorporates situational analysis, recognises side effects and long-distance effects, deals with interactional patterns and their dynamic feedback loops, avoids over-standardised solutions, is based on a substantial knowledge of intercultural management, and therefore justifies patience and self-effica-cy in dealing with intercultural management. By this, the decision horizon can be expanded. Such a meta-strategy will be helpful to implement a sys-tematic and non-erratic long-term approach to intercultural management. It provides for standardisation on an aggregated layer, but below that lay-er, more differentiated and individualised strategies can be implemented which fit to the specific situation.

3.3 System Relationships Perspective: Reliable

Behaving sustainably also refers to the system-environment-intersection. Outsiders expect sustainable behaviour to be predictable. In order to meet the international environment's legitimacy requirements as discussed be-fore, corporations can work on their reliability in intercultural manage-ment.

The international corporation can give weight to the continuity of its activities, based on the insight that few things are as damaging for a relationship as broken promises (e.g., Tomlinson/Dineen/Lewicki 2004). Giving a promise arouses expectations, and therefore, announcements – for example to behave sustainably in intercultural management – have to be authentical in the sense that the corporation has in the past provably kept its promises and that it gives credible signals that new promises will be kept in the future (e.g., Stein 2010, p. 202). Continuity supports sustainability by creating the perception of reliability which is an important legitimacy anchor for the external environment.

4. Intercultural Competitive Strategies as Framework for SIM

4.1 Overview

Concretising SIM calls for a meta-strategy which can be applied to everyday intercultural management, supporting corporations to sustainably reach their economic targets subject to the maintenance of the intercultural relationships.

At this point it has to be mentioned that the ecological responsibility of corporations (e.g., Young/Tilley 2006; Bazin 2009) is intendedly left out: While ecology is, of course, part of *international* management as a whole, the subdomain of *intercultural* management specifically concentrates on intercultural interactions.

The framework related to the intercultural challenge which seems to be highly appropriate is the "Intercultural Competitive Strategies" framework (Scholz/Stein 2013), because it contains a meta-strategy which aims at a behavioural pattern with a focus on continuity.

4.2 System Elements Perspective: Simplifying

Intercultural Competitive Strategies are based on pattern recognition, identifying typical behavioural patterns by which corporations and their employees aim to be successful in intercultural management. There are three traditional patterns (Scholz/Stein 2013, pp. 28-59):

- the majority of researchers and consultants in intercultural management plead in favour of behavioural assimilation in a foreign culture.

In keeping with the motto "When in Rome, do as the Romans do", corporations should give up their own cultural positions, adapt to the culture of the destination, and avoid attracting any negative attention. This pattern is called "cultural chameleon". However: The domiciled competitors know their cultural rules and conditions much better than the incoming corporation. Therefore, they are endangered to be "pulled over the barrel".

- some practitioners prefer not to adapt culturally at all. Instead, they transfer business strategies which proved successful in their home country to the markets abroad. This pattern is called "cultural cowboy". However, this type of ethnocentric strategy and cultural "bull in the china shop" does not go down well with everybody in the world, rather provoking rejection than supporting successful deals with business partners.

- in particular top-managers and top-consultants develop a pattern which allows them to find their way on the international scene regardless where in the world they are. Assuming that intercultural problems are overvalued in business life anyway, they do not concede them an important role: business is business, culture is culture. This pattern is called "cultural leveller". Not surprisingly, it leads on the surface to a negligence of cultural differences which in reality persist.

It is obvious that these patterns each are too single-sided in order to unlock competitive advantages for outperforming competitors in the foreign market and at the same time to avoid passing the "red lines" of acceptance of the foreign business partners.

Therefore, the newly defined pattern "cultural positivist" is an alternative and contemporary approach to intercultural management which combines the strengths of cultural chameleons, cultural cowboys, and cultural levellers, while at the same time avoiding their weaknesses (Scholz/Stein 2013, pp. 63-78). This meta-strategy calls for a considerable change in thinking and results in the country-specific application of three ways of behaving:

- there are cultural aspects where the local corporations in the foreign country are successful when strictly observing them. The cultural positivist should *adapt* to these cultural aspects as well for reasons of success orientation.

- there are cultural aspects where the local corporations in the foreign country are successful when purposely contrasting with them. Obvi-

ously, this is not only accepted but even approved. The cultural positivist should as well *counteract* these cultural aspects for reasons of
success orientation.

- there are cultural aspects which do not show any noticeable statistical
relationship with corporate success for the local corporations in the foreign country. It is safe to assume that the cultural positivist can as well
ignore these cultural aspects.

This underlying so-called "Competitive Acceptance" logic (described in
detail in Scholz/Stein 2002; 2010; 2012a; 2012b) is a decisive step in the
development of intercultural management increasing its sustainability. It
does not only explain successful intercultural management behaviour, but
also simplifies it and provides a major reduction of complexity. Instead of
dealing with any possible cultural aspect in a country, corporations are only supposed to concentrate on the few (usually two) most success-related
cultural aspects where *adapt* or *counteract* pay off.

As precondition, corporations have to acquaint themselves with the
country-specific patterns how to master the balance between cultural adaptation and cultural counteraction. They have to ensure that the considered
foreign culture is understood and assessed in regard to adaptation needs
and counteraction needs.

4.3 System Relationships Perspective: Consequent

Adding the continuity aspect, sustainability requires that contextualisation
and application of the cultural positivist meta-strategy at the boundary between system and cultural environment of the foreign country are performed in a non-erratic and credible manner. This will be accomplished if:

- the corporation as a whole with all its system elements strategically be-
haves according to the cultural positivist pattern which turned out to be
most functional in respect to intercultural management. The corporation develops respective intercultural competences for its employees
and trains their cultural positivist behavioural skills. Therefore, it will
no longer be an individual decision how to shape one's intercultural behaviour. It is a superior, overall corporate decision that intercultural
management behaviour follows the cultural positivist pattern.
- the chosen pattern is consequently kept for the future. It is not allowed
to skip back and forth between cultural chameleon, cultural cowboy,

and cultural leveller. Instead, the basic decision to behave according to the cultural positivist pattern is stable and imperative.

As a result, a substantial SIM can grow. The environment can build up trust towards the international corporation. In the end, the environment is the entity that assesses the corporation's behaviour and gives (or gives not) legitimacy, but the corporation strongly influences that.

5. Implementation Controlling as Sustainability Proof

5.1 Overview

Aiming at SIM is the one side of the coin – evaluating whether it has really been SIM is the other. This calls for a sustainability controlling in intercultural management, fittingly based on the Intercultural Competitive Strategies framework.

As multi-faceted SIM is, as multi-faceted is its controlling. SIM requires the acceptance of the sustainability *target*: the preservation of resources, people and environmental linkages in the sense of "non-consumption", i.e. long-term availability for own business success. SIM has different *performance* outputs, for example profits in international business. Of course, SIM implies a coordinated *planning* process. But foremost, SIM is an *activity* in the sense of generally implemented behavioural pattern. All these aspects – targets, performance, planning, and activities – can be controlled.

Differentiating content-related types of controlling in general, *target controlling* primarily controls sense and logical congruency of the target dimensions, *performance controlling* predominantly controls the output, *controlling of planning* chiefly controls the involved decision-making processes, and *activity controlling* especially controls the implementation of methods (Scholz 2000, p. 142).

Concentrating on SIM as an *activity*, activity controlling becomes most relevant. Therefore, it has to be assessed how far the implemented activities are taken according to the intended process and which progress is made in moving towards the state of sustainability in intercultural management.

5.2 System Elements Perspective: Competent

For a corporation involved in intercultural interaction, two competences are most important in order to act according to SIM: the overall corporate competences in regard to Intercultural Competitive Strategies for the respective countries, and the individual competences of the employees.

As far as the overall corporate competences in regard to Intercultural Competitive Strategies are concerned, corporations must have the country-specific knowledge on the cultural aspects to adapt and the cultural aspects to counteract. It is no longer sufficient only to know cultural dimensions of a country. As essential to know are the country-specific connections between these cultural dimensions and economic performance. Activity controlling, therefore, means assessing the richness of the knowledge base on strategic intercultural behaviour for different countries.

As far as the individual competences in regard to intercultural competitive strategies are concerned, every single employee who is involved in intercultural management has to know both the meta-strategy, i.e. how to become and stay a cultural positivist, and the cultural specificities of the respective country. Activity controlling, therefore, means assessing whether employees are undergoing an undirected preparation for intercultural management or not. It is not enough to postulate some "two years of international experience" for taking over responsibility in intercultural management if this is not accompanied by a reflection process (e.g., Daudelin 1996) which aims at intercultural as well as managerial performance. By this, it can turn into a principled experience which is coupled with ongoing reconsideration and critical abstraction of the own behavioural patterns.

5.3 System Relationships Perspective: Consistent

The intended process of SIM aims at infiltrating all interculture-related process chains in the corporation. Therefore, it will become necessary to adjust different activity areas to the Intercultural Competitive Strategies framework.

The first area where Intercultural Competitive Strategies will lead to sustainable performance is the *external* intercultural management. Business negotiations with customers, suppliers, or cooperation partners as well as corporate marketing can benefit from a consistent perception and implementation of the cultural self and the cultural other, and therefore, of needs to culturally adapt respectively to counteract.

The second area is the *internal* intercultural management. It is only consequent to apply it as well to internal fields such as human resource management, organisation, or the formation of corporate culture. In particular in leadership of employees from different countries, the Intercultural Competitive Strategies framework will as well support the implementation of a sustainable intercultural diversity management (e.g., Seymen 2006).

Taken together, the cultural positivist meta-strategy permeates the whole corporate intercultural management, leading to a consistency among external and internal intercultural management.

6. Conclusion: Definition of Sustainable Intercultural Management

This article aims at answering the initial question "What is Sustainable Intercultural Management?"

If staying on the surface, a definition of SIM is seemingly trivial, emphasising intercultural harmony and leaving out any (economic) conflict. But being more precise, the definition of SIM resembles nailing jelly to a wall, in particular if it should focus on "what exactly to do" rather than on "which results can be achieved".

Nonetheless, the systems approach allows becoming more accurate, and the Intercultural Competitive Strategies can serve as the guiding principle for sustainability in intercultural management. Therefore, the definition of SIM will be deduced as follows:

"Sustainable Intercultural Management (SIM) is

- an advanced, systemic type of intercultural management
- based on the contextualisation of the international environment according to the Intercultural Competitive Strategies framework
- with a corporate-wide consensus on behaving according to the complexity-reducing meta-strategy of the cultural positivist,
- controlled for consequent, competent, and consistent application throughout all areas of external and internal intercultural interaction,
- strategically aiming at business success as well as legitimacy in the intercultural environment".

References

AGYEMAN, J.; WARNER, K. (2002): Putting "Just Sustainability" into Place: From Paradigm to Practice, in: Policy & Management Review, Vol. 2, No.1, pp. 8-40.

ALDRICH, H.E.; PFEFFER, J. (1976): Environments of Organizations, in: Annual Review of Sociology, Vol. 2, No. 1, pp. 79-105.

ASHBY, W.R. (1956): An Introduction to Cybernetics, London.

BARMEYER, C. (2011): Interkulturalität, in: BARMEYER, C.; GENKOVA, P.; SCHEFFER, J. (Eds.): Interkulturelle Kommunikation und Kulturwissenschaft: Grundbegriffe, Wissenschaftsdisziplinen, Kulturräume, 2nd ed., Passau, pp. 37-77.

BARMEYER, C. (2012): Taschenlexikon Interkulturalität, Göttingen.

BAZIN, D. (2009): What Exactly is Corporate Responsibility Towards Nature? Ecological Responsibility or Management of Nature? A Pluri-Disciplinary Standpoint, in: Ecological Economics, Vol. 63, No. 3, pp. 634-642.

CARROLL, A.B. (1999): Corporate Social Responsibility: Evolution of a Definitional Construct, in: Business & Society, Vol. 38, No. 3, pp. 268-295.

CHILD, J. (1972): Organizational Structure, Environment and Performance: The Role of Strategic Choice, in: Sociology, Vol. 6, No. 1, pp. 1-22.

DAUDELIN, M.W. (1996): Learning From Experience Through Reflection, in: Organizational Dynamics, Vol. 24, No. 3, pp. 36-48.

DE LANGE, D.E.; BUSCH, T.; DELGADO-CEBALLOS, J. (2012): Sustaining Sustainability in Organizations, in: Journal of Business Ethics, Vol. 110, No. 2, pp. 151-156.

DÖRNER, D. (1976): Problemlösen als Informationsverarbeitung, Stuttgart.

DÖRNER, D. (1989): Die Logik des Mißlingens: Strategisches Denken in komplexen Situationen, Reinbek.

DOWNEY, H.K.; HELLRIEGEL, D.; SLOCUM JR., J.W. (1975): Environmental Uncertainty: The Construct and its Application, in: Administrative Science Quarterly, Vol. 17, No. 4, pp. 613-629.

DUNCAN, R.B. (1972): Characteristics of Organizational Environments and Perceived Environmental Uncertainty, in: Administrative Science Quarterly, Vol. 17, No. 3, pp. 313-327.

ELKINGTON, J. (1997): Cannibals with Forks: The Triple Bottom Line of 21st Century Business, Oxford.

HATCH, M.J. (1997): Organization Theory: Modern Symbolic and Postmodern Perspectives, New York.

HOFSTEDE, G. (2001): Culture's Consequences: Comparing Values, Behaviors, Institutions and Organizations Across Nations, 2nd ed., Thousand Oaks et al.

LEBLEBICI, H.; SALANCIK, G.R. (1981): Effects of Environmental Uncertainty on Information and Decision Processes in Banks, in: Administrative Science Quarterly, Vol. 26. No. 4, pp. 578-596.

MCWILLIAMS, A.; SIEGEL, D. (2001): Corporate Social Responsibility: A Theory of the Firm Perspective, in: Academy of Management Review, Vol. 26, No. 1, pp. 117-127.

MORGAN, G. (1983): Rethinking Corporate Strategy: A Cybernetic Perspective, in: Human Relations, Vol. 36, No. 4, pp. 345-360.

PALMER, J.; COOPER, I.; VAN DER VORST, R. (1997): Mapping Out Fuzzy Buzzwords: Who Sits Where on Sustainability and Sustainable Development, in: Sustainable Development, Vol. 5, No. 2, pp. 87-93.

PFEFFER, J.; SALANCIK, G.R. (1978): The External Control of Organizations: A Resource Dependence Perspective, New York et al.

POWELL, W.W.; DIMAGGIO, P.J. (Eds.) (1991): The New Institutionalism in Organizational Analysis, Chicago et al.

SCHEIN, E.H. (1992): Organizational Culture and Leadership: A Dynamic View, 2nd ed., San Francisco.

SCHOLZ, C. (2000): Personalmanagement: Informationsorientierte und verhaltenstheoretische Grundlagen, 5th ed., München.

SCHOLZ, C.; SCHRAMM-KLEIN, H.; STEIN, V.; ZENTES, J. (2011): Nachhaltigkeit: Wer hat eigentlich den Hut auf? Symposium organised on the 73rd VHB Conference (Verband der Hochschullehrer für Betriebswirtschaft), Kaiserslautern, June 17, 2011.

SCHOLZ, C.; STEIN, V. (2002): "Competitive Acceptance" in Cross-Cultural Interaction, in: SCHOLZ, C.; ZENTES, J. (Eds.): Strategic Management: A European Approach, Wiesbaden, pp. 283-304.

SCHOLZ, C.; STEIN, V. (2010): "Competitive Acceptance" in Cross-Cultural Interaction: A Long Path to a Fundamental Paradigm Shift. Paper presented at the 11th International HRM Conference, Aston Business School, Birmingham, June 10, 2010.

SCHOLZ, C.; STEIN, V. (2012a): From Cultural Chameleons to Cultural Intelligence: Teaching International Business in the Real World. Paper presented at the Academy of Management Annual Meeting in Boston, August 07, 2012.

SCHOLZ, C.; STEIN, V. (2012b): Die Competitive-Acceptance-Matrix, in: Personal.Manager HR International, Vol. 11, No. 4, pp. 46-49.

SCHOLZ, C.; STEIN, V. (2013): Interkulturelle Wettbewerbsstrategien, Göttingen.

SCOTT, W.R. (1991): Unpacking Insitutional Arguments, in: POWELL, W.W.; DIMAGGIO, P.J. (Eds.): The New Institutionalism in Organizational Analysis, Chicago et al., pp. 164-182.

SEYMEN, O.A. (2006): The Cultural Diversity Phenomenon in Organisations and Different Approaches for Effective Cultural Diversity Management: A Literary Review, in: Cross Cultural Management: An International Journal, Vol. 13, No. 4, pp. 296-315.

STEIN, V. (2010): Professionalisierung des Personalmanagements: Selbstverpflichtung als Weg, in: Zeitschrift für Management, Vol. 5, No. 3, pp. 201-205.

THOMAS, A. (2003): Das Eigene, das Fremde, das Interkulturelle, in: THOMAS, A. (Ed.): Handbuch Interkulturelle Kommunikation und Kooperation, Vol. 1: Grundlagen und Praxisfelder, Göttingen, pp. 44-59.

TOMLINSON, E.C.; DINEEN, B.R.; LEWICKI, R.J. (2004): The Road to Reconciliation: Antecedents of Victim Willingness to Reconcile Following a Broken Promise, in: Journal of Management, Vol. 30, No. 2, pp. 165-187.

TUNG, R.L. (1979): Dimensions of Organizational Environments: An Exploratory Study of Their Impact on Organization Structure, in: Academy of Management Journal, Vol. 22, No. 4, pp. 672-693.

VESTER, F. (1980): Neuland des Denkens: Vom technokratischen zum kybernetischen Zeitalter, Stuttgart.

VON BERTALANFFY, L. (1968): General System Theory: Foundations, Development, Application, New York.

WALGENBACH, P. (2002): Neoinstitutionalistische Organisationstheorie: State of the Art und Entwicklungslinien, in: SCHREYÖGG, G.; CONRAD, P. (Eds.): Managementforschung 12: Theorien des Managements, Wiesbaden, pp. 155-202.

YOUNG, W.; TILLEY, F. (2006): Can Businesses Move Beyond Efficiency? The Shift Toward Effectiveness and Equity in the Corporate Sustainability Debate, in: Business Strategy & the Environment, Vol. 15, No. 6, pp. 402-415.

ZUCKER, L.G. (1977): The Role of Institutionalization in Cultural Persistence, in: American Sociological Review, Vol. 42, No. 5, pp. 726-743.

The HR-Department as Driver for Sustainability

Christian Scholz and Stefanie Müller

Overview

1. Remembering the Past

When talking about the future of sustainability, it is helpful to start by looking into the past:

The first event we should remember is the explosion of the oil platform "Deepwater Horizon" in the Gulf of Mexico (e.g. Kurtz 2013). The BP oil disaster began in April 2010 and became the largest oil disaster in the history of the petroleum industry. The total discharge which went into the Gulf of Mexico is estimated at 4,9 million barrels. Until 2012 federal response costs amounted to 850 million Dollars, mostly reimbursed by BP. Furthermore BP is expected to invest at least 4 billion Dollars a year in oil and gas development in the Gulf of Mexico over the next 10 years (e.g. BP 2013).

The second event we should not forget easily is the breakdown of the financial system. Starting with the Lehman Brothers investment bank (2008) and the subprime crisis in 2007 (with the housing bubble), we have seen one of the largest failures of an investment bank, which was the trigger for the global financial and economic crisis from 2008 to 2010 (e.g. Cochrane 2009-2010). The consequences are known.

The third event is the mass layoff by Hewlett Packard in 2012, where 27.000 employees have been laid off worldwide (e.g. Brinkmann 2012). One reason for this radical move that was definitely not inline with the corporate culture of HP has been an uncompetitive product policy. Crucial trends in the IT environment, such as the tablet computer, have been ignored. At the beginning of 2011 the touchpad was presented, but in the summer of the same year the decision was reversed and HP left both the smartphone and tablet production. The consequences: layoffs and clear signs of a non-sustainable corporate strategy.

But why did all this happen? What are the reasons behind it and – even more important – the real reasons behind the obvious?

Looking at BP, we have not just to look at a mechanical failure, which happened by some strange random logic. We have to think about safety culture. But: If we assume, that BP has had a low safety-culture before and during the catastrophe then this is not only a factor contributing to the catastrophe, it is in particular a factor, which has something to do with people (e.g. Scholz 2010). And then we must ask who is responsible for that? Corporate culture is usually connected to Human Resource Management (HRM): A safety culture includes leadership, personnel development, recruitment, and many more aspects of Human Resource Management.

Looking at the Lehmann as a symbol for the financial crisis, we see, of course, the housing market in the U.S. as well as other obvious problems. We see greedy managers and greedy investment bankers, for whom this kind of making money appeared to be a natural part of their life. Therefore, we have to ask about incentive systems and have to look into the compensation systems that reward this kind of risky business by paying huge money for winning and have no penalty for loosing. It is obvious: Without such compensation systems with all its adverse selection of people and behaviour, the financial crisis would never have gone so much out of control. Who is responsible for that? And is not compensation a central part of HRM?

Looking at our third case and HP, we see the performance of a company depending on mismanagement of the CEO and a dramatic change of culture starting with the HR-policies of Carly Fiorina (e.g. Scholz 2003). The problem is that in that case employees are the victims of this mismanagement. Beside the social aspects of downsizing and layoffs, also, economic effect as human capital value reduction is to be noted. As we look at the case of HP, we can also discuss about management training or about management recruiting. And: layoff management, human capital management, management training, and management recruiting are parts of HRM.

We see three dimensions of sustainability: environmental (BP), economic (Lehmann), and social (HP). All three dimensions of sustainability have strong connections to HRM: We talk about the corporate culture of BP (where HR is responsible); we talk about employees' behaviour and compensation systems at Lehmann (where HR also is responsible) and we talk about leadership competencies at HP (where HR definitely is responsible).

Therefore, the ultimate questions for this article are: Assuming that HR-activities are relevant for sustainability, how can the HR-department as an organisational function ensure that sustainable behaviour will be part of all members of the company? How does the HR-department become a successful driver for sustainability?

In doing so, first we look at the literature and discuss the relevance of sustainability, the role of Human Resource Management in general and especially of Human Resource-department. Furthermore, we will show the barriers, which could exist in companies to anchor sustainability in the minds of the people. Finally, we show what HR-department can do to

move across these barriers and which implications result from these observations.

2. Looking Around the Corner

2.1 Obvious: Sustainability Is the Name of the Game

Sustainability is one of the most important issues currently facing our
world. This message has reached academia (e.g. Ambec/Lanoie 2008), as
well as the business context, which sees sustainability is not only an attitude, but also connected to financial performance: Reduction of energy
use can create cost savings, waste recycling can create new revenue
streams and sustainability initiatives can stimulate a culture of innovation
(Peloza et al. 2012, p. 74).

Sustainability is defined by the World Commission on Environment
and Development (WCED) as "the development that meets the needs of
the present without compromising the ability of future generations to meet
their own needs" (WCED 1987, p. 43). This understanding of sustainability refers to maintaining, renewing, or restoring something specific (Sutton
1998) and it includes an ethical dimension as fairness of trade-off between
current economic pressures and future needs of the environment (Wilkin-
son/Hill/Gollan 2001, p. 1492).

In research a wide range of definitions for sustainability exists. According to Elkington (1997) sustainability has three dimensions: "economic
prosperity, environmental quality and – the element which business had
preferred to overlook – social justice" (p. 70). Galdwin/Kennedy/Krause
(1995) showed the five principles connected to that field: (1) Inclusiveness, what means that sustainability embraces both environmental and human systems, both near and far, in both the present and the future. (2)
Connectivity, what means that sustainability demands an understanding of
the world's problems as systemically interconnected and interdependent.
(3) Equity, what means that sustainability deals with fair distribution of resource and property rights, both within and between generations. (4) Pru-
dence, what means, that sustainability calls for keeping life-supporting
ecosystems and interrelated socioeconomic systems resilient, for avoiding
irreversibilities, and for keeping the scale and impact of human activities
within regenerative and carrying capacities. (5) Security, what means, that

sustainability is a human-centered construct, aimed at ensuring a safe, healthy, high quality of life for current and future generations.

All over all, we find the so called triple bottom line, which consists of the whole set of values, issues and processes that companies must address in order to minimise harm resulting from their activities and to create economic, social and environmental value.

2.2 Less Obvious: Sustainability Needs Human Resource Management

Looking again at the three dimensions of sustainability, we see the need for HRM in the environmental, economic dimension and social dimension:

As to the environmental dimension, "Green HRM Management" as a specific line of research emerges: It involves rethinking and being more mindful of how organisations are operating with respect of the environment (e.g. Tran 2009, p. 24). In this context we find increasing support for the idea of "Green HRM", that analyses how and which HRM activities can support the success of environmental activities of the company (e.g. Wehrmeyer 1996). In doing so, Renwick/Redman/Maguire (2013) propose a framework that consists of (1) developing green abilities, (2) motivating of green employees, and (3) providing of green opportunities. All of these aspects include green activities, such as green issues in job descriptions, in employer branding, or training activities in green management. Muster/ Schrader (2012) make a suggestion for a green work-life balance concept, where the reconciliation of working and private life takes place with regards to environmental values, attitudes, and behaviour. Dubois/Dubois (2012) have showed how environmental sustainability can be linked to Strategic Human Resource Management with the aim of a paradigm shift for organisational members. In that context, the "German Journal of Research in Human Resource Management" published 2011 the special issue "Green Human Resource Management" (e.g. Jackson et al. 2011).

As we look to the social dimension, we find suggestions that result from a more soft HRM perspective. Especially when decisions relate to the shaping of employment relationships, social categories are relevant, as values, emotions, or traditions (Paauwe/Boselie 2008). This development is also triggered by the concept of Corporate Social Responsibility (CSR): Parkes/Borland (2012) argue that HRM's roots as a profession in promoting ethical and socially responsible behaviour enables it to take a progressive role in the most challenging issue for organisations, the lack of ecological sustainability. Within this social context there are issues as psychological contracts, work life balance, or safety and healthy working environment relevant.

Regarding to the economic dimension of sustainability and the link to HRM there exists in general a discussion about the idea, how HR becomes more analytical and able to document the benefits associated with effective HR policies and practices to firms and employees (Kochan 2008, p. 600). Following that line, the journal "Human Resource Management" had, in 2012, also published a special issue about sustainability and the role of HRM with theoretical and practical significance, as sustainability training programs (Vidal-Salazar/Cordón-Pozo/Ferrón-Vilchez 2012) or sustainable incentive programs for middle managers (Merriman/Sen 2012).

Comparing the information available to the three aspects of sustainability, we see strong support for Green HRM, which is aimed at the environmental dimension. However, in terms of the triple bottom line it is still unsolved, how HRM can contribute the social as well the economical as the environmental dimension. This means: The full potential of support for sustainability that could come from HRM has not yet been explored.

Therefore, companies encounter two types of pressure when dealing with sustainability (Wilkinson/Hill/Gollan 2001, p. 1494): first the commercial pressures from increasing environmental imperatives, second the internal pressures associated with the sustainability of human resources in an environment of increasing staff turnovers, declining firm loyalty, or increasing work hours and stress levels. Especially the second aspect emphasises the role of human resources and therefore the relevance of HRM. Basically "[…] they want corporations to reduce the externalities that burden future generations. Sustainability is not just good ethics; it is potentially good long-term economics. HR has an important role to play in sustainability." (Boudreau/Ramstad 2005, p. 134).

Accepting the conceptual fact that HRM could and should play an important role for all three aspects of sustainability and recognising the empirical fact that HRM is definitively in most companies not playing any of these roles at all, the question of "why is it this way" comes up. For this obvious question there is an obvious answer: "Because nobody is responsible for that."

2.3 Not at All Obvious: No Sustainability Without a Strong HR-Department

In a recent study the participants were asked, who is responsible for creating a sustainability strategy within their company: only 6% say that it is HR-department; 36% say it is a senior management team (SHRM 2011). It is of no surprise, that marketing claims responsibility for sustainability (e.g. Crittenden et al. 2012), but basically in the sense of sustainability as an image factor.

Sustainability is rather an issue of norms and values, of incentives, of leadership, and many other factors, which all ultimately result in influencing behaviour. Therefore, we not just talk about HRM in general; we are talking particular about the HR-department as the crucial factor of creating and keeping a culture of sustainability: The HR-department has the most potential to include the idea of sustainability in companies and it can be seen as the most effective driver of sustainable thinking.

However, only a few articles explicitly deal – as we have seen with the case of BP (e.g. Scholz 2010) – with the role of HR-department in the context of sustainability:

On one hand, they give some suggestions what HR's contribution could be for managing sustainability. Wirtenberg et al. (2007) analyse which qualities a sustainable company needs and what is HR's contribution to manage it. Here the role of HR-department is seen as developer, influencer, and helper for business leaders to build a foundation for sustainability strategy. In this context are activities as management of change processes, development of change competencies or support of workforce engagement to be noted.

On the other hand, the articles explore the roles that HR-departments might play to support all members of the company to operate within the framework of sustainability, what competencies they have to contribute or what strategic leadership role HR could play. Rimanoczy/Pearson (2010) argue that HR-department has the responsibility of providing information and educational resources to develop awareness among the workforce. They have to generate the conditions of dialogue, so that all employees understand and agree on what sustainability means, what the corporate goals are and how competencies and skills among all levels of management should be developed. They see the educational role of HR-department as one of the most important within the debate about sustainability, as a key support to the organisation learning to think and act within new paradigms.

Sustainability requires knowledge in a very wide range of topics: in a sustainable context companies need to know how they can prevent their resources from damage – not only natural resources, but also resources such as humans and both intellectual and financial capital.

3. Understanding the Barriers

3.1 Misconception of Sustainability

The first barrier preventing HR to be in the driver's seat for sustainability is a dramatic lack of understanding the meaning of sustainability by HR-professionals: When HR-practitioners do not really understand what sustainability means, they cannot accomplish the task.

A recent study (Institut für Managementkompetenz 2010) asks HR-professionals what they associate with the term sustainability: 48% see a general orientation like a mission statement, on which everyone's acting should base. These activities could lead to the the enhancement of employees' retention (79%) and to more motivation (71%). Only 34% consider the reduction of corporate risks as a relevant effect. Basically, these HR-professionals see sustainability as a message which sells.

Even though they understand that sustainability is a challenge for companies, they do not understand that sustainability requires changes in behaviour and in corporate culture.

As to HR, sustainability involves two crucial aspects: (1) Sustainability within HR-department means that the function by itself has to act sustainable. (2) Sustainability by HR-department means that the function provides knowledge and instruments on a corporate level to become a sustainable company.

3.2 Misconception of Capability

The second barrier relates to the capabilities necessary within the HR-department to ensure successful activities related to sustainability. This problem refers, between others, to the qualification of the managers working in the HR-department, who in many cases do not have a profound HR-background and therefore lack the necessary degree of professionalism.

In particular, it has to be understood, that sustainable HRM within the resource-based view of the firm can provide a competitive advantage (App/Merk/Büttgen 2012, p. 264). If these resources are valuable, rare, non-substitutable, and inimitable, they are considered as important and strategic. In this resource-based logic, sustainable HRM is "the pattern of planned or emerging human resource strategies and practices intended to enable organisational goal achievement while simultaneously reproducing the HR base over a long-lasting calendar time" (Ehnert 2009, p. 74).

Going one step forward, we lack orientation towards dynamic capabilities (e.g. Teece/Pisano/Shuen 1997), that combines the resource-based view with the market-based view and enriches the static perspective with a dynamic perspective of exploration of the future. Both aspects are essential for dealing with sustainability. Therefore, it is obvious that deficits in the HR-department related to these aspects account definitely for HR's incapability of dealing with sustainability.

3.3 Misconception of Responsibility

The third barrier relates to the meaning and the acceptance of the idea "to be responsible and accountable for something".

As Cohen (2011) described correctly, HR managers are usually focused on supporting management requirements while having the right set of employees needed to deliver business and keeping them "satisfied" and motivated; however, as the guardian of corporate culture, HR's role in embedding a sustainable mind-set in any business is crucial. She proposes that the human resource function has a responsibility to be proactive in leading the establishment of a sustainability-enabled culture within the business.

A similar observation has been made in connection with the study mentioned above (Institut für Managementkompetenz 2010): HR-professionals like to decide about sustainability issues and to control the sustainability budget, but they do not like to be responsible with all its consequences.

The concept of responsibility relates to accountability: Being "responsible" means "being accountable". This is in conflict with the traditional role of the HR-department. However, both responsibility and accountability are essential for dealing with sustainability. Therefore, it is obvious that the unwillingness of being measures for their performance related to sustainability accounts for the lack of real activities of the HR-department.

4. Moving Across the Barriers

4.1 Overview

For a strong sustainability alignment and moving across the barriers, companies need the connection to corporate and HR-strategy. This requires also the commitment of the top management. In the end HR-departments have to be responsible and accountable for corporate sustainable behaviour in enterprises, which calls for skills and decision-making power of the HR-professionals. Therefore the following seven steps are necessary in order to move the HR-department across the barriers.

4.2 Connecting Sustainabiliy with (HR-)Strategy

Sustainability must be part of the corporate strategy and of the HR-strategy: Explicit statements dealing with economic, environmental, and social aspects are required. Today most of stock listed companies have sustainability as part of their corporate strategy because their stakeholders (in particular, shareholders) demand sustainable behaviour.

In the sustainability report of Adidas for instance the following statement can be found: "One core aspect is about striking the balance between business needs and social and environmental demands. This requires integrating sustainability into our business strategy and our day-to-day operations." (Adidas Group 2013, p. 5) They formulate also sustainable aims as (1) Achieving environmental sustainability and managing scarce resources; (2) Respecting human rights and driving social compliance in our supply chain, or (3) Developing our employees.

For the inclusion of sustainability as part of the (HR-)strategy there are many interesting options, one of them being the idea of diversity: Having a company which is not biased towards specific age groups, sex, ethnographic backgrounds, or other characteristics, usually leads to a more stable strategy, since the variety of the strategy reflects the variety of the society the company belongs to.

In this case, it is important to understand that sustainability is not a task for a company which is successful and can afford to act in a responsible way: Going for sustainability is not caused by success. It is an explanation for success.

4.3 Commitment of the CEO as Condition

Before companies formulate, implement and execute a sustainable sustainability strategy, the top management including the CEO has to commit to sustainability as a must-be-behaviour.

This condition is necessary because of two reasons: (1) A CEO is responsible and accountable for the long-term oriented corporate performance. Some of German and international laws and rules demand sustainable behaviour as for instance the "Gesetz zur Angemessenheit der Vorstandsvergütung", where the remuneration of the CEO has to be in line with the ideas of a sustainable management. (2) A CEO acts as role model for all other employees. The sustainable behaviour of the CEO can be transferred to the whole members of the company. He gives the direction and the desirable behaviour.

4.4 Strong Chief-HR-Officer as Chief-Sustainability-Officer

Contrary to the existent trend, where companies (such as SAP) work without a specialised Chief-HR-Officer, companies need a strong Chief-HR-Officer, who is simultaneously the Chief-Sustainability-Officer. Strong means, that the Chief-HR-Officer (as Chief-Sustainability-Officer) has to be part of the "C-suite" as reinforcement of the corporate relevance of this role (e.g. Müller-Stewens 2012).

HR-related issues are crucial for many fields of sustainability, such as diversity, demographic developments, human rights and safety working conditions, long-term oriented training and development, compensation and benefits (as remuneration of management) and incentives policy. The relevance of that we saw in the first section of our article: These challenges include all three dimensions of sustainability.

Therefore, the Chief-HR-Officer needs decision-making power as part of the "C-suite" both for HRM issues and sustainability issues.

4.5 Sustainability-Assessment for the HR-Department

Sustainability within the HR-department needs a specification, what the triple bottom line means for core HRM activities (Table 1). For example, as we look to the activity "Recruitment & Selection" from an environmental perspective, companies can use green job descriptions and recruit employees, who are green aware. In an economic perspective (with effects on the environmental dimension) one part of selection process could be a video (skype) call (instead of local interview, where travelling is necessary).

Therefore, HR-department needs an assessment of how sustainable their processes, activities, and behaviours really are.

HRM activities	Triple bottom line sustainability		
	Economic	Environmental	Social
Planning & Forecasting			
Recruitment & Selection			
Staffing & Diversity			
Training & Development			
Performance & Appraisal			
Compensation & Benefit			
Leadership & Motivation			
Corporate Culture & Change			

Table 1: HRM Activities and their Connection to Triple Bottom Line

4.6 Role Clarification of the HR-Department with Respect to Sustainability

One necessary step for the HR-department to become more sustainable is to develop relevant and crucial competencies of the HR-professionals.

Competence must be interpreted as a two dimension model: They need competencies as skills and they need competencies as decision-making power. These two dimensions can be low or high. Putting these competencies together it results in the "Competence4HR-matrix", with its four roles for the HR-department (Figure 1). For sustainability in particular the fourth role "governance" makes sense, where HR-department has both, high decision-making power and high skills in Human Resource and Sustainability Management.

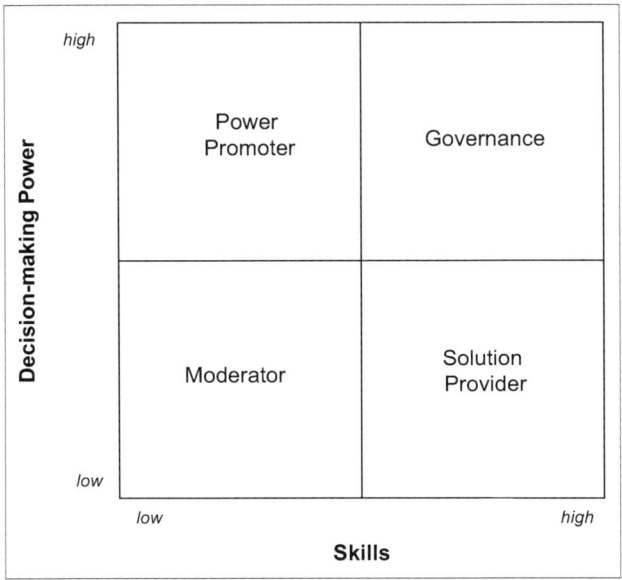

Figure 1:   Competence4HR-Matrix
(Source: Scholz 2011, p. 7)

Competencies as skills include: System thinking, knowledge and understanding about green HRM, knowledge about sustainable HRM instruments (e.g. incentive systems), knowledge about dynamic capabilities, or knowledge about measurement and controlling of sustainability. These skills relate to the core HRM activities with their manifestations in the triple bottom line.

Competencies as decision-making power include the following features: HR-department is a respected lobbyist for sustainability issues, is accountable for its sustainability activities, is responsible for corporate sustainability budget, as well as for internal and external communication dealing with sustainability.

4.7 Sustainability-Training for the HR-Department

HR-professionals need an extensive training in issues of sustainability. This training must increase awareness of the relevance of sustainability and the role of HR-department in becoming a sustainable company. In this training, HR-professionals also have to work on the two dimensions of competencies: skills and decision-making power. Finally the HR-department has to learn about strategy and business impact, in order to formulate and execute together with top-management a sustainability strategy.

4.8 Sustainability Management by the HR-Department

To implement sustainability into the "head and heart" of the organisation, a cultural change is necessary. This change is to be guided by the HR-department. A cultural change into the direction of sustainability requires communication with employees to provide knowledge and dialogue about this change, from corporate culture change to work system change and other opportunities.

Therefore, the whole management function (planning, governance, optimisation, measurement, and controlling) of all sustainability dimensions is to be structured by the HR-department, which eventually is not only responsible, but also accountable for corporate sustainability.

5. Getting Started Now!

In order to go for sustainability, it is tempting to transform "sustainability" into an external oriented communication message. For that, the communication department or the marketing department are potential institutions. But the real power of sustainability with respect to the ecological, economic and social environment unfolds itself only if it is really connected to real behaviour, which means, connected to the people in the company on all levels.

Therefore only the HR-department could be in the position to change employees' behaviour through organisational and personnel development. But we see huge barriers, which can only be crossed through cultural changes in their minds and in their behaviour. These barriers are far from being trivial. They explain why (beyond rhetoric) there is no real progress in dealing with sustainability. However, overcoming these barriers is without alternatives.

This idea of sustainability has to be a part of the guiding beliefs of the company and therefore of its culture. That is an HR-issue. To master it, we need the HR-department. Only then we can avoid cases such as BP, Lehmann and HP. And only then we will enter a sustainable way of dealing with sustainability.

References

ADIDAS GROUP (2013): Sustainability Progress Report 2012: Performance Counts.

AMBEC, S.; LANOIE, P. (2008): Does it Pay to Be Green? A Systematic Overview, in: The Academy of Management Perspectives, Vol. 22, No. 4, pp. 45-62.

APP, S.; MARK, J.; BÜTTGEN, M. (2012): Employer Branding: Sustainable HRM as a Competitive Advantage in the Market for High-Quality Employees, in: Management Review, Vol. 23, No. 3, pp. 262-278.

BOUDREAU, J.W.; RAMSTAD, P.M. (2005): Talentship, Talent Segmentation, and Sustainability: A New HR Decision Science Paradigm for a New Strategy Definition, in: Human Resource Management, Vol. 44, No. 2, pp. 129-136.

BP (2013): Gulf of Mexico Restoration, http://www.bp.com/en/global/corporate/gulf-o f-mexico-restoration/deepwater-horizon-accident-and-response.html, accessed on August 20, 2013.

BRINKMANN, B. (2012): 27.000 Entlassungen und viele verpasste Chancen, http://w ww.sueddeutsche.de/wirtschaft/hewlett-packards-weg-aus-der-krise-entlassungen-u nd-viele-verpasste-chancen-1.1365405, accessed on August 20, 2013.

COCHRANE, J.H. (2010): Lessons from the Financial Crisis, in: Regulation, Winter 2009-2010, pp. 34-37.

COHEN, E. (2011): Changing a Culture, in: Human Resources Manager International Issue, Vol. 1, pp. 7-9.

CRITTENDEN, V.L.; CRITTENDEN, W.F.; FERRELL, L.K.; FERRELL, O.C.; PINNEY, C.C. (2011): Market-Oriented Sustainability: A Conceptual Framework and Propositions, in: Journal of the Academic Marketing Science, Vol. 39, No. 1, pp. 71-85.

DUBOIS, C.L.Z.; DUBOIS, D.A. (2012): Strategic HRM as Social Design for Environmental Sustainability in Organizations, in: Human Resource Management, Vol. 51, No. 6, pp. 799-826.

EHNERT, I. (2009): Sustainable Human Resource Management: A Conceptual and Exploratory Analysis from a Paradox Perspective, dissertation, University of Bremen.

EISENHARDT, K.M.; MARTIN, J.A. (2000): Dynamic Capabilities: What are They?, in: Strategic Management Journal, Vol. 21, No. 10-11, pp. 1105-1121.

ELKINGTON, J. (1997): Cannibals with Forks: The Triple Bottom Line of 21st Century Business, Oxford.

GALDWIN, T.N.; KENNELLY, J.J.; KRAUSE, T.S. (1995): Shifting Paradigms for Sustainable Development: Implications for Management Theory and Research, in: Academy of Management Review, Vol. 20, No. 4, pp. 874-907.

INSTITUT FÜR MANAGEMENTKOMPETENZ (Ed.) (2010): Kompetenz4HR: Nachhaltigkeit in der Personalarbeit in Österreich, Saarbrücken.

JACKSON, S.E.; RENWICK, D.W.S.; JABBOUR, C.J.C.; MULLER-CAMEN, M. (2011): State-of-the-Art and Future Directions for Green Human Resource Management: Introduction to the Special Issue, in: Zeitschrift für Personalforschung, Vol. 25, No. 2, pp. 99-116.

KOCHAN, T.A. (2008): Social Legitimacy of the HRM Profession: A US Perspective, in: BOXALL, P.; PURCELL, J.; WRIGHT, P. (Eds.): The Oxford Handbook of Human Resource Management, Oxford, pp. 599-619.

KURTZ, R.S. (2013): Oil Spill Causation and the Deepwater Horizon Spill, in: Review of Policy Research, Vol. 30, No. 4, pp. 366-380.

MERRIMAN, K.K.; SEN, S. (2012): Incenting Managers Toward the Triple Bottom Line: An Agency and Social Norm Perspective, in: Human Resource Management, Vol. 51, No. 6, pp. 851-872.

MÜLLER-STEWENS, G. (2012): Die Corporate HR-Funktion: Bereit für einen Stammplatz in der "C-Suite"?, in: STEIN, V.; MÜLLER, S. (Eds.): Aufbruch des strategischen Personalmanagements in die Dynamisierung: Ein Gedanke für Christian Scholz, München et al., pp. 59-66.

MUSTER, V.; SCHRADER, U. (2012): Green Work-Life Balance: A New Perspective for Green HRM, in: Zeitschrift für Personalforschung, Vol. 25, No. 2, pp. 140-156.

PAAUWE, J.; BOSELIE, P. (2008): HRM and Social Embeddedness, in: BOXALL, P.; PURCELL, J.; WRIGHT, P. (Eds.): The Oxford Handbook of Human Resource Management, Oxford, pp. 166-184.

PARKES, C.; BORLAND, H. (2012): Strategic HRM: Transforming its Responsibilities Toward Ecological Sustainability: The Greatest Global Challenge Facing Organizations, in: Thunderbird International Business Review, Vol. 54, No. 6, pp. 811-824.

PELOZA, J.; LOOCK, M.; CERRUTI, J.; MUYOT, M. (2012): Sustainability: How Stakeholder Perceptions Differ from Corporate Reality, in: California Management Review, Vol. 55, No. 1, pp. 74-95.

RENWICK, D.W.; REDMAN, T.; MAGUIRE, S. (2013): Green Human Resource Management: A Review and Research Agenda, in: International Journal of Management Review, Vol. 15, No. 1, pp. 1-14.

RIMANOCZY, I.; PEARSON, T. (2010): Role of HR in the New World of Sustainability, in: Industrial and Commercial Training, Vol. 42, No. 1, pp. 11-17.

SCHOLZ, C. (2010): BP-Ölkatastrophe: Schuld der Personalabteilung?, http://derstand ard.at/1277338803917/Fuehrungskrise-BP-Oelkatastrophe-Schuld-der-Personalabte ilung, accessed on August 20, 2013.

SCHOLZ, C. (2011): Kompetenz4HR; Plädoyer für eine etwas andere Personalabteilung, in: SCHWUCHOW, K.; GUTMANN, J. (Eds.): Jahrbuch Personalentwicklung 2011: Ausbildung, Weiterbildung, Management Development, München et al., pp. 5-11.

SHRM/BSR/AUROSOORYA (2010): Advancing Sustainability: HR's Role: A Research Report.

SUTTON, P. (1998): The Sustainability-Promoting Firm, in: Greener Management International Journal, Vol. 23, pp. 127-152.

TEECE, D.J.; PISANO, G.; SHUEN, A. (1997): Dynamic Capabilities and Strategic Management, in: Strategic Management Journal, Vol. 18, No. 7, pp. 509-533.

TRAN, B. (2009): Green Management: The Reality of Being Green in Business, in: Journal of Economics, Finance and Administrative Science, Vol. 14, No. 27, pp. 21-45.

VIDAL-SALAZAR, M.D.; CORDÓN-POZO, E.; FERRÓN-VILCHEZ, V. (2012): Human Resource Management and Developing Proactive Environmental Strategies: The Influence of Environmental Training and Organizational Learning, in: Human Resource Management, Vol. 51, No. 6, pp. 905-934.

WCED (WORLD COMMISSION ON ENVIRONMENT AND DEVELOPMENT) (1987): Our Common Future, Oxford.

WEHRMEYER, W. (1996): Greening People: Human Resources and Environmental Management, Sheffield.

WILKINSON, A.; HILL, M.; GOLLAN, P. (2001): The Sustainability Debate, in: International Journal of Operations & Production Management, Vol. 21, No. 12, pp. 1492-1501.

WIRTENBERG, J.; HARMON, J.; RUSSELL, W.G.; FAIRFIELD, K.D. (2007): HR's Role in Building a Sustainable Enterprise: Insights from Some of the World's Best Companies, in: Human Resource Planning, Vol. 30, No. 1, pp. 10-20.

Part 2:
Macroeconomic Perspectives

The Rule of "No-Bail-Out" in the European Monetary Union: Why it Failed to be Sustainable

Heinz-Jürgen Axt

Overview

1. Introduction

When the Treaty of Maastricht laid the foundation for the European Monetary Union (EMU) in 1992, one of its core elements was the so called "no-bail-out clause". No Euro partner should be obliged to be liable for the debt of other states. Bundeskanzler Helmut Kohl appeased the public in Germany by arguing that no country could be forced to provide financial assistance to highly indebted states: "Meine Damen und Herren, nach der vertraglichen Regelung gibt es keine Haftung der Gemeinschaft für Verbindlichkeiten der Mitgliedsstaaten und keine zusätzlichen Finanztransfers" (Focus 2012). Reality, however, tells a different story. When the debt crisis started in Greece in October 2009 one "rescue umbrella" after the other was established to bail-out Greece and further Euro states. Actually financial assistance to the debt states is provided in the form of credits. However, it is disputed whether these loans will be repaid. If a new debt restructuring e.g. for Greece proves to be inevitable it would be the tax payer in the donor states who has to pay the bill, as more than 80% of Greece's foreign debt was financed by public authorities (see Jahn/Plickert 2013, p. 11).[1]

This article will analyse the reasons why the core element of the no-bail-out clause has been ignored and why this fundamental principle failed to be sustainable. For that purpose sustainability will be discussed from a political scientist's perspective, jurisprudential arguments are neglected. Another question will be to which extent the double-structure of the EMU – national competences in economic policy and European competences in monetary policy – had an influence. That implies the validity of the control mechanism which was established with the "Stability and Growth Pact" in 1997. As policy-makers were not inactive since the outbreak of the crisis it is necessary to assess the reforms of the Eurozone. Based on studies of the author in the past the basic argument offered here is that *contagion* of further Euro states was the main reason which undermined sustainability of the no-bail-out rule (Axt 2011, pp. 70). As financial markets had become extremely nervous since the outbreak of the debt crisis politicians did everything to calm down the markets. That leads to the main thesis as it has been formulated by experts of Bertelsmann Foundation recently: "While Greece defaulting on its sovereign debt and leaving the European Monetary Union would in and of itself have a relatively minor effect on the world economy, such a move could, however, undermine investor confidence in the Portuguese, Spanish and Italian capital markets and thus provoke not only a sovereign default in those states as well, but also a severe worldwide recession" (Bertelsmann Stiftung 2012).[2]

2. Public Debt and Sustainability

Max Weber has taught that modern and efficient structures of the economy and the administration are dependent on rules and durable institutions. That leads to legal authority and makes the difference to traditional or charismatic ruling (see Weber 1972). Rules are important to provide security on the behaviour of other actors, may it be individuals, organisations or states. When the no-bail-out clause has been fixed in the Maastricht Treaty the intention was that all members of the future Eurozone would handle debt rules in a coherent manner, so that negative processes of spill over could be avoided. The architects of the Treaty were aware of the dangers mismanagement of public debt in one country would have for other countries. With respect to public debt the centrepiece of sustainability becomes obvious. As far as economics is concerned, sustainability implies a careful management of resources which gives a guarantee that future generations can enjoy a good life. Or as the Brundtland Commission of the United Nations has put it in 1987: "Sustainable development is development that meets the needs of the present without compromising the ability of future generations to meet their own needs" (United Nations General Assembly 1987). This definition makes clear that sustainable development depends on ecological respect but should be understood in a broader sense.

As far as the well-being of future generations is concerned two aspects are of importance: *First*, mismanagement of public debt has negative consequences for the future. The actual generation may benefit when the state maximises public debt as it provides more finance for consumption. But future generations suffer when they have to pay the bill, i.e. raising interest rates, increasing dependence on creditors and shrinking means for consumption and securing life. Although there is a vivid discussion among economists about the effects of public deficit – Paul Krugman e.g. opposes the general assumption of negative effects (see e.g. Krugman 2012) – the liberal oriented Maastricht Treaty is more strict on debt limitation. *Second*, to avoid negative effects rules have been concluded. Among them the no-bail-out clause plays a prominent role as it intends to avoid that excessive debt leads to negative developments in the future. And only under the precondition that public debt is restricted to a certain maximum the functioning of a monetary union can be called to be sustainable. Therefore three questions must be answered: How did the EMU try to sustain a credible debt management? Why were the provisions neglected? And is there hope that reforms will solve the existing problems?

3. Debt Management Under the Maastricht Treaty

When the EMU was concluded in 1992 compromises had to be made. One of these compromises was the structure of the new project. Although it was named "Economic and Monetary Union" it was in fact a Europeanised Monetary but not a Europeanised Economic Union. Competences to handle all issues concerning the new currency "Euro" were handed over to the European level, mainly to the European Central Bank (ECB). Monetary policy – which deals with price stability and interest rates – is run independently by the ECB in the Euro area. It aims for stable and low consumer price inflation. The ECB's monetary policy's primary objective is to maintain price stability and to safeguard the value of the Euro. Contrary to that national governments were free in their choice of economic preferences as long as they meet the so called convergence criteria. Fiscal policy – which concerns decisions about taxation, spending and borrowing – is still the responsibility of the member states' governments. However, budgetary decisions taken in the member states can have an impact throughout the Euro area and the entire EU. These decisions must therefore conform to rules set at EU level, which put limits on government debt and deficit. Other economic policy making – such as decisions about the labour market, pension systems and other policy areas in the economy – is also the responsibility of the member states' governments.

The key EU instrument for coordinating and guiding economic policy making in

the member states is the Stability and Growth Pact. It sets two main rules:

The government debt may not exceed 60 % of GDP and the national deficit may not be greater than 3% of GDP. The main purpose of these criteria was to keep public deficit and debt under control and to avoid negative external effects. In defending this complicate structure the principle of subsidiarity can be advocated as freedom of action for national authorities was secured. Critics, however, argue that a monetary union without a centralisation of competences in the form of a "European Economic Government" would suffer from a constructional default.

The fact that an agreement was reached in Maastricht to transfer monetary but not economic policy jurisdiction to the supranational level was primarily due to the conflicting positions of France and Germany. Germany insisted that the ECB should be politically independent and maintain a commitment to price stability. France responded by demanding common economic governance. However, France's main concern was not to introduce supranational steering of economic policy, but to subject the ECB to the political influence of the governments of the Eurozone countries. As these countries no longer had recourse to the tool of "external" devaluation of their national currencies in order to improve their competitiveness vis-à-vis trade partners, their only remaining option was to resort to "internal" devaluation through adequate wage and price flexibility. Contrary to the German willingness at that time to resign on national competences and to establish a Political Union it was the French President Francois Mitterand who brought a different concept into the debate; it was the construction of a European Economic Government. This concept was by no means an equivalent to the Political Union. France was not in favour of a supranational Political Union but followed three targets: *First*, the influence of politics should be increased and the role of the markets decreased. *Second*, France preferred instead of a supranational concept an intergovernmental collaboration of governments. *Third*, France wanted to have a political counter-weight against the ECB.

How was it possible to achieve a sustain credible debt management? Under the Maastricht Treaty, every Eurozone country must adhere to the principles of sound financial and budgetary management and cannot expect its partners to take on liability for its debts. This no-bail-out clause is enshrined in Article 125 of the Treaty on the Functioning of the European Union (TFEU): "The Union shall not be liable for or assume the commitments of central governments, regional, local or other public authorities, other bodies governed by public law, or public undertakings of any Member State, without prejudice to mutual financial guarantees for the joint execution of a specific project. A Member State shall not be liable for or assume the commitments of central governments, regional, local or other public authorities, other bodies governed by public law, or public undertakings of another Member State, without prejudice to mutual financial guarantees for the joint execution of a specific project." Article 123 TFEU prohibits the European Central Bank from granting overdraft facilities to Member States. The ECB is not legitimated to purchase debt instruments directly from the member states or national central banks.

As we will see later, Art. 125 TFEU has not been interpreted consistently. As far as the words "shall not be liable" are concerned, we have to realise that there exist two different if not contradictory interpretations at least: The *first* one is wide-spread in the Northern part of Europe. "Shall not be liable" is understood here as "it is not allowed" to bail-out highly indebted Euro countries. The *second* interpretation can be heard quite often in the Southern part of Europe: "Shall not be liable" is interpreted in that way that no Euro partner is obliged to bail-out its highly indebted partners but it can do it if it wants. What is the background of these alternative interpretations? The Northern European understanding relied on the assumption that the no-bail-out clause would safeguard that all Euro members comply with the Maastricht criteria of maximum deficit and debt. By that way the stability of the Euro area would be guaranteed. The Southern European interpretation, on the other hand, was based on the assumption that bail-out transfers were nothing more than a justified compensation for less competitive economies, for development gaps, or for higher deficits in current account balances (see Tsoukalis 1997, pp. 137). (And to be frank, the Southern European interpretation in that case starts in France.)

4. How Rules Were Undermined – the Prehistory

The provisions of the Monetary Union were not taken seriously. Limits of deficit and debt have been ignored by many states. This was the case with Germany, France and Italy in the booster phase of the Monetary Union. The bad example was followed by other states. Although Germany was keen to ensure, with the Stability and Growth Pact, that the Eurozone countries adhered to sound budgetary management principles, Germany's own actions contributed to the softening of the Pact. In 2005, the Brussels European Council amended the Stability Pact and eased the criteria for defining what constitutes an "excessive deficit" (Axt 2010). Financial markets tolerated higher debt rates in the past but they became very suspicious and hyper nervous after 2008 when they demanded higher interest rates and credit default swaps from highly indebted countries. And lastly, the rating agencies also deserve criticism for failing to fulfil their responsibilities, particularly for their considerable delay in warning of the risks posed by Euro countries with a very high level of debt (see Belke/Burghof 2010). Instead of increasing international competitiveness the peripheral countries made use of the declining interest rates after they joined the Eurozone to increase wages especially in the public service.

5. Testing the Thesis: Fear of Contagion Eroded the No-Bail-Out Clause

In order to test the basic assumption that fear of contagion was the main reason why Euro partners decided to shelve the concerns with respect to the obligations stemming from the no-bail-out clause it proves to be helpful to discuss advantages and disadvantages of alternative attempts to solve the debt crisis in the Eurozone. By the way, the Government of Germany had to be extremely cautious as it was under permanent surveillance of its Constitutional Court. In order not to conflict with European or national law the Federal Government was in favour of bilateral "pooled" loans from the Eurozone countries instead of loans from the Euro area as a whole when it came to the first financial assistance package for Greece in May 2010 (for details see Bild 2010). The legal basis for the granting of these bilateral loans and credits was Article 122 TFEU, which states that "in a spirit of solidarity", where a Member State is in difficulties caused by "natural disasters or exceptional occurrences" beyond its control, the Union may grant financial assistance to the Member State concerned.[3]

What were the alternatives at hand in order to assist Greece and stabilise the Eurozone (see Axt 2011)? Five alternatives were under discussion: Following the first option Greece like other countries would leave the Eurozone and return to a national currency. The second solution would be a (hard) debt restructuring as it was done e.g. in the case of Russia in 2000, Argentine in 2005 or Ukraine in 2000. A "soft" debt restructuring as the third option would rely on the reduction of interest rates and/or an extension of the terms of loans given to Greece. Common loans of the Eurozone, so called Eurobonds, which would offer lower interest rates to heavily indebted countries, constitute the fourth alternative. And finally, the fifth option would be to assist countries like Greece with fresh money and putting back the regulations stemming from the no-bail-out clause.

To provide a more systematic analysis of what are the chances and risks of the options mentioned ten questions had to be be answered by the authorities:

1. What will be the reaction of *rating agencies* concerning the alternatives mentioned above? Although these agencies must be criticised as they had given positive credit ratings to institutions like the Lehman bank which led into the global financial crisis of 2008 and underestimated the critical situation in the Eurozone, it cannot be ignored that investors rely on these rating agencies when they decide where to invest their money.

2. A second question concerns the reactions of the *financial markets*. Will they provide acceptable conditions with respect to interest rates and credit default swaps when one of the alternative options is chosen?

3. What are the consequences for *domestic financial institutions*? Will banks e.g. have a chance to survive or will savers transfer their mon-

ey abroad, so that banks will no longer be able to provide credits to enterprises in the highly indebted states?

4. What are the consequences for *creditor banks*? Do they suffer from substantial losses when borrowing states do not fulfil their obligations? As it was mentioned before, private banks of the Eurozone have reduced their engagement in crisis states and loans are provided by other member states.

5. Every alternative option has to answer the question what the consequences for the *stabilisation of the country* with an excessive debt are. Will revenue of the state budget increase and expenditure decrease so that the deficit will be reduced in a shorter and the debt in a longer time period? Financial assistance is provided on strict conditions set by the Eurozone and the IMF.

6. As states try to avoid political costs it is inevitable that the reduction of excessive deficits and the implementation of stabilisation programmes are put under *surveillance*. Two alternatives are at hand: First, surveillance can be carried out by *political* mechanisms – among them the convergence criteria and the Stability and Growth Pact. Second, control can be accomplished by the *markets* in a very simple manner: Markets can sanction states with excessive deficits and debts by demanding higher interest rates and credit default swaps.

7. If stabilisation programmes of heavily indebted countries concentrate on expenditure reduction and revenue increase exclusively a major problem will not be tackled: These states have to strengthen *economic growth* and improve *competitiveness*. The more an economy grows the smaller the debt as a percentage of the GDP will become and the easier the access to fresh money will be.

8. As Greece is not the only country with an excessive deficit the risk is given that other states in the Eurozone like Portugal, Ireland, Italy, Spain, or even France could be infected. So, alternative options to solve the problems of Greece must intend to avoid *contagion*. That could happen when investors pull out of countries or raise interest rates significantly as they perceive measures taken to rescue Greece too negative.

9. *Financial costs* of every rescue package cannot be neglected. Nearly every country has been forced to consolidate public finances and to cut social expenditure. Under such circumstances it is a sensitive issue when financial assistance is provided to countries which ignored the principles of solid housekeeping.

10. And finally *political costs* might occur when dissatisfaction with rescue measures lead to growing nationalist tendencies and to national animosity.

6. Alternative Options: Chances and Risks

The first scenario, a country *leaves the Eurozone,* has to take into account that no country can be forced to do that as the treaties of the European Union do not foresee such an alternative. Positive implications of such a (more theoretical) scenario would be: As far as prices are concerned the country would become more competitive by the chance of devaluation of its currency. This would have a positive impact on growth rates and finally lead to more competitiveness. On the other hand the country's debt still would be signed in Euro. With its devalued national currency the country would not be in a position to pay its dues. The rating agencies would assume that a state cannot longer trust in "solidarity" of the Eurozone and therefore warn to invest in the country leaving the Euro area. Debt conditions would deteriorate. Banks in countries leaving the Eurozone would have no chance to survive as clients would deplete their accounts immediately. Creditor banks on the other hand would face problems if their credits would not be repaid. Whether a state follows a strict policy of consolidation is a critical question: If policy makers gain for some form of debt relief the will to follow a strict course of stabilisation could be weakened as governments try to avoid political costs. Although competitiveness can be improved under such conditions by devaluation it must be anticipated that depression would dominate for a long time. And contagion to other highly indebted countries would be probable.

The second option, a *debt restructuring,* is the favourite among economists, who argue that private creditors benefit from the financial crisis of Euro members as they realised high interest rates which are guaranteed by financial assistance of the Eurozone. In the case of a debt restructuring not only the tax payers but also the creditors would have to take over some costs of financial assistance for the heavily indebted states. For creditors a debt restructuring implies that they have to charge off at least parts of their credits. In such a case rating agencies would declare immediately a "default", consequently a country like Greece would no longer have access to the financial markets. Banks in Greece would go bankrupt as the exodus of capital would be the consequence. That is why partners from the Eurozone might think about financial assistance for these banks. To which extent creditor banks would face severe problems depends from the level of their financial investment in the country in question. Under such conditions the control over stabilisation programs would be executed by markets mainly. Without a convincing programme of consolidation the financial markets would be closed for states after a debt restructuring. A longer time of depression is unavoidable and can be shortened by drastic reforms only. The problem of contagion would be significant due to the reaction of rating agencies and financial markets which mistrust other heavily indebted states and anticipate a debt restructuring here also.

Whereas some economists prefer a "hard restructuring" many prominent policy makers are in favour of a "*soft restructuring*". To some extent the Euro partners have followed already the method of a soft restructuring when they extended the credit period for Greece from 3 to 7 ½ years and reduced the interest rates. The crucial question is: Will rating agencies come to negative assessments and will financial markets follow their estimations? If yes the soft restructuring would become a hard one. If not the soft restructuring had advantages especially as the risk of a contagion of other heavily indebted states would be reduced. On the other hand if the restructuring would be a soft one this could become very critical for domestic banks as they hold big parts of their states' debts. When creditor banks agree to a soft restructuring it is highly probable that they demand state guarantees for the security of the loans provided.[4] The pressure for severe programs of consolidation would be weaker than it would be in the case of a hard restructuring. The surveillance of such programs would be a political one with all the weaknesses mentioned above. Whether growth and competitiveness can be improved that depends from the course followed the government of the indebted state. The pressure to do it is limited as long as the perception prevails that getting fresh money is no problem.

The interest rates demanded from countries in the Eurozone differ significantly. Germany's interest rates tend to lower than 1% for a 10-year sovereign bond yield whereas markets demanded from Greece more than 30% in early 2012. That led to the idea whether it wouldn't be favourable when countries enjoying an excellent rating would take loans with favourable conditions and transfer these loans to countries in the Eurozone from which markets demand higher interest rates. That is the basic idea of "*Eurobonds*". One risk will be the perspective that rating agencies would downgrade the donor states as investments here are assessed to be more risky. Financial markets could follow and demand higher interest rates as they feel insecurity when Eurobonds are transferred to countries with lower credit standing. Negative effects could harm donor states but not the banks. Domestic as well as creditor banks had no reason to assess their investments in heavily indebted states as insecure. Under such conditions the pressure to follow a strict course of stabilisation and consolidation would be weakened. The lever that markets exercise control over these programs would be abolished. Improvement of growth and competitiveness would depend totally on the course of governments. The positive news, however, is that contagion to other massively indebted states would be restricted. Contagion would be a problem for countries with a positive rating. And the main question is whether Eurobonds are acceptable to the public in donor countries. When people in the European Union were asked about their attitude towards Eurobonds a mere 26% of the respondents in Germany responded positively.[5]

The last option is eliminating concerns with respect to the no-bail-out clause and providing "*fresh money*" for those countries which have no chance of re-financing their debt by the financial markets at acceptable conditions. In such a case the rating agencies' response is more or less neutral as they do not see any reason to downgrade or upgrade a country. The same should be anticipated from the markets' reaction. Financial markets surely would be calmed down. Interest rates would be kept on nearly the same – high – level. Perspectives of domestic as well as creditor banks should be positive as they do not have to be afraid of any sort of "haircut". It is not very likely that a government follows a strict course of consolidation if it can avoid it. As the control is carried out by political mechanisms exclusively bad experiences with the Stability and Growth Pact rise up once again. The chances for improving growth and competitiveness depend on the decisions taken by the government which enjoys financial assistance once again. As far as contagion is concerned the markets do not have convincing reasons to increase interest rates for other highly indebted countries. And policy makers intention to calm down financial markets could be met more probably.

Having discussed alternative options the questions arises: What is the price of these alternatives in financial terms? It is evident that such a calculation must be tentative and rough. Asked to calculate the costs for Germany if loans are not repaid the Federal Ministry of Finance gives the figure of 95,3 bn Euro as maximum. Other sources come to 122 bn Euro and the "Ifo-Instiut" in Munich assumes that 623 bn Euro would be realistic

(Jahn/Plickert 2013, p. 11). As mentioned above political costs have to be taken into account too. In the case of Greece and other highly indebted countries it might be a question of time when people throw governments out of office and political instability is the consequence. On the other hand people in the "donor countries" become more and more critical over financial assistance to the favour of highly indebted countries. Governments can come under pressure, animosities increase and lead into nationalist and anti-integrations movements.

7. Ignoring the Rules and Amending the Treaty

All alternatives discussed above have severe negative implications. A "silver bullet" out of the crisis is not in sight. So, a last question shall be answered: Which option is favourable to whom? *Banks in Greece* and other heavily indebted countries have to fear nearly every attempt to solve the crisis. Only in the case of fresh money and Eurobonds their future existence is not endangered. In all other cases they will survive only when state aid is guaranteed from the Eurozone. The same holds true with respect to *creditor banks*. For them, however, it is important to which extent they are engaged in the crisis states. As we have seen private banks have reduced their engagement and devalued their credits to Greece to the fallen market prices. Nevertheless, the more stable countries in the Eurozone are aware of the banks' request for rescue measures.

As far as *Greece and other states in trouble* are concerned the option of fresh money is the most favourable perspective for them: Refinancing their debt would be secured, own banks would not come under pressure and the control over the stabilisation program would be a political one, leaving some room of action. The pressure from the markets is limited. It is important to note that perspectives for growth and competitiveness are critical if not negative in all options. Only in the case that governments are in a position to implement substantial reforms even against massive protest positive prospects are in sight.

Contagion of other Euro members from the Greek drama is a core concern of policy makers in the Eurozone. From this perspective two alternatives – Greece leaves the Eurozone and a hard debt restructuring is executed – are the most dangerous cases of all. Economists perceive it to be helpful that markets define the rules of the game. For politicians that has negative implications of contagion. For them fresh money, Eurobonds and soft restructuring are less risky to infect other countries. Under such circumstances the no-bail-out clause had to come under pressure and was no longer the absolute priority. *At first, the no-bail-out rule has been ignored and afterwards the treaty has been revised and complemented.* A new article 136 of the TFEU allows bail-out activities when the Eurozone is endangered as a whole . With the establishment of the *European Stability Mechanism* (ESM) and the completion of *Art. 136 TFEU* the way has been paved to permanent financial transfers in the Eurozone. The newly added text reads as follows: "Member States whose currency is the Euro may establish a stability mechanism to be activated if indispensable to safeguard the stability of the Euro area as a whole. The granting of any required financial assistance under the mechanism will be made subject to strict conditionality" (Official Journal of the European Union 2011).

What has been done to stabilise the Euro area (see European Commission 2012a)? A *"sixpack"* of legal acts has sharpened the Stability and Growth Pact. Surveillance has been strengthened and sanctions became a little bit more automatically. The "European semester" has been introduced. The *"Euro-Plus-Compact"* is demanding more international competitiveness and employment. The *Fiscal Compact* has obliged all participating states (not the United Kingdom and the Czech Republic) to establish debt brakes preferably in their constitutions. Although this is an intergovernmental agreement it was made possible to integrate the ruling of the European Court of Justice. And the *"Twopack"* obliges the member states to follow common rules of their budgets which are supervised by independent agencies. Future will show whether these reforms will make rules more "weather-proof" when contagion will threat the Euro area once again. The option that states could become insolvent and that this could help to make norms and rules more sustainable was not considered seriously.

8. Conclusions: Subsidiarity of Rules

What are the lessons with respect to the principle of subsidiarity? The case chosen here demonstrates that at least three factors may be relevant for the sustainability of rules: weighting of risks, time and pressure from the public. When heads of Euro states decided to bail-out Greece and further states afterwards the risks were numerous: breaching the EU Treaty, endangering the stability of the Euro area, challenging the Common Market and the European economic integration as as whole, unmanageable financial transfers. Policy-makers came to the conclusion that despite all hazards the option to ignore the no-bail-out rule – or to be more precise: to switch to article 122 TFEU in a more than dubious manner (see above) – would imply the least risky solution. Action was perceived as unavoidable as the convergence criteria were not taken seriously in the past and ignoring the rules did not lead to substantial sanctions.

Time was the next crucial factor. The important question is: when will the consequences of decisions taken today become noticeable? The more they can be displaced to the future the better it is for all who assume responsibility. In our case it was made easier by the fact that the financial packages for the highly indebted states were provided as loans. They are given in anticipation to be repaid in the future. If this is the case and when interest rates are high enough a donor state could profit. However, the decisive question remains whether the highly indebted states will ever be able to repay the loans. As the answer is not clear it has been made easier to legitimate the loans with the assumption to defend the Euro area – even by ignoring the fundamental rule of no-bail-out. When interest rates of the loans for Greece were reduced and when the government gave up to share the earnings of the ECB the German Minister of Finance was forced to cut down revenues of the national budget by 730 million Euro at the end of 2012 (Zeit Online 2012). This, however, did not lead to a bigger controversy in the country.

Whether costly and legally disputable political decisions can be taken or not has to do with public opinion and political culture. As long as there is a consensus among leading politicians that rescuing the Euro area does legitimate ignoring essential rules this will happen and sustainability of norms will be undermined. As soon as political polarisation prevails the situation may alter. The Prime Minister of Slovakia was forced to resign, when the country was asked to participate in the bail-out of Greece.[6] Colleagues of her do not have to be afraid of such a fate as long as the political consensus on the Euro policy prevails.

Notes

[1] Many analysts and economists estimate that a debt restructuring will be unavoidable after the elections in Germany in September 2013, may it

be as a partial disclaimer or reduction of interest rates or extension of the credit term (see Jahn/Plickert 2013, p. 11).

2   It was estimated that economic growth would be reduced by a total of 17.2 trillion Euro in the world's 42 largest economies in the lead-up to 2020.

3   Referring to the Greek debt crisis in the term of natural disasters or exceptional occurrences was not convincing, as the European Commission itself confirmed in February 2010 (see Commission of the European Communities 2009).

4   As mentioned before, due to massive financial rescue packages from the Eurozone the external debt of the crisis states shifted to state and not private loans.

5   Not astonishing, respondents in other Euro states have been more favourable to Eurobonds. 63% of the Greeks, 56% of the Portuguese, 56% of the Italians, 54% of the Irish, 51% of the Spanish, and 51% of the French responded positively. However, the Belgians (67%) and the Luxemburgers (51%) were in favour of Eurobonds too (see European Commission 2012b).

6   The opposition in Slovakia requested a motion of confidence as a precondition for the parliament to vote on the financial rescue package for Greece. The parliament agreed with with the package but the Prime Minister had to leave office (see Die Welt 2011).

References

AXT, H.-J. (2010): Griechenlands Schuldenkrise: Gefahr für den Euro? Das Dilemma von vertragskonformen oder politisch opportunen Lösungen, http://www.uni-due.de /imperia/md/content/politik/axt/gr_euro_axt_sog_20100307__1_.pdf, accessed on August 16, 2013.

AXT, H.-J. (2011): Turmoil in the Euro-Zone: No Lifeline without Major Risks, in: Unikate: Berichte aus Forschung und Lehre, Vol. 40, pp. 70-79.

BELKE, A.; BURGHOF, H.-P. (2010): Jedes Land für sich selbst, http://www.ftd.de/p olitik/konjunktur/:eu-schuldenkrise-jedes-land-fuer-sich-selbst/50175118.html, accessed on August 16, 2013.

BERTELSMANN STIFTUNG (2012): Economic Impact of Southern European Member States Exiting the Eurozone, http://www.bertelsmann-stiftung.de/cps/rde/xbcr/ SID-A9BF786A-EDBDBFE1/bst_engl/xcms_bst_dms_36656__2.pdf, accessed on August 15, 2013.

BILD (2010): BILD.de zeigt die geheimen Griechen-Verträge, http://www.bild.de/BIL D/politik/wirtschaft/2010/05/24/griechenland-hilfe-deutschland-milliarden-euro/sch warz-auf-weiss-die-dokumente.html, accessed on August 16, 2013.

COMMISSION OF THE EUROPEAN COMMUNITIES (2009): Report from the Commission Greece, http://ec.europa.eu/economy_finance/ economic_governance/sgp/pdf/30_edps/104-03/2009-02-18_el_104-3_en.pdf, accessed on August 16, 2013.

DIE WELT (2011): Wie sich Iveta Radicova für den Euro opferte, http://www.welt.de/ politik/ausland/article13705524/Wie-sich-Iveta-Radicova-fuer-den-Euro-opferte. html, accessed on August 19, 2013.

EUROPEAN COMMISSION (2012a): Economic and Monetary Union and the Euro, http://europa.eu/pol/emu/flipbook/en/files/economic_and_mone- tary_union_and_the_euro_en.pdf, accessed on August 16, 2013.

EUROPEAN COMMISSION (2012b): Europeans, the European Union and the Crisis, http://ec.europa.eu/public_opinion/archives/eb/eb78/eb78_cri_en.pdf, accessed on August 16, 2013.

FOCUS (2012): Von Währungsunion zur Haftungsunion in 14 Jahren, http://www.foc us.de/finanzen/news/staatsverschuldung/von-waehrungsunion-zur-haftungsunion-in -14-jahren-grosse-mehrheit-fuer-griechen-hilfspaket-im-bundestag-kommentar_420 6341.html, accessed on August 15, 2013.

JAHN, J.; PLICKERT, P. (2013): Deutsche Haftung höher als Schäuble angibt, in: Frankfurter Allgemeine Zeitung, August 16, 2013, p. 11.

KRUGMAN, P. (2012): On the Non-Burden of Debt, http://krug- man.blogs.nytimes.com/2012/10/12/on-the-non-burden-of-debt/?_r=1, accessed on August 16, 2013.

OFFICIAL JOURNAL OF THE EUROPEAN UNION (2011): European Council De- cision of 25 March 2011, http://eur-lex.europa.eu/LexUriServ/LexUriServ.do? uri=OJ:L:2011:091:0001:0002:EN:PDF, accessed on August 20, 2013.

TSOUKALIS, L. (1997): The New European Economy Revisited, New York.

UNITED NATIONS GENERAL ASSEMBLY (1987): Report of the World Commis- sion on Environment and Development: Our Common Future, http://www.un-docu- ments.net/wced-ocf.htm, accessed on August 15, 2013.

WEBER, M. (1972): Wirtschaft und Gesellschaft: Grundriß der verstehenden Soziolo- gie, Tübingen.

ZEIT ONLINE (2012): Griechenland-Hilfe belastet Bundeshaushalt millionenschwer, http://www.zeit.de/wirtschaft/2012-11/griechenland-hilfe-kosten-deutschland, accessed on August 19, 2013.

Sustainability of Currency Unions: What Went Wrong in EMU and How to Fix it?

Ansgar Belke and Florian Verheyen

Overview

1. Introduction

As there has been no historical precedent for a European Monetary Union (EMU) (Eichengreen 2008), opposing views about the desirability of a common currency in Europe have emerged as an immediate consequence. In the run-up of the introduction of the single currency in eleven countries of the European Union (EU) in 1999, there have been enthusiasts as well as skeptics about this ambitious political and economic project. For example, Rose's (2000) famous analysis suggests that trade among member countries might triple due to the abolishment of national currencies. Others feared that a monetary union without a fiscal union may not prove sustainable in the end (Bean 1992). Teulon (2011) concludes in the same vein that monetary unions do only survive if they are preceded by a political union. If there is only a "naked" monetary union, history shows that such an arrangement is unsustainable.

The aforementioned debate actually exhibits the contrasting economic views of the so-called monetarists on the one hand who believe that monetary integration is followed by economic and political integration. The opposing view is held by the economists. They argue that integration has to be run the other way round: political integration has to precede monetary integration.

With the benefit of hindsight, it has to be feared that the sceptics may end up being right. The Rose effect of heavily increasing trade volumes did not materialise and the issue of political stability of the Eurozone is at stake more than ever before. Scenarios of a breakup of the Eurozone (Belke/Verheyen 2013) as well as a two-speed Europe with a North and a South (Belke 2013) are considered. Furthermore, various proposals of how to further integrate EMU or how to overcome the debt crisis are in the making (see, for example, Delpla/von Weizsäcker 2010 or Schmidt/Weigert 2013).

Accordingly, it seems natural to pose the question whether the Eurozone is sustainable or not. In other words, one could ask, for example, which adjustments of the prevailing institutional framework are necessary to render EMU sustainable. But to be able to find setscrews for improvements one has to carefully analyse the flaws of the current framework to begin with. These and other issues will be tackled in this contribution.

In general, sustainability of currency unions is referred to quite often from a fiscal (policy) perspective. Theoretical investigations of the sustainability of EMU yield different results. While Wickens (2007) concludes that considerable changes especially regarding the fiscal framework have to be made, Alho (2013) questions Wickens' (2007) results and states that the unsustainability presumption does not hold in general. However, sustainability can be achieved if there are fiscal transfers from high-inflation countries to low inflation-countries. However, these are unlikely to be put in place due to heavy resistance of the governments in the donor countries. Furthermore, high-inflation countries are usually smaller in size than low-inflation countries. It is incidental then, that the transfers to be effective would be far too large to be borne by the small countries (Wickens 2007). Empirically, recent results of, for example, Bajo-Rubio et al. (2009) or Afonso and Rault (2010) yield more favourable results and mark public finances in EMU countries as sustainable.

Another dimension of sustainability of currency unions refers to intra-union imbalances with regard to the current account in which cross-border income and trade flows are booked. Thus, the current account measures the amount of foreign debt or surplus of a country. For example, Keynesians like, for instance, Schoder/Proaño/Semmler (2012) find that the introduction of the single currency lead to unsustainable current account balances in the Euro area.

And a final dimension of sustainability which is a matter for EMU countries can be found in the debate brought up by Sinn/Wollmershäuser (2011) about the imbalances regarding the interbank payment system called TARGET2.

Precisely, the structure of this contribution is as follows. We will first give a brief survey of the path towards and history of the EMU which is followed by a sketch of the optimum currency area theory of Mundell (1961). Against this background, we describe the EU convergence criteria. Afterwards, we will take a closer look at the sustainability of public finances in EMU. It will turn out that fiscal policy has reached its limits so that the European Central Bank (ECB) remains the only player able to act. Accordingly, we will spend a few words on the ECB's role during the crises. Before concluding, we will outline possible scenarios for the future of EMU and elaborate on which institutional changes might be necessary to render the currency union sustainable.

2. The Path Towards Monetary Union in Europe

The process of European integration started after the end of World War II. In 1951 the European Coal and Steel Community (ECSC) was founded by Belgium, France, Germany, Italy, Luxembourg and the Netherlands. With this agreement, the founding nations created a first supranational institution in Europe which had the right to enact rules for the coal and steel production. For example, it entailed the reduction of tariffs which should strengthen the trade among member countries.

This clearly shows that the process of European integration has of course been driven by economic forces. However, reducing the process of European integration only to an economic dimension would be far too simple. European integration after World War II has to be seen always as a political, peacebuilding and peacekeeping process which was rewarded recently in 2012 when the EU received the Nobel Peace Prize. And it will turn out in this contribution that the future of the EMU depends largely on the political willingness to continue the road of European integration. Eichengreen/Frieden (1993) even go one step further and conclude after their analysis that EMU is a result of much more political than economic considerations.

The six ECSC states signed the Treaty of Rome in 1957 which established the European Economic Community (EEC). One main goal of this agreement was to create a single European market. 30 years later, in 1987 the Single European Act (SEA) can be seen as the first major revision of the Treaty of Rome. By then, twelve European Economies agreed upon the competences of European institutions and formulated several objectives for further integration. Among them were the erection of the Single European Market which just celebrated its 20th anniversary in the year 2013 and the creation of the EU. The following treaties of Amsterdam, Nice and Lisbon all build up on the SEA.

Another milestone was set in 1992 with the Maastricht Treaty also known as the Treaty on the EU (TEU). Regarding the way towards a monetary union the TEU proposed a three-step procedure which should finally lead to the introduction of a single currency on January, 1st 1999 at the latest. And indeed, at that date, eleven countries of the EU introduced the Euro as their new currency and the responsibility for monetary policy decisions changed over from the national central banks to the ECB headquartered in Frankfurt on the Main. Since then, the ECB is put in charge to deliver price stability for the countries of the EMU.

In 2001, Greece joined EMU so that when the Euro notes and coins were introduced in 2002, altogether twelve countries held new money for their payments in their hands. In the following years, five more countries entered the monetary union and the accession of Latvia on January, 1st 2014 is agreed upon.

Generally, the EU has become the largest single market in the world with respect to the gross domestic product (GDP) and the Euro has established on international financial markets. Behind the US dollar it is the second most important reserve currency in the world. Furthermore, across EMU the ECB has been successful in delivering price stability. While these achievements are certainly notable, EMU finds itself actually in its severest crisis and no solution has been found yet. To understand why such an existence-threatening crisis could build up, one should take a brief look at the economic considerations which led politicians chose the option of a monetary union in Europe and the mistakes that have been made therewith.

3. Theory of Optimum Currency Areas

From an economic point of view, the question whether a country should abandon its currency and join a monetary union is typically analysed in the framework of the so-called theory of optimum currency areas (OCA) which has been established by Mundell (1961). The OCA theory elaborates on the size of a monetary union and on the conditions under which an accession is favourable. While the abolishment of an own currency comes along with costs and benefits, such a far-reaching decision should not be taken easily.

Regarding the number of countries which should introduce a single currency, there is a trade-off which becomes obvious when one considers the costs and benefits of a common currency. The benefits due to, for example, increasing trade flows and the omission of currency exchange increase with the number of countries that take part in the currency area. In contrast, an increasing number of countries is equivalent to more heterogeneity across the countries. In consequence, a common monetary policy will become less advantageous. Mistaking regarding the right number of countries might, of course, lead to instability and unsustainability of the currency union.

Taking now a more thorough look at the costs and benefits of a currency union, one important prerequisite for a country to join a monetary union is a high degree of factor mobility. Factor mobility thereby refers to factors like capital or labour that can freely flow between countries. Accordingly, factors flow (or at least should flow) to the countries where they are rewarded best. This mobility is important in order to cushion asymmetric shocks that might hit a single country of the currency union. Ideally, in a situation of an asymmetric shock, for example if only one country of a monetary union faces a rapid decline in demand which goes along with increasing unemployment, the workers would move to another country where unemployment is lower. While this tends to hold for the United States which is often put as the role model of an OCA, such a high degree of labour mobility is absent in Europe. For example, regulatory issues or simply different languages hamper the resettlement of laid off workers.

Generally, the decision to enter a monetary union has to be taken by weighing costs and benefits. The main benefits arise from the omission of currency exchange when trading with currency union members or when simply travelling around the union. These costs of currency exchange are all but negligible. According to Bean (1992), a traveller that visits all at that time ten countries of the European Community would lose 50% of its purchasing power simply because of converting notes and coins. Furthermore, price transparency and comparison becomes easier as there is no need to convert currencies. And finally, there is no need to hedge the currency risk anymore. All this yields considerable efficiency gains. However, a precise quantification of these benefits is probably impossible. Nevertheless, these should be all the larger the more intense the interrelations of the accessing country and the existing monetary union are.

As said in the introduction, Rose (2000) estimates the trade effects of a currency union to be extraordinarily large. He concludes that trade might triple within a monetary union. However, this number and the way it was obtained have been heavily criticised and other researchers came to much smaller and probably much more plausible estimates. For example, Micco/ Stein/Ordoñez (2003) expect an increase in trade volumes of only around 10%.

The costs that have to be taken into account when joining a currency union arise especially from surrendering the own autonomous monetary policy. Consequently, an accessing country loses one important policy instrument for stabilisation issues. From that day on, monetary policy and the adjustment of the nominal exchange rate is no longer feasible. For example, in a situation of an economic downturn in solely one country of the monetary union, the common central bank might not lower interest rates to foster growth as this would be inappropriate for all the other countries. Accordingly, a "one size fits all" monetary policy is, of course, inferior to an autonomous one. However, this statement does no longer hold when a country's monetary policy is lacking credibility. If so, a country can even benefit from surrendering its currency as it can import credibility of the currency union's central bank which could stabilise inflation expectations. Thus, at the end, the accessing country can be better off with a common monetary policy compared to a situation with autonomous monetary policy.

Again, the costs of the loss of the monetary policy instrument are not seriously calculable. However, these will be less relevant when the entering country is very similar to the countries which are already part of the currency union. This is because a high degree of similarity reduces the likelihood of asymmetric shocks.

Summing up these considerations of the OCA theory, when deciding about entering a monetary union; a certain degree of integration with the member countries has to be achieved. Otherwise, the costs might surpass the benefits and the accession becomes unfavourable. The integration thereby arises as a consequence of intensive trade relationships and factor mobility.

The challenges for the policymakers in the run-up of EMU were then to operationalise this framework. How should the OCA theory be transferred into criteria which are applicable to European countries in order to decide whether these countries are suitable for a common currency or not? This has been a challenging task as the aforementioned trade-off between size and similarity had to be taken into account. Further difficulties arose as the OCA theory might be appropriate only for very small countries that adopt a larger country's currency (Goodhart 2007). Additionally, economists like Frankel and Rose (1998) argue that OCAs are endogenous. This means that the optimality arises not before the establishment of the monetary union but over time of its existence.

Finally, the European authorities decided to announce four so-called convergence criteria which had to be passed before a country was allowed to join the single currency. These criteria and the Stability and Growth Pact (SGP) were meant to assure that EMU proves to be sustainable.

4. Operationalising the OCA Theory: the Four EU Convergence Criteria and its Flaws

The first criterion addresses national inflation rates. An accessing country's inflation rate may according to the criterion not be higher than the average of the inflation rates of the three EU member countries with the lowest inflation rates plus 1.5 percentage points. This kind of inflation convergence is necessary because otherwise a common monetary policy will not be feasible. In general, this criterion has been passed by all countries as inflation rates converged during the 1990s. This was at least partly due to the European exchange rate mechanism (ERM). As Germany with its extremely anti-inflationary policy had a leading role in the ERM, the other countries had to mimic the German monetary policy which led to a credibility import that reduced inflation rates across Europe. Furthermore, even after accession, inflation rates remained similar during the first ten years of EMU.

The second convergence criterion claims that a country has to participate in the ERM without any tension two years before the accession. The ERM is a system which provides narrow bands between which the European currencies could fluctuate. As the inflation criterion, all founding members had no problems with this criterion.

The third criterion states that long-term interest rates of a country had to be no larger than the average of the long-term interest rates of the three EU member countries with the lowest inflation rates plus 1.5 percentage points. Interest rate convergence was seen as an indication whether public finances were sustainable or not. While this criterion had not been a problem at the end of the 1990s because interest rates converged in line with inflation rates, the picture has changed considerably yet. Since the beginning of the European debt crisis, long-term interest rates heavily diverged in EMU. Countries of the South like Greece, Italy, Portugal or Spain have to pay much higher interest rates for their sovereign bonds than the countries of the North. These developments represent one main threat for the sustainability of EMU.

The other menace stems from the evolution of fiscal debt and deficits in Europe which are formulated in the fourth convergence criterion. For a candidate country the public deficit may not be larger than 3% of GDP and the public debt may not surpass 60% of GDP. After the accession this debt criterion should be continuously met and the SGP even claimed that public budgets should be balanced on average. While this criterion has not been met by all of the member countries of EMU on accession, the situation has now turned even worse. Due to the economic stimulus packages in the aftermath of the financial crisis, all debt levels heavily increased and today only Finland and Luxembourg exhibit debt ratios below 60%.

One failure that has been made was that the economic convergence criteria were not consequently adhered to. For example, Belgium, Greece and Italy had debt ratios far beyond 60% in 1999. Nevertheless, these countries were allowed to enter EMU anyway, probably because a monetary union without the ECSC founding counties Belgium and Italy was politically inacceptable. Thus, political reasons seem to have been more important than economic ones.

Furthermore, the annual deficits surpassed the allowed level of 3% in many countries of the EMU. For example, Germany and France reported too large deficits in the mid-2000s. While generally these non-compliances should be sanctioned according to the treaties, none of these countries actually has been punished yet. It turned out that the institutional framework had one severe flaw. The decisions about sanctions were taken by all countries of the union, including the sinners themselves. What is more, no country wanted be the one who claimed strict sanctions, well aware of the fact that this could bite back when one also reports to large deficits. Accordingly, the SGP was not able to guarantee sustainable public finances.

Moreover, two more points regarding the debt criterion and the SGP have to be mentioned. First, critics of these (see, for example de Grauwe 1996 or Coeuré/Pisani-Ferry 2005) argue that these are completely at odds with the OCA theory. Buiter et al. (1993) even state that "the fiscal convergence criteria [...] are badly motivated, poorly designed and apt to lead to unnecessary hardship if pursued mechanically." When entering a currency union, a country gives up the monetary policy instrument. Thus, only fiscal measures remain for stabilising business cycles and domestic demand in a Keynesian way. However, prescribing strict fiscal rules as it is done by the debt criterion and the SGP erodes more or less also the second policy instrument. A member country hit by an asymmetric shock is left without any means to stimulate its economy. Instead of providing sustainability for a currency union, these rules would lead to destructive forces and endanger the cohesion of the monetary union. What is more, EMU is still lacking a common fiscal transfer mechanism and bail-outs are forbidden as no country has to stand in for another country's debt. Such a fiscal transfer mechanism is one main point to think about when setting the course for the future of EMU and several proposals have been made yet. First steps in this vein are already made with the European stability mechanism (ESM). We will come back to the issue of institutional changes later on.

The second critique is even more general. Balassone/Franco/Zotteri (2006) argue that the indicators for the fourth convergence criterion of public finances do not really measure what they should do. For example, the debt and deficit measures can be improved via one-time items which do not improve the sustainability of public finances at all. Furthermore, the deficit indicator is not available in a timely manner because it is prone to considerable revisions. Accordingly, one can assess the compliance to the rules only ex post and adjustments may then come too late. Unfortunately, Balassone/Franco/Zotteri (2006) have to admit that there is no better means available. Consequently, many more indicators should be considered in order to judge whether the fiscal pace is appropriate or not.

5. *Sustainability of Public Finances*

As mentioned before, the sustainability issue is often considered by taking a look at public finances. Precisely, Bohn (1998) proposed a neat way to test whether public finances are sustainable or not. He defines sustainability in the following way: If the government's primary balance, which is a government's revenues minus its expenditures without interest payments on its debt, reacts positively to the debt-to-GDP ratio, public finances are said to be sustainable. While Bohn's (1998) investigation for the US finds that the US primary balance reacts positively to the debt ratio there are several author's which applied this methodology to European data.

For example, Haber/Neck (2006) investigate the sustainability of Austrian public finances. Generally, they find that Austrian public finances are sustainable. However, they also detect a break in the relationship. The primary balance still reacts positively to higher debt ratios in recent times but the effect becomes smaller. Greiner/Köller/Semmler (2007) investigate this question for France, Germany, Italy and Portugal. Their results suggest that public finances of these four EMU countries are also sustainable. However, future challenges arise due to demographic changes. Lastly, Bajo-Rubio/Díaz-Roldán/Esteve (2009) include eleven EMU countries in their investigation. Once again, with the exception of Finland, sustainability of public finances cannot be rejected. Ironically, Finland is actually among the two EMU countries which reports lower debt ratios than 60%. Accordingly, before the outbreak of the financial crisis, public finances still seemed to be sustainable although the rules of the SGP had been violated frequently.

While these results might seem strange from today's point of view with rising debt levels all across EMU, obviously none of the aforementioned studies included the recent years of the financial market turmoil and the recent crisis. However, Hauptmeier/Sanchez-Fuentes/Schuknecht (2011) conclude their analysis with the finding that in all EMU countries except Germany, the fiscal path has been expansionary even before the crisis. Thereby, the worsening the public debt was due to rising expenditure ratios rather than shrinking revenues. These results question the sustainability of public finances in Europe as suggested by the aforementioned investigations.

Accordingly, we performed a regression analysis according to Bohn (1998) including data from 1995 to 2012 for the twelve EMU countries that adopted the Euro notes and coins in 2002. In a panel framework we were not able to obtain a positive relationship between the debt ratio and the primary balance. In contrast, while controlling for business cycle effects with the inclusion of the output gap which measures GDP deviations from trend, we received significant negative values for the debt ratio coefficient in various specifications. This indicates that higher debt ratios come along with more negative primary balances. Therefore, public finances in EMU do not seem to be sustainable in the sense of Bohn (1998) any longer.

This holds all the more if one keeps in mind that we only considered the primary balance. Recent developments on financial markets led to increasing interest rates spreads across EMU countries. For example, Greece or Portugal have to pay much higher interest rates when issuing new sovereign bonds to refinance their debt. Thus, debt service becomes increasingly costly which aggravates the unsustainability of public finances. And these developments surely have contributed to the behaviour of the ECB during the financial crisis. However, the ECB consequently denies this conclusion.

6. The ECB's Role and its Political Implications

It has been said before that the SGP led to a situation that limits the stabilising role of fiscal policy in times of asymmetric shocks. This is all the more relevant in recent times when debt ratios increased and the leeway for fiscal stimuli is restricted. As a matter of fact, the ECB is left as the last player that can counteract the recession in the Eurozone.

Consequently, since May 2010, the ECB is more and more involved in quasi fiscal actions. Since then, the ECB has bought sovereign debt of more than 200 billion € in the so-called securities market programme (SMP). Thereby, the SMP is legally at least questionable. According to the treaties, the ECB is not allowed to finance any country of the monetary union via printing money. However, by buying sovereign bonds, the ECB lowers interest rates on financial markets which alleviates the roll-over of public debt. It is important to mention that the purchases have been executed only on the secondary market which means that the ECB did not buy new bonds but papers that were already available on the market. Thus, one could argue that the ECB does not violate the treaties. However, the sovereign bonds purchased by the ECB are taken on the ECB's balance sheet. Accordingly, all countries of EMU stand in for the risks associated with these papers. Whether this is in line with the treaties has not yet been answered. In Germany for example, the constitution court is actually concerned to answer the question whether the outright monetary transactions (OMT) programme announced by the ECB complies with the treaties or not. The OMT programme which was announced in 2012 stands for unlimited sovereign bond purchases. However, up to now, the ECB has not bought any paper within this program. A decision of the court is expected for September 2013, probably right after the federal elections in Germany.

The ECB defends the OMT program and also the SMP with the argument that these assure a proper functioning of the monetary transmission mechanism and is thus completely in line with the ECB's mandate. While there is no final answer if the measures taken by the ECB are in line with the treaties or not, it definitely shows that institutional frameworks in EMU are altering. Before the crisis, the common notion was that monetary and fiscal policies have to be strictly separated and central banks should be independent. With the bond purchases, the ECB has lost at least some of its independence and we cannot draw a clear line between monetary and fiscal policy any longer. Furthermore, European rescue funds and the ESM can be seen as a starting point for further European integration with respect to fiscal coordination.

7. Towards Sustainability: Scenarios for EMU in the Next Years

What has to be done, to render EMU sustainable? This question can be answered in several ways. For example, if one answers in accordance with the OCA theory one could elaborate on which sub-group of countries of EMU really represent an OCA. Accordingly, a secession of one or more countries from EMU could be considered. We will briefly give an indication of possible consequences here. For a more thorough analysis, please refer to Belke/Verheyen (2013).

When a country secedes from EMU one should distinguish between the two distinct cases if a fiscally sound country or a highly indebted one leaves. A weak country seceding from EMU would have to return to its own currency with the effect that the new currency would probably strongly devaluate which means that international competitiveness increases immediately. The country's products will become cheaper for foreigners and thus demand should increase. Thus, a seceding country would regain the instrument of independent monetary policy. Nominal exchange rate adjustments would become possible immediately. However, an exit will imply also considerable costs. For example, if the country's liabilities remain denominated in Euro, these liabilities will strongly increase in value and repaying these becomes far more complicated. Furthermore, with a secession, the fiscal imbalances will not be solved either. Therefore, an exit of a weak country does not seem favourable from the weak country's point of view.

If a strong country leaves, the effects are mirror-imaged. The new currency should appreciate with negative consequences on foreign trade while the repayment of liabilities in Euro is facilitated. However, an additional thing has to be kept in mind. While a currency union might cope with an exit of a weak country comparably easily, the secession of a strong country could lead to a considerable destabilisation of the whole union and a breakup becomes more likely.

While such an exit is in principle an option, it does not seem as if this is really considered right now. First, according to the treaties, secession is not possible. And second, the agreement that Latvia will enter EMU in 2014 can be seen as a clear statement in favour of EMU. Additionally, ECB president Mario Draghi (European Central Bank 2012) has stated that the ECB will do everything in line with its mandate so that the Euro will survive. Therefore, instead of a breakup, the EMU enlargement continues as it was planned right from the start: Countries that satisfy the convergence criteria have to join the currency union.

However, a possibility which is somewhat in between a breakup and an enlargement scenario is a North South division of the Euro area. This might seem intuitively plausible as the OCA theory describes that countries should be sufficiently similar when forming a monetary union. And the past years have shown that economic conditions have diverged somewhat between the South and the North of Europe. Nevertheless, even these thoughts are damaging the EU and the Eurozone. While the South claims for pooling at least some of the debt and an end of the excessive austerity programs the North believes that banks have to be saved first because otherwise pressure to undergo structural reforms is removed.

8. *Changing the Institutional Framework of EMU*

From what we have seen so far it seems more likely that the policy of small steps will be continued. This will probably come along with a deeper integration in Europe; even fiscally. The no bail-out clause of the Maastricht Treaty will possibly be more and more relaxed. The erection of the ESM can be interpreted as a first step in this direction. The ESM represents a guarantee scheme that provides emergency assistance to highly indebted countries under strict conditionality. This means that aid is only provided if the country agrees to structural reform and austerity programs. Regarding the capitalisation of the ESM, each country contributes to it according to its economic size. Germany has to pay in about 22 billion € and guarantees for another 168 billion €. The whole volume of the ESM amounts to 700 billion €.

Such a fiscal transfer mechanism is of course politically and economically controversial. When designing such a mechanism one has to take care that it does not give wrong incentives. The strict conditionality points in this direction. Finally, it all depends on the political willingness to continue the process of European integration. Fiscal transfer schemes are already established for example in Germany on a national level. And even on the national level, there is a debate whether such mechanisms are sensible or not. Thus, it cannot come as a surprise that a fiscal union for the whole Eurozone yields heated discussions.

Beck/Prinz (2012) suggest that EMU finds itself actually in a situation which they call «another impossible trinity". Generally, such a trilemma describes a situation in which from three different goals only two can be met at a time. The three goals of a monetary union are a politically independent monetary policy, national fiscal sovereignty and a no-bail out rule. Beck/Prinz (2012) conclude that for EMU it is most likely that fiscal sovereignty will be surrendered. However, this will not be an easy step because as history has shown, the SGP which actually tried to limit excess deficits and debt did not work. The countries were unwilling to accept fiscal restrictions. Therefore, they propose an institutional framework which is able to handle sovereign defaults.

Such a framework could be a European Monetary Fund (EMF) – a European analogon to the International Monetary Fund (IMF). One detailed proposal into that direction has been developed by Gros/Mayer (2010). The main advantage of such an institution would be that there is a clear framework how to deal with sovereign default. Instead of taking decisions in a hurry, an EMF would give clear guidance of how to proceed in case of fiscal distress. Furthermore, these fiscal problems could be solved by a fiscal institution instead of abusing the ECB for this purpose.

Other proposals of how to overcome the European debt crisis are, for example, the emission of so-called Eurobonds. With such kind of bonds the whole union instead of a single country would guarantee a country's debt. Thus, according to the proponents of these proposals, the rating of such bonds would be quite high (maybe even as high as the best rating of a single country). Consequently, the issuance of debt would be less costly as the interest rate to be paid would be lower. One way of how to design such Eurobonds is provided by Delpla/von Weizsäcker (2010). Generally, there is a fundamental problem when giving assistance to countries that did not stick to the rules in the past. Helping these could lower the incentives for complying to the treaties in the future. This phenomenon is usually referred to as moral hazard. However, leaving the countries alone is probably not an option as well because, as we have seen on international financial markets, there is a valid threat of contagion. Consequently, Delpla/von Weizsäcker (2010) propose to differentiate between red and blue bonds. The blue bonds guarantee the whole union's debt which is below the 60% Maastricht threshold. For all debt above the 60% debt ratio, a country is responsible for on its own and this debt has to be financed by red bonds. With such a design, a country with a high debt level would benefit from the sound countries while still considerable incentives for fiscal consolidation remain. However, the German government still rejects the emission of Eurobonds in some way or other.

Another proposal has been made by the German Council of Economic Experts (see, for example, Schmidt/Weigert 2013). They recommend implementing a so-called European Redemption Pact (ERP) as a compromise between structural reforms and fiscal solidity. In order to give the right incentives for fiscal consolidation, the ERP claims structural reforms from participating countries. Furthermore, debt brakes should be written down into the national constitutions to guarantee long-run sustainability of public finances. If a country credibly promises to adhere to these commitments it would get access to a European Redemption Fund (ERF) which aims at lowering refinancing costs of over-indebted countries. A certain amount of debt would be transferred to the ERF and this amount is then refinanced by the ERF for which all countries of the union are liable. However, this proposal is probably not an instrument to solve the immediate problems of the European debt crisis. It is rather a means that could be implemented in the long-run. Furthermore, countries like Greece, Ireland or Portugal are probably unlikely to qualify for the ERP.

As it seems unlikely that neither the pure Northern nor the mere Southern view will be realised, a compromise is probably the best one can aim at. Such a compromise could look like a fiscal federalism as can be found in Canada, Switzerland or the US. While the states face the risk of insolvency they have a strong incentive to take corrective measures to avoid a default. However, for such a framework to be efficient one has to separate the fate of banks and sovereigns. Accordingly, instead of a fiscal union one now has to go (only) for a banking union in Europe. This would be a less drastic measure compared to a fiscal union and national governments would not have to surrender as many competences to the European level as in a fiscal union. Nevertheless, a banking union would require a resolution authority which has to be endowed with capital to rescue large cross-border banks. According to the German view, these resources should come at least partly from the banking sector.

Thus, a banking union could separate the banking from the debt crisis. Insolvent banks would no longer endanger the stability of the whole EMU. Accordingly, no Eurobonds will be needed.

9. Conclusion

We have seen that the process of European integration has already started after World War II. Over time, considerable steps have been taken and now an EU with 28 member countries and an EMU with 17 economies has been installed. While this is surely a huge achievement which lead to prosperity and peace within Europe, the Eurozone and its institutions actually find themselves in its deepest crisis. Some of these problems are home-made and we are actually coping with these due to an ill-designed fiscal framework. Thus, the process of European integration is all but finished yet. Moreover, it seems as it has arrived at a crossroads and it is to decide about to continue or to dismiss this process. It finally turned out that the sceptics proved right: A monetary union without a fiscal union is unsustainable.

Probably, everyone accepts that there is a strong need for adjustments regarding the institutional framework if the decision is to further follow the road of more and deeper integration in Europe. However, how these adjustments should look like in detail is heavily disputed and various proposals have been made. Finding a solution to this is, however, much less an economic question but rather a political one. In this context, Jonung (2002) mentions that the whole EU and EMU project generally lacks political legitimacy. Citizens do not feel as Europeans, they still identify with national symbols like flags or anthems instead of European ones although there is also a European flag and an anthem. If no improvement in this direction is made, it will be particularly difficult to justify fiscal transfer schemes in whatever way in Europe. Especially in times like these when crises hit the economy everyone falls back to a national perspective instead of fostering the common beliefs. Generally, a union without or endowed with only limited solidarity suffers from a considerable weakness. Actually, it seems as if this is a major flaw in the Eurozone.

For a positive outlook for EMU it will be particularly important to break the vicious circle of high refinancing cost for the Southern EMU countries, a fragile banking system and poor growth perspectives which self-enforce each other (Schmidt/Weigert 2013). Unfortunately it seems unlikely that there will be a big hit. Especially in the run-up of the German federal elections, no real solution seems possible. Instead, harsh incisions like a second debt haircut in Greece will be postponed so that the policy of small steps will continue. Of course, calling for political solutions which lead to a political or fiscal union might seem naïve. But in our view these are necessary to put EMU on a sustainable level. Unfortunately, as we have seen in the past, political decisions regarding the EU are always delicate. Remember, for example, the referendums about the Lisbon Treaty. Thus, there will be no quick and especially no easy solution to the European debt crisis. Moreover, the policy of small steps might continue. However, we believe that the political will is finally large enough to take the decisions that have to be taken in order to keep EMU and put it on a sustainable trajectory.

References

AFONSO, A.; RAULT, C. (2010): What Do We Really Know About Fiscal Sustainability in the EU? A Panel Data Diagnostic, in: Review of World Economics, Vol. 145, No. 4, pp. 731-755.

ALHO, K.E.O. (2013): How to Restore Sustainability of the Euro, in: Revue de L'OFCE, Vol. 127, No.1, pp. 303-340.

BAJO-RUBIO, O.; DÍAZ-ROLDÁN, C.; ESTEVE, V. (2009): Deficit Sustainability and Inflation in EMU: An Analysis from the Fiscal Theory of the Price Level, in: European Journal of Political Economy, Vol. 25, No. 4, pp. 525-539.

BALASSONE, F.; FRANCO, D.; ZOTTERI, S. (2006): EMU Fiscal Indicators: A Misleading Compass?, in: Empirica, Vol. 33, No. 2, pp. 63-87.

BEAN, C.R. (1992): Economic and Monetary Union in Europe, in: Journal of Economic Perspectives, Vol. 6, No. 4, pp. 31-52.

BECK, H.; PRINZ, A. (2012): The Trilemma of a Monetary Union: Another Impossible Trinity, in: Intereconomics, Vol. 47, No. 1, pp. 39-43.

BELKE, A. (2013): Debt Mutualisation in the Ongoing Eurozone Crisis: A Tale of the "North" and the "South", in: DURLAUF, S.N.; BLUME, L.E. (Eds.): The New Palgrave Dictionary of Economics, Online Edition.

BELKE, A.; VERHEYEN, F. (2013): Doomsday for the Euro Area: Causes, Variants and Consequences of a Breakup, in: International Journal of Financial Studies, Vol. 1, No. 1, pp. 1-15.

BOHN, H. (1998): The Behavior of U.S. Public Debt and Deficits, in: Quarterly Journal of Economics, Vol. 113, No. 3, pp. 949-963.

BUITER, W.; CORSETTI, G.; ROUBINI, N.; REPULLO, R.; FRANKEL, J. (1993): Excessive Deficits: Sense and Nonsense in the Treaty of Maastricht, in: Economic Policy, Vol. 8, No. 16, pp. 57-100.

COEURÉ, B.; PISANI-FERRY, J. (2005): Fiscal Policy in EMU: Towards a Sustainability and Growth Pact, in: Oxford Review of Economic Policy, Vol. 21, No. 4, pp. 598-617.

DE GRAUWE, P. (1996): The Economics of Convergence: Towards Monetary Union in Europe, in: Weltwirtschaftliches Archiv, Vol. 132, No. 1, pp. 1-27.

DELPLA, J.; VON WEIZSÄCKER, J. (2010): The Blue Bond Proposal, Bruegel Policy Brief 2010/03.

EICHENGREEN, B. (2008): Sui generis EMU, NBER Working paper 13740, Cambridge.

EICHENGREEN, B.; FRIEDEN, J. (1993): The Political Economy of European Monetary Unification: An analytical Introduction, in: Economics and Politics, Vol. 5, No. 2, pp. 85-104.

EUROPEAN CENTRAL BANK (2012): Speech by Mario Draghi, President of the European Central Bank at the Global Investment Conference in London 26 July 2012, http://www.ecb.europa.eu/press/key/date/2012/html/sp120726.en.html, accessed on July 29, 2013.

FRANKEL, J.A.; ROSE, A.K. (1998): The Endogeneity of the Optimum Currency Area Criteria, in: The Economic Journal, Vol. 108, No. 449, pp. 1009-1025.

GOODHART, C.A.E. (2007): Currency Unions: Some Lessons from the Euro-Zone, in: Atlantic Economic Journal, Vol. 35, No. 1, pp. 1-21.

GREINER, A.; KÖLLER, U.; SEMMLER, W. (2007): Debt Sustainability in the European Monetary Union: Theory and Empirical Evidence for Selected Countries, in: Oxford Economic papers, Vol. 59, No. 2, pp. 194-218.

GROS, D.; MAYER, T. (2010): How to Deal with Sovereign Default in Europe: Create the European Monetary Fund now!, CEPS Policy Brief No. 202, Brussels.

HABER, G.; NECK, R. (2006): Sustainability of Austrian Public Sebt: A Political Economy Perspective, in: Empirica, Vol. 33, No. 2, pp. 141-154.

HAUPTMEIER, S.; SANCHEZ-FUENTES, A.J.; SCHUKNECHT, L. (2011): Towards Expenditure Rules and Fiscal Sanity in the Euro Area, in: Journal of Policy Modeling, Vol. 33, No. 4, pp. 597-617.

JONUNG, L. (2002): EMU and the Euro - The First Ten Years: Challenges to the Sustainability of the Euro Area – What Does History Tell Us?, EUI Working Paper No. 2002/46, San Domenico.

MICCO, A.; STEIN, E.; ORDOÑEZ, G. (2003): The Currency Union Effect on Trade: Early Evidence from EMU, in: Economic Policy, Vol. 18, No. 37, pp. 315-356.

MUNDELL, R. (1961): A Theory of Optimum Currency Areas, in: American Economic Review, Vol. 51, No. 4, pp. 657-665.

ROSE, A. (2000): One Money, One Market: The Effect of Common Currencies on Trade, in: Economic Policy, Vol. 15, No. 30, pp. 7-45.

SCHMIDT, C.M.; WEIGERT, B. (2013): Weathering the Crisis and Beyond: Perspectives for the Euro Area, CEPR Discussion Paper No. 9414, London.

SCHODER, C.; PROAÑO, C.R.; SEMMLER, W. (2012): Are the Current Account Imbalances Between EMU Countries Sustainable? Evidence from Parametric and Non-Parametric Tests, IMK Working Paper 90, Duesseldorf.

SINN, H.-W.; WOLLMERSHÄUSER, T. (2011): Target Loans, Current Account Balances and Capital Flows: The ECB's Rescue Facility, CESifo Working Paper No. 3500, Munich.

TEULON, F. (2011): EMU: The Sustainability Issue, in: International Journal of Business, Vol. 16, No. 3, pp. 272-288.

WICKENS, M.R. (2007): Is the Euro Sustainable?, CEPR Discussion Paper No. 6337, London.

Part 3:
Stakeholder Perspectives

The Problem of Consumer Sovereignty and the Concept of Consumer Democracy

Andrea Gröppel-Klein

Overview

1. Consumers' Sovereignty – Illusion or Fact?

The problem of citizen sovereignty has a long history in state philosophy and politics and is of great importance in discussions on the law of nature. Supporters of the law of nature, such as Locke and Rousseau, stress sovereignty and freedom as natural states common to all human beings. Political rights and duties derive from citizen sovereignty. However, the reality is very different, and supporters of the law of nature have come to the conclusion that this sovereignty and freedom are seldom realised and therefore need to be attained through human education.

According to political science, consumer sovereignty is essentially perceived as a myth, and citizens are hardly involved in the creation of their political environment. They are passive, reacting to a greater or lesser extent to environmental stimuli. Thus they can be highly influenced by political (or other) authorities. Representatives of formal models of democracy do not regard the ideal of sovereignty as worthwhile. They have given up on the belief in sovereign citizenship and have long distanced themselves from the norm of a sovereign citizen (Zimpel 1972). However, the concept of a sovereign citizen has been maintained in economics, where belief in sovereign citizens and the normative claim for sovereign consumers is strongly defended. With regard to their behaviour, the consumer might be more sovereign in the field of economics than in politics.

This view is supported by many experts, such as Schumpeter. He explains this phenomenon by arguing that consumers act more rationally when their immediate (or existential) interests are affected. At such a time, consumers' goals are more concrete, and knowledge based on past experiences can be used to pursue the goal. Nevertheless, the factual and the normative concepts of sovereign citizens do not match: consumer behaviour is only partially rational, and is far removed from the normative view of sovereignty (Schwan 2009).

Although actual experiences suggest the opposite, the concept of sovereign consumers is still maintained. The reason why it is perpetuated is clear: the concept of a sovereign consumer serves mainly ideological purposes. It is stated that consumers themselves are the ones who select products and decide whether to follow marketing activity. Thus, consumers are stylised to be independent judges who decide which products are consumed and released to the market. Commercial companies only meet consumers' needs and plan production accordingly.

In this case, the following justification comes into effect: if consumers are sovereign, they are in charge of accepting or refusing offers. This affects all kinds of offers such as informational offers or offers for consumer goods. Consumers are responsible for their behaviour, and commercial companies just satisfy consumers' needs. As a result, companies cannot be blamed for any of the consequences of marketing, since they only act according to consumers' demands and preferences.

The same justification is also welcomed by other organisations, politicians and trade unionists. First they influence the voter and later they state that the votes only represent voters' wishes.

Such an ideological justification and deliberate disregard of problems seems implausible. The implausibility arises from the contradiction between the arguments that are used for defending the normative concept of a sovereign consumer and the findings from behavioural sciences.

The constraints of consumer sovereignty and the manipulation of consumer behaviour are often seen as analogous concepts. Since the term "manipulation" contains strong inferences and is normally used in ideological situations, it is appropriate to replace the term with a more neutral term, such as behavioural control or behavioural modification.

Marketing mechanisms to influence behaviour can be defined as intentional external influences on behaviour that are often not cognitively controlled by the person concerned. This is the case when:

- consumers do not see through the advertising and therefore do not consciously notice what is happening to them. For instance, this is sometimes the case when consumers are confronted with advertorials and misinterpret them as editorial reports and independent (neutral) "third party" comments.
- consumers see through the advertising but cannot resist the influence because they like it too much. For instance, consumers realise that the advertising campaign that was styled as an editorial report is an advert, but they love the idea that if they use the advertised product they could lose 20 pounds in weight within two weeks.
- advertisements have quasi-compulsive effects on consumers so that they cannot resist the influence. The advertised message evokes an immediate or automatic reaction. For instance, the image of an ice cream on a huge billboard poster looks so delicious and tempting that the consumer cannot help but buy one from the ice cream seller next to it.

Some more or less general rules explain the efficiency of these mechanisms.

In some cases, personal opinions can be influenced more effectively by distracting from the actual intention to influence. This technique is called distracting communication. Distraction can be carried out by choosing a narrator with an erotic or exotic accent in commercials, or showing pictures that don't necessarily fit with the claims being made. Another example is showing attractive images of landscapes while arguing for a certain brand of car. Distraction can particularly influence consumers who have an indifferent attitude towards the advertised brand.

In these examples, consumers consciously process the information. However, the presentation of distracting stimuli interrupts their information processing in such a way that their resistance is weakened and they often do not understand the marketers' intentions and practices. If consumers were to be asked if they are happy with a deliberate intention to influence their behaviour, they would probably not agree and may be highly indignant about the attempt to deceive them.

From a psychological perspective, many techniques are used that aim to influence consumers in this way. These techniques control consumers' information processes and behaviour as they don't consciously notice what is happening to them. Taking this into consideration, it is highly problematic to talk about consumers' sovereignty or self-determination.

If a certain automatic behaviour is triggered, the consumer cannot easily withdraw. Consumers react to stimuli without cognitively controlling their behaviour. One technique is emotional conditioning: the repeated presentation of a neutral brand name in combination with a pleasant stimulus (e.g. young children, erotic appeal or romantic pictures of the olden days) can create a positive attitude towards the neutral brand name. In other words, an indifferent attitude can be transformed into a positive attitude towards a certain product – without conscious elaboration. Remarkably, it is not necessary to use a piece of factual information to bring about such a transformation in attitude.

Appealing to innate reaction patterns and the systematic use of principles based on learning theory can influence consumer behaviour in such a way that fits with marketers' goals. This view is supported by behavioural scientists who deal with innate reaction patterns (such as Eibl-Eibesfeldt 1995, pp. 63ff.) or learning abilities.

When stating the case for sovereign and sensible humans, it is important to consider genetic ancestry. From an evolutionary perspective, the central nervous system maintains the functionality of the organism. It controls human behaviour from simple stimulus–reaction links. We like to think that every erotic arousal, for instance, is the result of a consciously controlled human affection, but we forget the fact that hormone release and reactions driven by physical urges are innate and of a subconscious nature. Modern social sciences in particular, such as comparative human science or psychobiology, put a strong emphasis on genetic behaviour and sensory reactions.

Marketing techniques that constrain consumers' sovereignty are commonly used by marketers. It would be very difficult to attempt to regulate these practices in marketing.

With regard to consumer policy measures, these will only be effective if they are based on consumers' actual behaviour and properly coordinated with innate and learned behavioural patterns. To put it another way, the true concept of a sovereign consumer must be based on behavioural sciences. Consumer protection needs to consider actual behaviour rather than normative desired behaviour in order to establish effective measures.

One method to measure actual buying behaviour or information-processing is the recording of eye-movements. Eye-tracking gives evidence that consumers only take a very brief glance at products when they do their normal shopping.

2. Case Study Showing Consumers' Actual Buying Behaviour at the PoS

Visual attention can be measured accurately via eye-tracking devices. Königstorfer and Gröppel-Klein (2012, also see Gröppel-Klein/Königstorfer 2013), for instance, conducted an eye-tracking study (head-mounted eye-tracking technology) in a retailer's laboratory store (3,000 sq m, 4,500 different products). Some of the results of this study help to shed some light on realistic consumer behaviour at the point of sale. They show that consumers access products immediately and normally do not consciously seek elaboration with regard to product quality.

The initial goal of our study was to find out whether nutrition information on the products is observed at all and whether this information could be improved and made more relevant by changing the nutrition label.

We first conducted a benchmark study to measure attention given to existing nutrition labels. After recruiting participants of various age, income, and education groups, and some variations in body mass (BMI between 18.2 and 34.6kg/sq m), the eye tracking device was fixed. We used the monocular, pupil cornea-reflection based system from SMI which has a sampling rate of 25 Hz and allows free movement. However, we had to restrict consumers' movements in the store to some extent to guarantee the validity of the data recordings. Participants were asked to walk on a 40cm wide carpet at all times in order to regulate the distance to the shelves at 60cm (the distance during calibration).

After the calibration, participants received a shopping list. They were told that we were interested in how they orient when buying a packet of muesli, a packet of biscuits and a ready meal according to their preferences. The available products differed in nutritional value, which was assessed via the products' SSAg/1 scores ranging from 0 (healthiest product) to 15 (unhealthiest product). After the shopping trip, the calibration was controlled for.

For the comparative study (four weeks later), using the same design as in study 1, new product packages with a new label were created. This new label had previously been controlled for comprehensibility and understanding in lab studies. The mock-ups were perceived as original products.

The results demonstrate first of all that the total gaze duration on the product packages was extremely low (around 1-2 seconds, see Figures 1 and 2), irrespective of the nutrition labelling system, and that consumers spent only fractions of a second looking at nutrition information. Socio-demographic variables had no impact on label attention. However, attention increased when the new label was used, and the share of attention to the labels increased significantly from study 1 to study 2 (cereals 1.23% to 3.93%; biscuits 0.83% to 4.71%; ready meals 0.75% to 4.96%; $p < 0.05$).

The results of these studies are both encouraging and sobering. The introduction of the new label led to a significant increase in attention. We further found that the new label improved consumers' ability to buy healthier food.

However, we also have to admit that nutrition information still is more or less irrelevant for consumers at the point of purchase: the share of attention is still less than 5 per cent. Most of the time is spent looking at the product/brand name and the picture. On average, consumers only glance 1 or 2 seconds at the product package indicating that most purchases are either habitual or without cognitive effort – this is realistic buying behaviour.

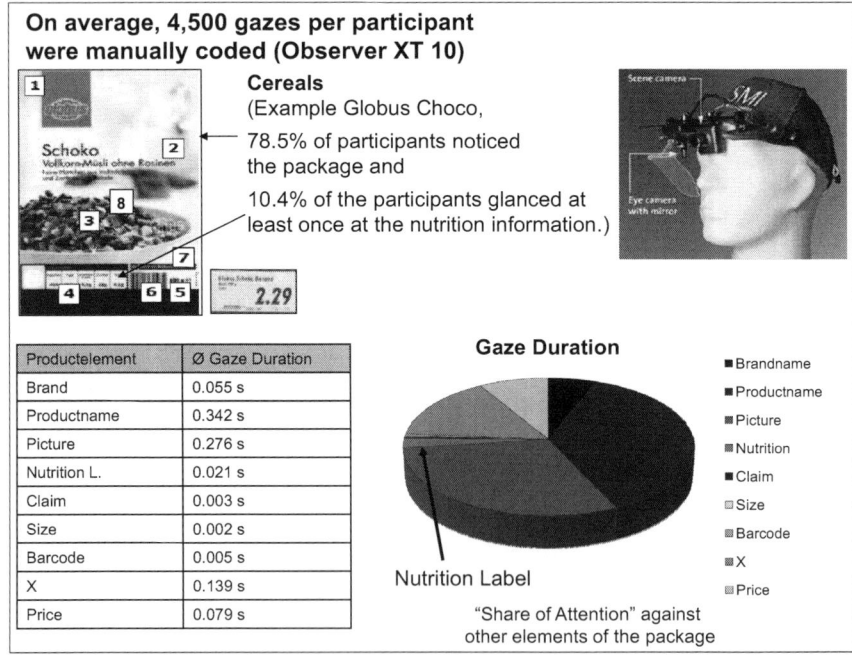

Figure 1: Share of Interest

114

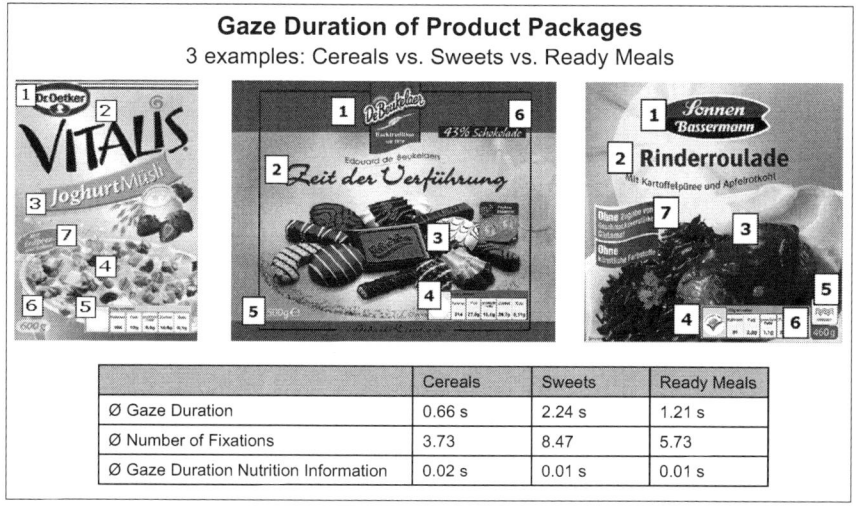

Gaze Duration of Product Packages
3 examples: Cereals vs. Sweets vs. Ready Meals

	Cereals	Sweets	Ready Meals
Ø Gaze Duration	0.66 s	2.24 s	1.21 s
Ø Number of Fixations	3.73	8.47	5.73
Ø Gaze Duration Nutrition Information	0.02 s	0.01 s	0.01 s

Figure 2: Average Gaze Durations

Figure 2 also shows that the picture on the product package is often the most important source of information. So, for instance, when the consumer sees a jar of marmalade on the shelf with a picture of apricots, and also sees the slogan "70% fruit", the consumer automatically assumes that the marmalade contains 70 per cent apricots. If, in fact, half of the fruit is apple, the consumer will feel cheated and can make the issue known at "Lebensmittelklarheit".

"Lebensmittelklarheit" is a new internet portal organised by the German Ministry for consumerism. It helps consumers to discover products that mock high-quality food ingredients, pretend to be healthy or make claims to be nutritional via misleading pictures or slogans on product packages (see Figure 3).

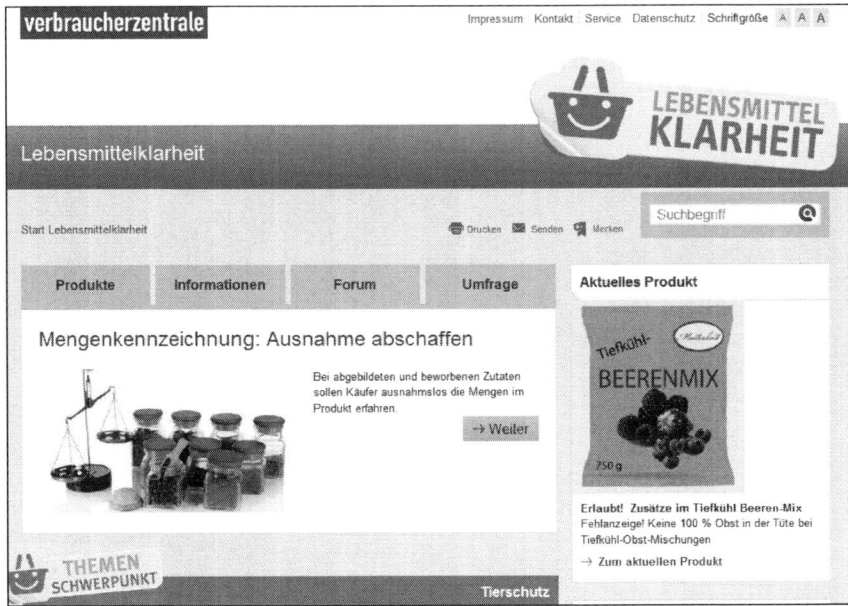

Figure 3: Portal "Lebensmittelklarheit"

On the one hand, this initiative helps to discover the "black sheep" in the food industry, but on the other hand perhaps more important is that it helps reputable companies to change their product packages when the information and/or the design are misleading.

The initiative will check the accusation and, if it is upheld, will instruct the company concerned to change either the picture or the ingredients. The examples show that consumers can feel cheated by exaggerated product promises. However, via internet communities they can also pillory companies that play dirty.

Thus the question arises: how do consumers evaluate their sovereignty?

3. How Do Consumers Evaluate Their Sovereignty?

Recently, consumer behaviour has changed as an increasing number attach great importance to sustainable products, compliance with social standards and fair trade with producers (Heidbrink/Schmidt/Ahaus 2011). In addition, corporate social responsibility has become an important issue for consumers (Stötzel 2010, pp. 163ff.) and they are now requesting companies to guarantee production standards. However, can consumers force companies to obey the standards, or do they simply have to trust in what companies pretend to do, even though organisations risk media scandals when unfair, illegal and exploitative behaviour is revealed? One should keep in mind previous public discussions about scandals such as BSE, horsemeat in lasagne, dioxin in eggs or the unauthorised filming of employees.

This problem can be discussed from two perspectives:

Perspective A:

Digital information and communication technologies have provided consumers with direct opportunities for inclusion (Lamla 2011). They can be informed about products through use of a barcode scanner or they can use their smartphones to log in to different networks and read up on product recommendations, download test reports, browse the standpoints of non-governmental organisations (NGO) or watchdogs in order to check whether the products meet their needs and values In addition, consumers can join together, pillory companies via the internet or upload parodies of advertisements on YouTube. Finally, it could be said that we live in a direct consumer democracy in which consumers determine the success or failure of a product.

In the last few years, a variety of books dealing with consumer policy have become available, ranging from Naomi Klein's bestseller "No Logo" (2000) to Peter Unfried's entertaining book "Öko: Al Gore, der neue Kühlschrank und ich" (2008) (Lamla 2011, p. 103). Also the portal "Lebensmittelklarheit.de" (initiated by the Federal Ministry of Food, Agriculture and Consumer Protection) caused a furore with the following revelations: veal sausages were actually made from pork, cheese didn't contain milk and confectionery contained pure sugar instead of the advertised vitamins. Consumers were outraged by these deceptions. Even consumer advocates underestimated consumers' anger towards the food industry. The internet homepage "Lebensmittelklarheit.de" broke down immediately after its activation: up to 20,000 clicks per second were registered on the home page by the Federation of German Consumer Organisations (vzbv) on the Wednesday afternoon (FocusOnline, 2011). However, is consumer democracy an efficient system that is able to replace state control, or is consumer democracy a burden for consumers as they are indirectly held responsible for any negative consequences?

Perspective B:

According to consumer behaviour research, a number of consumers do not see through the unconscious processes that are responsible for behavioural control. It is illusionary to think that consumers actually inform themselves about products – for instance, via barcode scanners – during every shopping trip to find out whether they can rely on the product promises. Consumers are not just constrained by money but also by time. Research points out that very few daily purchases are performed with high cognitive involvement (Kroeber-Riel/Gröppel-Klein 2013); consumers just take a quick glance at individual products (see also the above-mentioned eye-tracking study) and make decisions within seconds. A consumer who would actively reflect on every decision they make during the day would end up with a cognitive overload.

Thus, "rationality" in consumer behaviour should not be considered or discussed in isolation. It might be that "irrational" behaviour is beneficial for other areas of life. For instance, habitual quick shopping trips without thorough comparisons of different offers can lead to more time for leisure or with the family. This can be more valuable for the consumer than carefully selected products. Representatives of consumer policy might point out that consumers don't take the bad with the good. Reasonable consumer performance includes the thorough consideration of goals and personal advantages gained by certain choices. In other words, the consumer needs to choose between more leisure time or more time for shopping.

In addition, consumers are often overtaxed by the appraisal of the "integrity" of offers of financial services (Oehler/Reisch 2012) and fast-moving consumer goods. Organisations increasingly take a stand on claims for marketing purposes and in support of consumers' decision making processes. Claims can be very helpful for consumers, as findings on the acceptance of Stiftung Warentest claims proved. In the meantime, a large number of claims mushroomed, and the newspaper Bild published the following headline: "The madness with claims! Who is really making sense of this?" and added the different variants (see Figure 4).

Figure 4: Information Overload via Claims

Consumers are also easily influenced by (initial) comments published on the internet. In this way they demonstrate herd behaviour, as Campbell et al. (2011) verified. This herd behaviour often leads to panic or other irrational reactions that might be harmful for consumers.

In this way, it is likely that consumers adopt the opinions of others without verifying them. Consequently, people or brands are unjustly criticised. To avoid such situations, the editorial department of the portal "Lebensmittelklarheit.de" asks the criticised companies in turn to release a written statement. In addition, the editorial staff assesses the situation from both perspectives. After the these assessments are finished, the consumer complaints, the company's written statement and the additional assessments by the office are published online (FocusOnline 2011). This contributes to a climate in which companies are willing to change and make amendments.

Finally, empirical studies have emphasised that consumers' boycotts are fiercely debated in public, but change little about the situation itself. Koku (2012, p. 20) summarises his empirical findings as follows: "The results show that consumer boycotts launched by individuals on the internet are ineffective in inflicting economic harm on the targeted firm." In the analysis, 63 appeals to boycott were counted. The findings might be perceived as disillusionment by supporters of consumer democracy.

4. Conclusion

So how do we conclude? On the one hand, it is beneficial that opportunities for inclusion and therefore consumer sovereignty have increased. Consumers intend to take more responsibility. In addition, some consumers are tired and frustrated with the EU's overregulation in the area of consumer protection and they fear that they will lose more and more responsibility.

On the other hand, different findings based on consumer behaviour research stress the fact that direct consumer democracy is not always efficient and doesn't always deliver immediate results. Certain state-run organisations and regulations are urgently needed in order to guarantee suitable consumer protection. Companies, in particular, are in favour of state regulations as they protect and assure competitiveness as well as prohibit unfair competition. Therefore, a balance between essential protection and overregulation needs to be established.

The overriding aim to protect consumers from non-transparent marketing techniques is difficult to achieve, and certain techniques are still used to control consumer behaviour. Providing consumers with information and raising their awareness of these marketing techniques cannot prevent any behavioural control, as many of these techniques activate automatic responses. Once they are activated, consumers cannot suppress their responses, even though they are informed about the influence and use of these techniques. Consequently, it is necessary to increase consumer protection in order to avoid a lack of transparency and deliberate behavioural control, as consumers cannot fully protect themselves against these techniques.

References

CAMPBELL, C.; PITT, L.F.; PARENT, M.; BERTHON, P. (2011): Understanding Consumer Conversations Around Ads in a Web 2.0 World, in: Journal of Advertising, Vol. 40, No. 1, pp. 87–102.

EIBL-EIBESFELDT, I. (1995): Der vorprogrammierte Mensch. Das Ererbte als bestimmender Faktor im menschlichen Verhalten, Kiel.

FOCUSONLINE (2011): Online-Pranger für Lebensmittel kollabiert, http://www.focu s.de/finanzen/recht/lebensmittelklarheit-de-online-pranger-fuer-lebensmittel-kollabi ert_aid_647774.html, accessed on March 25, 2013.

GRÖPPEL-KLEIN, A.; KÖNIGSTORFER, J. (2013): Nutrition Information and Consumer Behaviour at the Point-of-Sale, in: SCHOLDERER, J.; BRUNSO, K. (Eds.): Marketing, Food and the Consumer, Festschrift für Klaus Grunert, Aarhus, pp. 173-188.

HEIDBRINK, L.; SCHMIDT, I.; AHAUS, B. (Eds.) (2011): Die Verantwortung der Konsumenten: Über das Verhältnis von Markt, Moral und Konsum, Frankfurt et al.

KLEIN, N. (2000): No Logo: Taking Aim at the Brand Bullies, New York.

KOKU, P.S. (2012): On the Effectiveness of Consumer Boycotts Organized through the Internet: The Market Model, in: Journal of Services Marketing, Vol. 26, No. 1, pp. 20-26.

KÖNIGSTORFER, J.; GRÖPPEL-KLEIN, A. (2012): Wahrnehmungs- und Kaufverhaltenswirkungen von Nährwertkennzeichnungen auf Lebensmitteln, in: Marketing ZFP - Journal of Research and Management, Vol. 34, No. 3, pp. 213-226.

KROEBER-RIEL, W.; GRÖPPEL-KLEIN, A. (2013): Konsumentenverhalten, 10th ed., München.

LAMLA, J. (2011): Verbraucherdemokratie: Ein Zwischenbericht zur Politik der Konsumgesellschaft, in: HEIDBRINK, L.; SCHMIDT, I.; AHAUS, B. (Eds.): Die Verantwortung der Konsumenten: Über das Verhältnis von Markt, Moral und Konsum, Frankfurt et al., pp. 93-112.

OEHLER, A.; REISCH, L.A. (2012): Sie lebt! Zur Verbraucherforschung im deutschsprachigen Raum: Eine empirische Analyse, in: Journal für Verbraucherschutz und Lebensmittelsicherheit, Vol. 7, No. 1, pp. 105-115.

SCHWAN, P. (2009): Der informierte Verbraucher? Das verbraucherpolitische Leitbild auf dem Prüfstand: Eine Untersuchung am Beispiel des Lebensmittelsektors, Wiesbaden.

STÖTZEL, C. (2010): Corporate Social Responsibility: Adipositas als Herausforderung für Nahrungsmittelhersteller: Marketingmaßnahmen zwischen Gewinn und Gewissen, Hamburg.

UNFRIED, P. (2008): Öko: Al Gore, der neue Kühlschrank und ich, Köln.

ZIMPEL, G. (1972): Selbstbestimmung oder Akklamation: Politische Teilnahme in der bürgerlichen Demokratietheorie, Stuttgart.

How Sustainable is Sustainability? The Impact of Corporate Social Irresponsibility on Consumer Behaviour in Retailing

Hanna Schramm-Klein and Sascha Steinmann

Overview

1. Introduction

In the past, many companies have implemented several activities from the field of corporate social responsibility (CSR) to be perceived as a good corporate citizen as well as to gain a sustainable competitive advantage from corresponding business practices (Chabowski/Mena/Gonzales-Padron 2010; Wagner/Bicen/Hall 2008). These business practices include activities such as ethical sourcing, cause-related marketing, socially responsible employment or corporate philanthropy. The concept of corporate social responsibility has not only been introduced and intensified by manufacturing companies or service providers, but has also become a relevant topic as well as a strategic success factor for retail companies.

The concept of corporate social responsibility is by no means new in the academic and practice oriented literature. The concept and the discussion about the necessity and relevance of socially responsible and sustainable business practices date back to the 1930s. Dodd (1932, p. 1149) argued that a company has to be socially responsible and sustainable because it is "permitted and encouraged by the law, primarily because it is a service to the community, rather than because it is a source of profit to its owners". Therefore, managers should not only act profit oriented and are not only responsible to the shareholders of their company, but also to the society as a whole, including e.g., its suppliers, its employees, its customers as well as the government. From then on, the concept has been extended by several domains of corporate responsiveness leading to a more robust and comprehensive understanding of corporate social responsibility. For example, McGuire/Dow/Archgeyd (2003) classified CSR into the four domains of *community support, employee relations, environmental support* and socially responsible and sustainable *product and business practices*, the latter one also covering ethical sourcing. Furthermore, it was argued by Mahoney/Thom (2006) that *diversity* as well as *international company efforts* have to be included as additional domains in the concept of corporate social responsibility. Overall, a company's (CSR) activities should therefore not only relate to making profit; rather, corporations should strive to further some social good that goes beyond the interests of the firm as well as the requirements of the law and thus, positively influence the society as a whole (Lindgreen/Swaen/Johnston 2009; McWilliams/Siegel/Wright 2006).

Because of the potential positive effects of socially responsible and sustainable corporate behaviour, the concept of corporate social responsibility has broadly been discussed and analysed in academic research. (e.g. Carroll 1999; De Bakker/Groenewegen/Den Hond 2005). Many of these studies are focused on the issue whether activities in the different domains of CSR could be considered as strategic success factors for a company and will lead to sustainable competitive advantages. This research question has mainly been addressed from a company perspective; specifically, the impact of CSR activities on corporate performance e.g., the market value of a company or its financial performance (for an overview see Orlitzky/Schmidt/Rynes 2003 and Wu 2006). The potential positive effects of CSR on corporate performance could only be realised if consumers are aware of such efforts and if the corporate social behaviour is evaluated as credible by the potential and actual customers. This will positively influence consumer beliefs regarding the CSR activities of a company and also could foster consumer attitudes towards the firm (Bhattacharya/Korschun/Sen 2009; Luo/Bhattacharya 2006; Schuler/Cording 2006).

Regarding its topicality in retail practice, few studies have comprehensively analysed the role of CSR in retailing (Pirsch/Gupta/Grau 2007). Especially for retail companies the correct management of CSR to become good corporate citizens in from the consumers' point of view is not an easily realised task. Consumer perceptions of the ethically and socially responsible behaviour of retailers depend not only on the retailer's CSR activities, but also on socially responsible behaviour of manufacturing companies as well as other parties in the supply chain. Thus, one would expect negative carry-over and spill-over effects in consumer perceptions of retailers from socially irresponsible behaviour by producers, which could have a negative impact on the overall performance of the retailer in the marketplace. Therefore, a comprehensive understanding of the impact of CSR activities as well as of the effects of unethical corporate behaviour on long-term consumer behaviour is of great relevance in the field of retailing.

While mostly the discussion on the potential impact of ethically and socially responsible corporate behaviour is centred on "positive" CSR activities of retailers, whether these findings can be transferred to "negative" CSR remains undetermined. It might be plausible to conclude that a so-called "scandal", e.g., violations of social norms, especially (with regard to our study) in an unethical and socially irresponsible manner, by a retail company or supplier (e.g., due to offering unhealthy products or due to an unethical employee treatment), could have negative effects on consumer loyalty toward the retailer and would be therefore, also reflected in consumer purchasing behaviour (Sen/Bhattacharya 2001) as well as in consumer store choice decisions (Klein/Smith/John 2004).

But, one might conclude, if past CSR activities of the retailer were perceived as credible by the consumers and have led to a positive attitude towards the retail company that the negative effects of a scandal might only occur in the short-run and that the company will be rewarded for its past CSR efforts, especially when the retailer is not the direct responsible party for the occurrence of a scandal.

Thus, this article implicitly addresses whether CSR activities of retail companies contribute to retailer performance and how this performance is affected due to the occurrence of a scandal. The remainder of this article is organised as follows. First, we introduce the relevant aspects of CSR by reviewing the relevant literature, focusing on possible effects of CSR activities on consumer behaviour. Next, based on a data set from a German household panel, which details the purchasing behaviour at different retailers over one year, we show that unethical corporate behaviour, e.g., violating human rights or offering harmful products, could have a negative effect on the purchase behaviour of consumers, resulting in decreasing purchases of regularly priced products and decreasing purchases of private label brands. Finally, we conclude with a summary of our findings.

2. Corporate Social Responsibility and Irresponsibility in Retailing

2.1 Corporate Social Responsibility: Definition and Domains

According to Schuler/Cording (2006, p. 544) CSR could be defined as "a voluntary [...] business action that produces social (third-party) effects". These business actions cover three main elements: social outcomes, market and social behaviour, and voluntary behaviours. Therefore, CSR is closely related to corporate citizenship (Carrol 1998; Matten/Crane 2003), corporate social performance (Luo/Bhattacharya 2006), corporate environmental performance (Russo/Fouts 1997) and stakeholder management (McWilliams/Siegel/Wright 2006). Overall, with regard to Mohr/Webb/Harris (2001) the concept of corporate social responsibility refers to the commitment of a company to eliminate and minimise any deleterious influences as well as to maximise its beneficial impact on society in the long-run. In this context, the discussions about a successful implementation of CSR activities were focused on what activities or domains should be included as components of CSR to gain a sustainable and long-term competitive advantage.

With regard to the "pyramid of corporate social responsibility" introduced by Carroll (1979)[1], several attempts have been made to categorise different domains of ethical and social responsible corporate behaviour (e.g., Maignan/Ferrel/Ferrel 2005; Wagner/Bicen/Hall 2008). For example, according to Brunk (2010) the CSR activities should include efforts to positively influence e.g., the consumers' perception of the company, the motivation of the employees to work for the company, to minimise a potentially negative impact of the environment, the local economy and community, the overseas community as well as the business community.

Sen/Bhattacharya (2001) analysed the CSR activities of 600 companies and classified them into six more or less similar domains: community support, diversity, employee support, environment, non-domestic operations, and products. Furthermore, based on their findings these authors also provide examples for successful CSR efforts in the different mentioned domains which could lead to a positive perception of the company from the consumers' perspective and therefore should also have a positive impact on attitude formation. For example, with regard to community support a company has the opportunity to introduce or to engage in health programs or to support educational initiatives (e.g. sponsoring of text books for schools or universities). In the domain of diversity family-, gender-, and disability-based initiatives should also have a positive impact on the consumers' evaluation of the CSR activities of a company.

2.2 The Role of Corporate Social Responsibility in Retailing

To be perceived as a good corporate citizen, a company's socially responsible behaviour should include activities in each of the six domains introduced by Sen/Bhattacharya (2001). For example, in the retail sector, CSR closely relates to the combination of products offered (e.g., organic and fair trade products and private labels), ethical sourcing (e.g., sustainable farming, no child labour), product quality, pricing, services, employee treatment and support (e.g., fair-minded wages and health safety protection) and community support. Today, retailers consider these activities to be important elements of their overall marketing strategy (e.g., Walmart's Global Responsibility Report 2012). Therefore, it is increasingly common for retailers to spend money, time and effort on CSR-related activities to influence the overall perceptions of customers and non-customers about the store's position as a good corporate citizen and to achieve a long-term sustainable growth. Moreover, increasing public criticism of socially "irresponsible" practices is driving retailers to behave as good corporate citizens through efforts with regard to CSR (Wagner/Bicen/Hall 2008). Stakeholders, such as governments (through regulations), non-governmental organisations, media, investors, and financial markets, have offered these criticisms. Furthermore, pressures from consumers drive retailers toward socially responsible behaviours (Piacentini/MacFayden/Eadie 2000).

But, to gain the potential positive effects of ethical and social responsible behaviour, retail companies have to ensure that the consumers are aware of the several efforts due to an effective and efficient marketing communication. Retailers communicate their socially responsible behaviour to society (e.g. Wal-Mart's Global Responsibility Report 2012; TESCO Corporate Responsibility Review 2012) to improve their image as well as their overall performance in the marketplace (Cochran/Wood 1984; Gupta/Pirsch 2008; Margolis/Walsh 2003).

However, being perceived by consumers as a good corporate citizen is a complex and difficult goal, especially for retailers. Because of the specific role of retailers as an intermediary – a gatekeeper – between the supplier and the consumer, consumer perceptions of the ethically and socially responsible behaviour of retailers not only depend on the CSR activities of retailers but also on the socially responsible behaviour of suppliers and other parties in the retailer's supply chain. Thus, if a supplier demonstrates a socially irresponsible behaviour in the production process, e.g., non-ethical sourcing or human rights violations, one would expect a spill-over effect of this unethical behaviour in consumer perceptions of the retailer. In the context of ethically and socially responsible retail, offering products associated with irresponsible behaviour might have a negative impact on retailer image, consumer loyalty toward the retailer, and consumer purchasing behaviour at the retailer which in turn will have an negative effect on the retailer's performance in the marketplace (Schramm-Klein et al. 2013).

Surprisingly, only a few studies have analysed the impact of CSR activities from the consumer perspective, even though consumers are one of the key stakeholders because their purchase decisions directly affect a company's revenue and overall financial performance. In general, it could be expected that consumers reward CSR activities with positive attitudes and beliefs toward the company and/or with favourable purchasing behaviour (Brown/Dacin 1997; Folkes/Kamis 1999). Additionally, the fit between a company's social marketing activities on the one hand and its products (or services) and the motivation of consumers on the other hand is of considerable importance (Barone/Norman/Miyazaki 2007). Aggressive and insincere CSR practices or activities, perceived as deleterious or illegitimate, foster negative consumer attitudes and reactions in terms of purchasing behaviour (Sen/Bhattacharya 2001). In this context, findings from academic research showed that the perceived motivation, orientation and credibility of CSR initiatives are also relevant to the purchasing intentions of consumers (Barone/Minard/Romeo 2000; Scholder Ellen/Webb/Mohr 2006). Therefore, consumers seem to challenge the ("true") intentions of companies to engage in CSR and their CSR orientation (Chabowski/ Mena/Gonzales-Padron 2010). Hence, unethical activities should negatively influence the ethical assessment of the retailer and further might have a negative effect on the satisfaction with the provided products (e.g., private labelled brands and services).

2.3 Unethical and Socially Irresponsible Corporate Behaviour in Retailing

While most of the previous mentioned studies focused on "positive" CSR activities of retailers, whether these findings can be transferred to "negative" CSR remains undetermined. It might be plausible to conclude that a so-called "scandal", e.g., violations of social norms, especially (with regard to our study) in an unethical and socially irresponsible manner, by a retail company or supplier (e.g., due to offering unhealthy products or due to an unethical employee treatment), could have negative effects on consumer loyalty toward the retailer and could, therefore, also affect consumer purchasing behaviour (Sen/Bhattacharya 2001; Webb/Mohr 1998). Such a scandal could also result in a consumer boycott against the unethical retail company (Klein/Smith/John 2004; Kozinets/Handelmann 1998). The effects of such scandals might be reflected in a decrease of purchases in a single shopping trip to the involved retailer or in a decreased purchase value in a consumer's purchases. In this context, unethical and socially irresponsible corporate behaviour would decrease the retailer's sales volume and revenue.

In the last years, several incidents of unethical and socially irresponsible behaviour occurred in the German retail sector. These scandals were released to the public and discussed intensively in the German media. For example, one of the largest discount retail chains in the German food sector was found to be responsible for the violation of human rights in developing countries by not paying fair wages and for unhealthy conditions of workers of producers in the retailer's supply chain. Furthermore, the systematic observation and recording of the behaviour of employees of several German retail chains during working hours, e.g., by using surveillance cameras, as well as their activities in their spare time and the illegal storage of the personal data of employees were also discovered recently. Moreover, retail companies inhibited the formation of worker councils by their employees and also prohibited employee membership in labour unions using so-called Yellow-dog employment contracts or by pressuring employees with several negative consequences for such engagements. In addition to those instances of illegal and unethical treatment of employees, several retailers in the German food sector displayed irresponsible social behaviour by offering contaminated, harmful products to customers. In some cases, the consumption of such food items even led to the death of consumers.

All of the previously mentioned examples were discovered and broadly discussed by German TV, newspapers and news magazines during the one-year study period. In some of these reports, consumers were called to boycott the unethical and socially irresponsible retail companies.

In line with the occurrence and publication of these violations of social norms, the retailers affected by or responsible for scandals undertook considerable communication efforts to mitigate potentially negative effects in sales volume and revenues, potentially negative perceptions in society, potentially negative effects on consumer loyalty, and potentially negative impacts of future consumer purchasing behaviour.

3. An Analysis of the Impact of Unethical and Social Irresponsible Corporate Behavior on Consumer Behaviour in Retailing

To assess the previously discussed assumptions, we evaluated the impact of unethical and socially irresponsible behaviour of retailers by analysing consumer purchasing behaviour at different retailers in Germany. We used a data of a German household panel reflecting a household's purchasing behaviour (i.e., purchase data) over a one-year time period. The data set includes full information on household purchasing behaviour in the fast moving consumer goods (FMCG) sector, including information on the retail companies chosen for each shopping trip, the number of purchased products for each shopping occasion, the purchase value of the different shopping trips, as well as the percentage of private labelled brands purchased in each single shopping trip. Furthermore, the data reflects the share of specially priced products bought and the share of purchases of other sales promotions (e.g., "buy one get one free") in purchases with respect to a single shopping trip.

We analysed the potential effects of the previously discussed scandals on consumer purchasing behaviour by using regression analysis (Draper/ Smith 1998) with the number of purchased products in a single shopping trip at a specific retailer, the purchase value, the percentage of private labelled brands purchased and the percentage of specially priced products purchased in a single shopping trip at specific retail companies involved in or affected by a scandal as dependent variables.

We conducted our analyses for different discount retail chains (discounter 1, discounter 2, discounter 3) as well as for different retailers (retailer 1, retailer 2, retailer 3, retailer 4) involved in or affected by a scandal during the covered one-year time period of the household panel data.

As expected, the findings of our analyses show that for each of the considered discount retail chains, as well as for each considered retail chain, the occurrence of a scandal has a small but significant negative impact on the percentage of purchases of a retailer's private labelled brands during each shopping trip. But, this negative effect is much stronger if a discount retail chain is involved in a scandal, compared to a situation in which a non-discount retail chain is affected by unethical and socially irresponsible corporate behaviour. In general, one might conclude that a plausible reason for this negative impact could be a negative spill-over effect of the consumer perceptions of the retail brand or a specific retailer and the evaluation of the private label brands of the retailer, which is reflected in the consumers' brand choice behaviour at the point-of-sale in the time period after the occurrence of a scandal. Furthermore, products offered by a discount retail chain as well as private label brands are often evaluated as being of lower quality than other brands (Semeijn/Van Riel/Ambrosini 2004). Therefore, especially if the scandal relates to the sale of harmful food items by the retailer, another possible reason for the obtained negative effect might be that customers are trying to decrease the perceived risk of consuming unhealthy products by changing their brand choice behaviour from private label brands to other brands which are not involved in the scandal and, therefore, perceived as secure and not harmful products.

Contrary to our expectations, our results showed that the occurrence of a scandal does not have negative effects on consumer purchasing behaviour or store choice behaviour in general. For example, for each of the considered discount retail chains and for each of the affected retail chains, scandals had a positive effect on the percentage of specially priced products bought during a single shopping. One might conclude that especially price sensitive consumers are less affected in their store choice behaviour due to the occurrence of a scandal, while it seems that less price sensitive consumers penalise the retailer by choosing retail brands which are not affected by unethical and irresponsible corporate behaviour. Hence, the share of price sensitive consumers of the retail chain involved in the scandal increases, which in turn increases the percentage of specially priced products bought in a single shopping trip.

Furthermore, we found several positive effects on the number of purchased products in a single shopping trip and the purchasing value of the purchases in the time period after the scandal. In this context, these positive effects mainly occur if the scandal was triggered by a supplier of specific unhealthy or harmful products offered in the retailer's stores and therefore, the retailer was not the party directly responsible for the occurrence of the scandal. With regard to that, it seems suitable for a retail company to implement a communications strategy that weakens the potential negative effects of this kind of unethical and socially irresponsible corporate behaviour for their image in society, e.g., by cautioning their customers about the consumption of the contaminated food items by providing the information on posters in their stores or on the retailer's website, as well as by giving their customers the opportunity to return these products in an uncomplicated way, free of charge. Such activities could emphasise the authenticity of retailer intentions to be good corporate citizens with regard to the credibility of their overall CSR initiatives, which is rewarded by the customers in terms of positive attitudes toward the retailer and favourable purchasing behaviour (Folkes/Kamins 1999; Murray/ Vogel 1997). Furthermore, these positive effects could be explained due potentially positive consumer perceptions and evaluations of past CSR activities and CSR communication on the loyalty of the consumers which could positively influence patronage behaviour towards a specific retail company.

However, we also obtained negative effects on the number of purchased products in a single shopping as well as on the purchase value, especially when a discount retail chain was involved in the occurrence of a scandal. But, these negative influences only were obtained for retail companies that were directly responsible for the unethical and socially irresponsible incident. Interestingly, negative influences of a scandal mainly occur when the retailer was involved in the systematic observation and recording of the behaviour of employees during working hours, e.g., by using surveillance cameras. This kind of observation could affect consumers privacy concerns and therefore, have an impact on consumer's store choice decision, because such observation techniques could also be used to observe customers while they visiting the store.

4. Discussion and Implications

The findings of our analysis show that CSR activities seem to be of considerable importance for consumer behaviour and have to be maintained by retailers to ensure continued impact on long-term consumer purchasing behaviour. In this context, the conclusions drawn from the findings of the household panel analysis let us conclude that potential long-term positive and sustainable effects of CSR activities positively influences consumer loyalty towards a retailer as well as consumer purchasing behaviour, especially when the retail company is not directly responsible for the occurrence of a scandal. But, if a scandal occurs a negative effect on purchases of private labelled brands of the involved retailer has to be expected. Moreover, the findings let us conclude that consumer store choice decisions could also be affected due to the occurrence of a scandal. It seems that especially less price sensitive consumers will switch from the retailer or retail brand involved in unethical and socially irresponsible behaviour to another non-involved retailed brand after the scandal was discovered and broadly discussed in the media.

However, there is still the question what drives the identified relationships of our analyses. With regard to the findings of Schramm-Klein et al. (2013), we conclude that these effects could mainly be driven by the overall store image due to the consumers' perception of different retailer attributes, like the overall customer service, value for money, the retailer's in-store design, as well as the assortment (see also Mazursky/Jacoby 1986). The perception of the retailer's attributes has especially positively affects not only customer loyalty, but also purchasing behaviour. Those results indicate that consumers rely more on retailer (or store) attributes to decide on future purchasing intentions, which affect the current and future purchasing intensity of consumers and are only less affected by the occurrence of a scandal, especially when the retailer is not directly responsible for the socially irresponsible incident. Based on the results of Schramm-Klein et al. (2013), we assume that the consumers' perception and evaluation of CSR activities of a retailer which could have a positive impact on consumer loyalty as well as on consumer purchasing behaviour could be a reason for the identified effects of analysis. Therefore, if consumers are aware of the retailer's CSR activities, a single scandal might only have a negative effect in the short-run, while in the long-run the retail company is rewarded by the consumers' perception of its "true-intentions" of several CSR activities (e.g., sponsoring of local sports and cultural events, local sourcing, fair employee treatment, environment protection). Therefore, the credibility of past and current CSR activities is also of crucial relevance for a retailer to minimise the potential negative effects of the occurrence of a scandal on consumer behaviour in the short-run and especially in the long-run (Newell/Goldsmith 2001). In general, the results of Schramm-Klein et al. (2013) indicate that retailer CSR activities are less important in terms of influences on purchasing behaviour, while influences on attitudinal dimensions, such as loyalty, are more strongly and directly impacted by perceived CSR. Overall, these findings provide reasonable explanations especially for the obtained positive effects of the occurrence of a scandal in our analysis. We conclude that the strength of the customers' loyalty towards the retailer, which is positively affected by the CSR activities of a specific retailer, is an important influencing factor which has a high potential to weaken the potential negative effects due to patronage behaviour (Pan/Zinkhan 2006) of the consumers if a scandal occurs.

Overall, the results imply that (ongoing) communication of CSR activities, highlighting different CSR domains, both at the point of sale and in the form of general marketing communication, is important for keeping consumers informed about company activities, especially in the period after a scandal that could negatively affect consumer perceptions of the retailer, even when the retailer is not directly responsible for the occurrence of the scandal. We assume that honesty, sincerity and credibility of communication activities are of key importance for a retailer's success.

However, as a limitation of our study we evaluated the influence of unethical and socially irresponsible behaviour on consumer behaviour in the context of CSR, using analyses of household panel data but without regarding consumer perceptions of the different scandals during the covered time period. Therefore, we could not derive detailed information on the trade-offs between perceived CSR activities and specific retail marketing-mix instruments, such as price or convenience, and their influence on consumer behaviour.

Furthermore, in our analysis of the household panel data, we only evaluated the impact of the occurrence of a scandal on single dependent variables, but we did not analyse potential interdependencies or interaction effects between the effects of a scandal, for example, on consumer store choice behaviour. We also did not differentiate diverse forms of socially or ethically irresponsible behaviour, but our findings imply that different kinds of scandals will differ in their strength and direction of the impact on consumer behaviour as the positive and negative effects on the number of purchased products as well as on the purchasing value of a single shopping trip have shown. Positive effects were obtained for situations when the retailer was not the responsible party for the occurrence of a scandal. If the retailer is directly responsible for the unethical on socially irresponsible behaviour e.g., due to unfair employee treatment, this will have a negative impact on consumer purchase behaviour at this retailer.

These limitations clearly indicate areas for future research. A possible limitation of our study could also be the specific retail context (Germany) of our study. As German customers are well known for price-oriented behaviour and for a specific consciousness for CSR issues, reactions within other cultural contexts might be interesting. Thus, the relationships between CSR and consumer behaviour should be tested in other sectors and in other countries. Last but not least, changes in the environmental conditions, especially in the economic conditions, might have an impact on the consumers' perceptions and reactions of different CSR activities of a retailer. This implies a longitudinal study on the impact of environmental conditions on the perception of CSR activities of a retailer as well as on their credibility and CSR orientation of the consumers over time.

Notes

1 According to Carroll (1979), corporate social responsibility could be conceptualised as four expectations that society has of organisations: the economic domain ("being profitable"), the legal domain ("obeying the law"), the ethical domain ("being ethical") and the philanthropic domain ("being a good citizen").

References

BARONE, M.J.; MINIARD, P.W.; ROMEO, J.B. (2000): The Influence of Positive Mood on Brand Extension Evaluations, in: Journal of Consumer Research, Vol. 26, No. 4, pp. 386-400.

BARONE, M.J.; NORMAN, A.T.; MIYAZAKI, A.D. (2007): Consumer Response to Retailer Use of Cause-Related Marketing: Is More Fit Better?, in: Journal of Retailing, Vol. 83, No. 4, pp. 437-445.

BHATTACHARYA, C.B.; KORSCHUN, D.; SEN, S. (2009): Strengthening Stakeholder Company Relationships through Mutually Beneficial Corporate Social Responsibility Initiatives, in: Journal of Business Ethics, Vol. 85, No. 2, pp. 257-72.

BROWN, T.J.; DACIN, P.A. (1997): The Company and the Product: Corporate Associations and Consumer Product Responses, in: Journal of Marketing, Vol. 61, No. 1, pp. 68-84.

BRUNK, K.H. (2010): Exploring Origins of Ethical Company/Brand Perceptions: A Consumer Perspective of Corporate Ethics, in: Journal of Business Research, Vol. 63, No. 3, pp. 255-262.

CARROLL, A.B. (1979): A Three-Dimensional Conceptual Model of Corporate Performance, in: Academy of Management Review, Vol. 4, No. 4, pp. 497-505.

CARROLL, A.B. (1998): The Four Faces of Corporate Citizenship, in: Business and Society Review, Vol. 100, No. 1, pp. 1-7.

CARROLL, A.B. (1999): Corporate Social Responsibility, in: Business and Society, Vol. 38, No. 3, pp. 268-295.

CHABOWSKI, B.; MENA, J.; GONZALES-PADRON, T. (2010): The Structure of Sustainability Research in Marketing, 1958-2008: A Basis for Future Research Opportunities, in: Journal of the Academy of Marketing Science, Vol. 39, No. 1, pp. 55-70.

COCHRAN, P.L.; WOOD, R.A. (1984): Corporate Social Responsibility and Financial Performance, in: The Academy of Management Journal, Vol. 27, No. 1, pp. 42-56.

DE BAKKER, F.G.A.; GROENEWEGEN, P.; DEN HOND, F. (2005): A Bibliometric Analysis of 30 Years of Research and Theory on Corporate Social Responsibility and Corporate Social Performance, in: Business and Society, Vol. 44, No. 3, pp. 283-317.

DODD, E.M. (1932): For Whom are Corporate Managers Trustees?, in: Harvard Law Review, Vol. 45, No. 7, pp. 1145-1163.

DRAPER, N.R.; SMITH, H. (1998): Applied Regression Analysis, 3rd ed., New York.

FOLKES, V.S.; KAMINS, M.A. (1999): Effects of Information About Firms' Ethical and Unethical Actions on Consumers' Attitudes, in: Journal of Consumer Psychology, Vol. 8, No. 3, pp. 243-259.

GUPTA, S.; PIRSCH, J. (2008): The Influence of Retailers Corporate Social Responsibility Program on Re-Conceptualizing Store Image, in: Journal of Retailing and Consumer Services, Vol. 15, No. 6, pp. 516-526.

KLEIN, J.G.; SMITH, N.C.; JOHN, A. (2004): Why We Boycott: Consumer Motivations for Boycott Participation, in: Journal of Marketing, Vol. 68, No.3, pp. 92-109.

KOZINETS, R.V.; HANDELMAN, J.M. (1998): Ensouling Consumption: A Netnographic Exploration of Boycotting Behavior, in: Advances in Consumer Research, Vol. 25, No. 1, pp. 475-480.

LINDGREEN, A.; SWAEN, V.; JOHNSTON, W.J. (2009): Corporate Social Responsibility: An Empirical Investigation of U.S. Organisations, in: Journal of Business Ethics, Vol. 85, No. 2, pp. 303-323.

LUO, X.; BHATTACHARYA, C.B. (2006): Corporate Social Responsibility, Customer Satisfaction, and Market Value, in: Journal of Marketing, Vol. 70, No. 4, pp. 1-18.

MAHONEY, L.S.; THORN, L. (2006): An Examination of the Structure of Executive Compensation and Corporate Social Responsibility: A Canadian Investigation, in: Journal of Business Ethics, Vol. 69, No. 2, pp. 149-162.

MAIGNAN, I.; FERRELL, O.C.; FERRELL, L. (2005): A Stakeholder Model for Implementing Social Responsibility in Marketing, in: European Journal of Marketing, Vol. 39, No. 9/10, pp. 956-977.

MARGOLIS, J.D.; WALSH, J.P. (2003): Misery Loves Companies: Rethinking Social Initiatives by Business; in: Administrative Science Quarterly, Vol. 48, No. 2, pp. 268-305.

MATTEN, D.; CRANE, A. (2005): Corporate Citizenship: Toward an Extended Theoretical Conceptualization, in: Academy of Management Review, Vol. 30, No. 1, pp. 166-179.

MAZURSKY, D.; JACOBY, J. (1986): Exploring the Development of Store Images, in: Journal of Retailing, Vol. 62, No. 2, pp. 145-165.

MCGUIRE, J.B.; DOW, S.; ARCHGEYD, K. (2003): CEO Incentives and Corporate Social Responsibility; in: Journal of Business Ethics, Vol. 45, No. 4, pp. 341-359.

MCWILLIAMS, A.; SIEGEL, D.S.; WRIGHT, P.M (2006): Corporate Social Responsibility: International Perspectives, in: Journal of Business Strategies, Vol. 23, No. 1, pp. 1-12.

MOHR, L.A.; WEBB, D.J.; HARRIS, K.E. (2001): Do Consumers Expect Companies to Be Socially Responsible? The Impact of Corporate Social Responsibility on Buying Behavior, in: Journal of Consumer Affairs, Vol. 35, No. 1, pp. 45-72.

MURRAY, K.B.; VOGEL, C.M. (1997): Using a Hierarchy-of-Effects Approach to Gauge the Effectiveness of Corporate Social Responsibility to Generate Goodwill Toward the Firm: Financial versus Nonfinancial Impacts, in: Journal of Business Research, Vol. 38, No. 2, pp. 141-159.

NEWELL, S.J.; GOLDSMITH, R.E. (2001): The Development of a Scale to Measure Perceived Corporate Credibility, in: Journal of Business Research, Vol. 52, No. 3, pp. 235-247.

ORLITZKY, M.; SCHMIDT, F.L.; RYNES, S.L. (2003): Corporate Social and Financial Performance: A Meta-Analysis, in: Organization Studies, Vol. 24, No. 3, pp. 403-441.

PAN, Y.; ZINKHAN, G.M. (2006): Determinants of Retail Patronage: A Meta-Analytical Perspective, in: Journal of Retailing, Vol. 82, No. 3, pp. 229-243.

PIACENTINI, M.G.; MACFADYEN, L.; EADIE, D.R. (2000): Corporate Social Responsibility in Food Retailing, in: International Journal of Retail and Distribution Management,Vol. 28, No. 11, pp. 459-469.

PIRSCH, J.; GUPTA, J.; GRAU, S.L. (2007): A Framework for Understanding Corporate Social Responsibility Programs as a Continuum: An Exploratory Study, in: Journal of Business Ethics, Vol. 70, No. 2, pp. 125-140.

RUSSO, M.V.; FOUTS, P.A. (1997): A Resource-Based Perspective on Corporate Environmental Performance and Profitability, in: Academy of Management Journal, Vol. 40, No. 3, pp. 534-559.

SCHOLDER ELLEN, P.; WEBB, D.J.; MOHR, L.A. (2006): Building Corporate Associations: Consumer Attributions for Corporate Aocially Responsible Programs, in: Journal of the Academy of Marketing Science, Vol. 34, No. 2, pp. 147-157.

SCHRAMM-KLEIN, H.; ZENTES, J.; STEINMANN, S.; SWOBODA, B.; MORSCHETT, D. (2013): Is Retailer Corporate Social Responsibility Relevant to Consumer Behavior?, in: Business and Society, Vol. 53 (forthcoming).

SCHULER, D.A.; CORDING, M. (2006): A Corporate Social Performance-Corporate Financial Performance Behavioral Model for Consumers, in: Academy of Management Review, Vol. 31, No. 3, pp. 540-558.

SEMEIJN, J.; VAN RIEL, A.C.; AMBROSINI, A.B. (2004): Consumer Evaluations of Store Brands: Effects of Store Image and Product Attributes, in: Journal of Retailing and Consumer Services, Vol. 11, No. 4, pp. 247-258.

SEN, S.; BHATTACHARYA, C. B. (2001): Does Doing Good Always Lead to Doing Better? Consumer Reactions to Corporate Social Responsibility, in: Journal of Marketing Research, Vol. 38, No. 2, pp. 225-243.

TESCO PLC (2012): It's at the Heart of What We Do: Tesco Corporate Responsibility Review 2012, Cheshunt.

WAGNER, T.; BICEN, P.; HALL, Z.R. (2008): The Dark Side of Retailing: Towards a Scale of Corporate Social Irresponsibility, in: International Journal of Retail and Distribution Management, Vol. 36, No. 2, pp. 124-142.

WEBB, D.J.; MOHR, L.A. (1998): A Typology of Consumer Responses to Cause-Related Marketing: From Skeptics to Socially Concerned, in: Journal of Public Policy and Marketing, Vol. 17, No. 2, pp. 226-238.

WEBB, D.J.; MOHR, L.A.; HARRIS, K.E. (2008): A Re-Examination of Socially Responsible Consumption and its Measurement, in: Journal of Business Research, Vol. 61, No. 2, pp. 91-98.

WAL-MART STORES, INC. (2012): Beyond 50 Years: Building a Sustainable Future, Global Responsibility Report 2012, Bentonville.

WU, M.-L. (2006): Corporate Social Performance, Corporate Financial Performance, and Firm Size: A Meta-Analysis, in: Journal of American Academy of Business, Vol. 8, No. 1, pp. 163-171.

Firm-NGO Alliances as a Proactive Approach to Credible Corporate Social Responsibility

Stefan Kolb and Joachim Zentes

Overview

1. Introduction

Non-governmental organisations (NGOs) have taken a permanent place in international business research (Lambell et al. 2008). The growing interest in NGOs is caused by their rapid growth both in number and influence (Bendell 2000; Teegen 2003). In the past, the relationship between companies and NGOs was often characterised as comparatively hostile (Elkington/Beloe 2010) and early literature often described NGOs as opponents of MNEs (Corlette 1989; Frooman 1999). However, the number and intensity of collaborations between firms and NGOs has risen substantially during the last 30 years (Graf/Rothlauf 2012; Lucea 2010) and recent literature describes NGOs more and more as legitimate partners of actors within the second sector (Lambell et al. 2008). This article focuses on CSR-alliances between NGOs and companies, including all facets of cooperative engagements aiming at corporate CSR-strategies. Environmental approaches, sometimes referred to as "green alliances" (Stafford/Hartman 1996; Arts 2002), and social approaches, sometimes called "social alliances" (Berger/Cunningham/Drumwright 2004), can be part of what we call a CSR-alliance. The advantages of CSR-alliances for business include new business opportunities, improved environmental performance and enhanced reputation. NGOs benefit from a greater impact on environmental and social gains, compared to cooperation with governments (Glasbergen/Groenenberg 2001).

2. Literature Review

As CSR-alliances have become an important tool for companies as well as for NGOs (Argenti 2004), the literature has increasingly started to focus on these kinds of relationships (Andreasen 1996; Austin 2000; Seitanidi/Crane 2009).

Several different research themes can be identified regarding the relationship between NGOs and companies. While some authors study the different strategies of NGOs and their impact on sustainability approaches of companies (Doh/Guay 2006; Joutsenvirta 2011), others focus on NGOs in a functional or institutional context (Brumley 2010; Doh/Teegen 2002). Another important research-stream entails the analysis of the various forms of collaboration between companies and NGOs, e.g. in terms of dialogue and partnerships (Argenti 2004; Austin 2000; Rondinelli/London 2003; Seitanidi/Crane 2009).

Graf/Rothlauf (2012) draw the conlusion that the literature lacks consensus on whether or not partnerships between companies and NGOs should be analysed analogously to firm-firm collaborations. Some authors point to obvious and compelling differences (Rondinelli/London 2003; Wymer/Samu 2003), while others, like Teegen/Doh/Vachani (2004, p. 476) argue, that "explorations of collaboration between NGOs and MNEs can be informed by lenses commonly used to examine partnering and alliances among firms." We address this research-gap in analysing partnerships between companies and NGOs using theories that focus traditionally on firm-firm collaborations, with minor adjustments to the peculiar nature of NGOs, and test our hypotheses with a quantitative database of 96 firm-NGO cooperations.

3. Theoretical Background and Hypotheses

There is no generally accepted definition of NGOs in the literature. The acronym itself contributes only little on explanation, as it makes clear what these organisations are not, rather than what they are (Vakil 1997). This paper follows the definition of Teegen/Doh/Vachani (2004, p. 466), who define NGOs as "private, not-for-profit organisations that aim to serve particular societal interests by focusing advocacy and/or operational efforts on social, political and economic goals, including equity, education, health, environmental protection and human rights." NGOs can be classified according to the benefits they aim to create: While membership NGOs focus on creating benefits for their members, social purpose NGOs intend to promote social interests (Teegen/Doh/Vachani 2004). This paper focuses exclusively on the latter.

With regard to the underlying theories, we follow Teegen/Doh/Vachani (2004), who suggest that a firm's competitive advantage caused by a firm-NGO-cooperation can be explained by theories commonly used in a firm-firm context. Starting from the stakeholder theory which has several implications relating to the formation of CSR-alliances, our model is based mainly on the relational view (RV) that is derived from the resource-based view (RBV).

Stakeholder theory argues that all legitimate individuals or groups affected by the activities of a firm will demand certain benefits. Referring to Freeman (1984), a stakeholder can be defined as "any group or individual who can affect or is affected by the achievement of an organisation's objectives". Secondary stakeholders like NGOs are relevant to this theory, as they are able to influence primary stakeholders (Phillips/Freeman/Wicks 2003), such as customers. This contributes to explaining the formation of CSR-alliances between companies and NGOs, as these partnerships focus on reducing the pressure imposed by a firm's stakeholders with regard to certain company activities.

A leading paradigm in strategic management, which aims at explaining the competitive advantage of a firm is the RBV, arguing that differential firm performance is due to firm heterogeneity, rather than to industry structure (Barney 1991). Complementary to the RBV, the RV builds on this notion but considers the dyad/network, instead of the individual firm (Chen/Paulraj 2004). This approach can therefore provide further insights into the creation of a competitive advantage through alliances, as here, an inter-firm focus is established explicitly (Duschek 2004). The RV is based mainly on the work of Dyer/Singh (1998). According to this theory, the main drivers of valuable relationships are investments in relationship-specific assets, a substantial knowledge exchange, the combination of complementary, but scarce resources or capabilities and more effective governance mechanisms (Dyer/Singh 1998).

Based on the above elements, we develop our conceptual model (see Figure 1), which contains minor adaptions to the specific nature of business-NGO-alliances. Based on the RV, an initial explanation of a competitive advantage derives from "idiosyncratic interfirm linkages" (Dyer/Singh 1998, p. 661) in the form of idiosyncratic resources. The model furthermore contains several elements originally rooted in the theory of social contracts (MacNeil 1980) and often used in the relationship marketing literature (Morgan/Hunt 1994; Hunt/Lambe/Wittmann 2002), such as cooperation (Dwyer/Schurr/Oh 1987; Morgan/Hunt 1994), trust (Achrol 1991), commitment (Berry/Parasuraman 1991), shared values (Dwyer/Schurr/Oh 1987; Nevin 1995) or the absence of opportunistic behaviour (John 1984) – which contribute self-enforcing agreements and accordingly treat effective government mechanisms as substantial promoters of knowledge exchange within relationships, from the perspective of the RV. In terms of an explorative analysis, the impact of the level of aggression of the partnering-NGO, as a moderating variable, is tested with regard to the relationships of the dependent and independent variables within the model.

Starting with the antecedents of the factors proposed as leading to a competitive advantage, opportunism can be defined as "self-interest seeking with guile" (Williamson 1975, p. 6). Concordant with Hunt/Lambe/Wittmann (2002), we propose a negative relationship between the opportunistic behaviour of an NGO and trust of a company in CSR-alliances:

H1: The more opportunistic the behaviour of an NGO, the lower the trust of the cooperating company in the NGO.

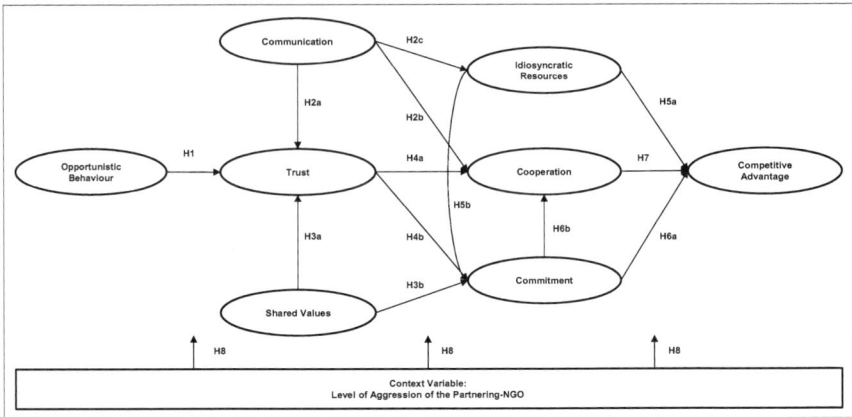

Figure 1: Conceptual Model

Communication can be understood as the "formal as well as informal sharing of meaningful and timely information between firms" (Anderson/ Narus 1990, 44). We assume a positive relationship between communication and trust in CSR-alliances, on the basis that the exchange of ideas and information between NGOs and companies helps to solve disputes and aligns expectations (Anderson/Narus 1990). Furthermore, as Hunt/Lambe/ Wittmann (2002) propose, communication directly promotes effective cooperation, which requires extensive interactions among partners. With regard to idiosyncratic resources, we assume that partner-specific knowledge is one of the most important resources in firm-NGO cooperations, and thus also assume a positive relationship between communication and idiosyncratic resources. Accordingly:

H2: The more communication between the NGO and the company,
   • the greater the trust of the cooperating company (H2a)
   • the greater the cooperation between both partners (H2b)
   • the more the idiosyncratic resources are built up over the course of the alliance (H2c).

Following the argumentation of Hunt/Lambe/Wittmann (2002), shared values can be understood as common beliefs in what is important or unimportant, appropriate or inappropriate and right or wrong. A positive relationship between shared values and trust, as well as shared values and commitment, is posited both in the marketing literature (Dwyer/Schurr/Oh

1987) and in that of organisational behaviour (Chatman 1991). According to the findings of the qualitative pre-study, we propose:

H3: The more shared values between the cooperating organisations,
- the greater the trust of the company in the NGO (H3a)
- the greater the commitment of the company (H3b).

As suggested by Dyer/Singh (1998), in the course of the RV, trust can be seen as a self-enforcing governance mechanism. Trust can be defined as the confidence of an alliance member in the integrity and reliability of the partner (Morgan/Hunt 1994). A positive relationship between trust and co-operation is supported, for example, by Anderson/Narus (1990). Further-more, a positive relationship between trust and commitment is underlined by social exchange theory and relationship marketing (Morgan/Hunt 1994). We therefore propose:

H4: The greater the trust of the cooperating company,
- the more the cooperation between both partners (H4a)
- the more the commitment towards the NGO (H4b).

Coming to the direct effects of competitive advantage, idiosyncratic re-sources are created by relation-specific investments or a combination of the resources of partner companies. They are developed by the alliance partners during the alliance and are useful only to the alliance, with little or no value outside the cooperation (Anderson/Weitz 1990; Jap 1999). Jap (1999) argues that alliance success results from partners developing idiosyncratic resources. Furthermore, we assume a positive effect of these resources on the commitment of the partners, which can be defined as "a desire to develop a stable relationship, a willingness to make short-term sacrifices to maintain the relationship, and confidence in the sustainability of the relationship" (Anderson/Weitz 1990, p. 19), as idiosyncratic re-sources lead to ligation. Therefore we argue:

H5: The more the idiosyncratic resources built up over the course of the alliance,
- the greater the competitive advantage of the cooperating company (H5a)
- the greater the commitment of the cooperating company (H5b).

Commitment is one of the key factors in alliances with regard to relation-ship success (Morgan/Hunt 1994). Furthermore, partners with high com-mitment to the alliance are more likely to cooperate and be willing to work hard for its success (Nevin 1995). Therefore, commitment is considered to have direct effects on competitive advantages generated by the CSR-alliance, as well as on cooperation, so that we assume:

H6: The greater the commitment of the cooperating company,
- the greater the competitive advantage of the cooperating company (H6a)
- the greater the cooperation between both partners (H6b).

Another factor that is commonly related to the success of alliances is cooperation. Anderson/Narus (1990, p. 45) define cooperation as "similar or complementary coordinated actions taken by firms in interdependent relationships to achieve mutual outcomes or singular outcomes with expected reciprocation over time." Das/Teng (1998) postulate that one of the main reasons why alliances fail is a low level of cooperation. Therefore we argue:

H7: The greater the cooperation between both partners, the greater the competitive advantage of the cooperating company.

NGO-strategies range from cooperative to confrontational (Valor/Diego 2009), and especially confrontational approaches are a common method of NGOs in pointing out business problems (Kong et al. 2002). In some cases, NGOs represent uneasy cooperation partners (Jamali/Keshishian 2009). Taking this into account, we assume that the level of aggression of the cooperating NGO has a moderating influence on the relationship between the factors in our model. Thus:

H8: The level of aggression of the cooperating NGO influences the relationship between the factors leading to a competitive advantage of the cooperating company in CSR-alliances.

4. Methodology

To investigate our research question, we gathered data from two different studies. First, we carried out a qualitative pre-study amongst international retail companies, consumer goods manufacturers, service companies and international NGOs. The purpose of these face-to-face expert interviews with CEOs and top managers of companies, as well as representatives of NGOs, was to pre-test the questionnaire for the quantitative survey, as well as to discuss the model and the underlying hypotheses.

Taking the findings of the qualitative pre-study into account, in a second step, we gathered quantitative information through a questionnaire survey, focusing explicitly on retail and service companies, as well as on consumer goods manufacturers in Germany, Switzerland and Austria. The companies maintained at least one CSR-alliance with an NGO. This questionnaire was pretested and finally adjusted by a group of eight research experts. A total of 2.600 questionnaires were sent out by e-mail, of which 98 were returned. A total of 96 questionnaires could finally be used for the calculation of our model. This yields a response rate of around 3.7%, which is satisfactory with regard to the specificity of our research-topic and displays a sufficient sample size to test our model with a PLS-analysis (Henseler/Ringle/Sinkovics 2009). The study contains 50 respondents from retail companies, 29 consumer goods manufacturers and 17 service companies. Each of the companies was asked to focus their answers on one single cooperation-project with an NGO. The projects described by the respondents have been in existence for more than five years on average, ranging from loose cooperations to more intense forms of alliance, like joint product development.

5. Measures

We used 7-point Likert scales to measure the indicators of our variables (Liu 2012). The model was tested by applying partial least squares structural equation modeling (PLS-SEM) (Simonin 2004), using SmartPLS, a powerful instrument for analysing small samples (Nijssen/Douglas 2008) which is well suited to an analysis of comparatively new research topics (Tsang 2002). Except for the level of aggression of the partnering-NGO, we used existing reflective scales, and translated and adapted them to our research context, based on our qualitative pre-study and the pre-test.

Opportunistic behaviour is operationalised according to Morgan/Hunt (1994), supplemented by an item developed by MacMillan et al. (2005) (see Table 1). Communication is conceptualised according to MacMillan et al. (2005), and was measured using scales developed by Anderson/Lodish/Weitz (1987) and MacMillan et al. (2005). The operationalisation of shared values and trust also follows the ideas of MacMillan et al. (2005). Idiosyncratic resources are mainly operationalised according to Lambe/Spekman/Hunt (2002). The operationalisation of commitment integrates "attitudinal commitment" (item 1) and "continuance commitment" (items 3-5) according to Kumar/Scheer/Steenkamp (1995) as well as "instrumental commitment" (item 2) according to Stanko/Bonner/Calatone (2007). Cooperation is conceptualised according to Anderson/Narus (1990). We operationalised cooperation according to Vázquez/Iglesias/Álvarez-González (2005), with minor adjustments by our experts. Regarding the competitive advantage of a company, generated by the cooperation with an NGO, we adopt the ideas of Jap (1999; 2001), supported by the expert interviews. As a moderating variable, we integrated the level of aggression of the partnering-NGO, referring to the general degree to which an NGO acts aggressively within the company's competitive environment. The operationalisation is based on the expert interviews.

The construct measures as well as the reliability and validity assessment of the reflective measured constructs are shown in Table 1 and confirm that the values for each construct are satisfactory. Construct validity includes the sub-dimensions of content, convergent and discriminant validity. Content validity is augmented both by a thorough literature review and the pretesting with a panel of experts comprising academics as well as practitioners, while convergent and discriminant validity are shown in Tables 1 and 2.

Items	Factor loadings	t-value	Cronbachs Alpha	Composite reliability	AVE	Corrected Item-to-total correlation
Dimension: Opportunistic Behaviour			0.7788	0.8639	0.68	
To accomplish her own objectives, the NGO sometimes alters the facts slightly.	0.8880	5.37241				0.572
To accomplish her own objectives, the NGO sometimes promises to do things without actually doing them.	0.9063	6.42022				0.764
The NGO generally tries to get the upper hand when they deal with us.	0.6626	2.76858				0.532
Dimension: Communication			0.8829	0.9278	0.81	
In our relationship, the NGO keeps us informed about new developments.	0.9192	49.10826				0.837
The NGO provides us with information that is relevant to us.	0.9334	51.22447				0.855
Even when things do not develop according to plan, the NGO does its best to listen to us.	0.8468	25.62870				0.643
Dimension: Shared Values			0.9025	0.9390	0.83	
In general, the opinions and values of the NGO are a lot like ours.	0.8641	19.23798				0.739
We like and respect the values of the NGO.	0.9191	46.63424				0.780
We share a very similar set of values.	0.9594	85.00403				0.891

Items	Factor loadings	t-value	Cronbachs Alpha	Composite reliability	AVE	Corrected Item-to-total correlation
Dimension: Trust			0.8992	0.9297	0.76	
The NGO will be thoroughly dependable, especially when it comes to things that are important to our organisation.	0.8594	31.03252				0.718
The NGO will be reliable in the future.	0.9012	44.86418				0.791
The NGO will always be willing to offer our organisation the support it may need.	0.9038	41.76133				0.843
The NGO would never let us down.	0.8393	23.36133				0.748
Dimension: Idiosyncratic Resources			0.8184	0.8918	0.73	
Both of us have created capabilities that are unique to this alliance.	0.9146	56.26325				0.696
Together we have developed a lot of knowledge that is tailored to our relationship.	0.9333	54.94479				0.795
If this relationship were to end, we would be wasting a lot of knowledge that is tailored to our relationship.	0.7071	9.39416				0.524
Dimension: Commitment			0.8589	0.9007	0.64	
We are planning to sustain the cooperation with the NGO for a long time.	0.8348	25.83842				0.712
We are planning to extend the relationship with the NGO.	0.7378	11.93555				0.593
Even if we could, we would never quit the relationship with the NGO, as we feel like working together with them.	0.8852	36.98170				0.777
We want to keep on working with this NGO, as we feel comfortable about the relationship with them.	0.8953	39.29065				0.805
Our good relationship with the NGO is one of the main reasons why we work together with them.	0.6530	8.78217				0.521

Items	Factor loadings	t-value	Cronbachs Alpha	Composite reliability	AVE	Corrected Item-to-total correlation
Dimension: Cooperation			0.8419	0.8886	0.61	
To achieve the goals of our cooperation, the NGO and us work closely together.	0.8156	25.93602				0.625
In the course of our cooperation, we have regular meetings.	0.8301	23.59759				0.728
We often jointly attune details in the course of our cooperation.	0.7957	15.96558				0.689
Our communication is strongly formalised, i.e. we often share information in official project meetings.	0.6521	5.82610				0.512
We work intensively together in the course of our cooperation.	0.8913	43.50082				0.770
Dimension: Competitive Advantage			0.8385	0.8909	0.67	
The cooperation with the NGO leads to a positive reputation of our company.	0.7568	9.60335				0.675
The cooperation with the NGO leads to a competitive advantage over our competitors.	0.8871	17.59535				0.886
Due to our relationship with the NGO, we are more successful within the market.	0.9115	15.82579				0.865
Due to our cooperation with the NGO, we have won many new customers.	0.7099	7.18362				0.835

Items	Factor loadings	t-value	Cronbachs Alpha	Composite reliability	AVE	Corrected Item-to-total correlation
Moderating Variable: Level of Aggression of the Partnering-NGO			0.8920	0.9200	0.81	
The NGO we are working with is generally known for making companies a public example in case of detecting a grievance.	0.9270	16.177				0.821
The NGO we are working with is generally known for attacking other market participants in case of not acting according to the ideals of the NGO.	0.9370	15.977				0.847
The NGO we are working with accounts campaigns as a suitable instrument for inducing companies to change their policies.	0.8590	17.192				0.706

Note: Cronbachs Alpha is considered acceptable with a minimum value of 0.70 concerning to Nunnally (1967), composite reliability is also confirmed by a minimum value of 0.70 (Chin 1998a; b). The average variance extracted (AVE) as well as the corrected item-to-total-correlation should exceed 0.50 (Fornell/Larcker 1981; Chin 1998a; b). Convergent validity is given if the factor loadings are greater than 0.50 (Davis/Rivard/Huff 1988).

Table 1: Construct Measures, Reliability and Validity Assessment

Table 2 reports correlations between the constructs and the analysis of discriminant validity according to Fornell/Larcker's (1981) criterion. The results indicate that none of the constructs shares more variance with another construct than with its own indicators. Thus, each construct has a sufficient level of discriminant validity.

		(1)	(2)	(3)	(4)	(5)	(6)	(7)	(8)
(1)	**Commitment**	**0.64**	0.34	0.24	0.05	0.37	0.38	0.11	0.25
(2)	**Idiosyncratic Resources**	0.59**	**0.73**	0.24	0.0001	0.19	0.12	0.07	0.36
(3)	**Communication**	0.49**	0.49**	**0.81**	0.04	0.32	0.19	0.07	0.32
(4)	**Opportunistic Behaviour**	-0.23*	0.01	-0.19	**0.68**	0.04	0.05	0.0009	0.02
(5)	**Shared Values**	0.61**	0.44**	0.57**	-0.21*	**0.83**	0.27	0.07	0.18
(6)	**Trust**	0.62**	0.35**	0.44**	-0.23*	0.52**	**0.76**	0.01	0.11
(7)	**Competitive Advantage**	0.33**	0.26**	0.27**	0.03	0.26*	0.11	**0.67**	0.08
(8)	**Cooperation**	0.50**	0.60**	0.57**	-0.14	0.42**	0.34**	0.29**	**0.61**

Note: Diagonal terms (in bold) are the average variance extracted (AVE). The lower triangle of the matrix provides the correlations (** $p < .01$, * $p < .05$) and upper triangle of the matrix the shared variances. The discriminant validity of the constructs is tested according to Fornell/Larcker's (1981) suggestions, i.e. that AVE should be greater than the square of the correlations between the constructs.

Table 2: Correlations and Discriminant Validity of the Constructs

6. Hypotheses Testing

Figure 2 shows the results of our PLS analysis. The Q2 values are consistently higher than zero, indicating that the prerequisites of predictive relevance for the model are fulfilled (Chin 1998b). With an R^2 of 0.25 for idiosyncratic resources, 0.32 for trust, 0.39 for cooperation, 0.60 for commitment and 0.14 for competitive advantage, the explanatory power of the model is sufficient. Effect sizes (f2) are acceptable, except for H4a and H5a. Prediction accuracy was measured by a Stone-Geisser-test.

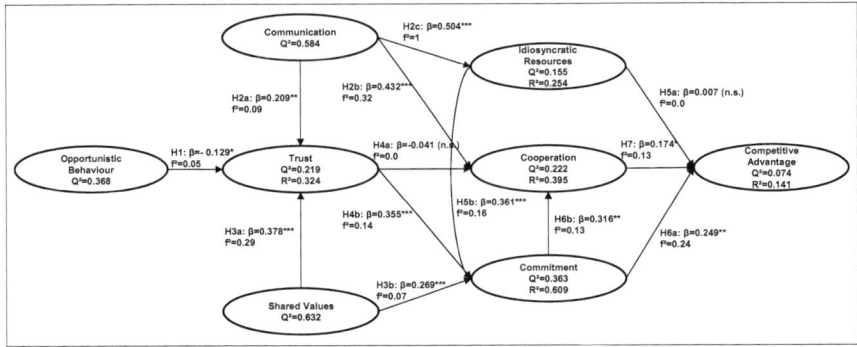

Note: Bootstrapping: n=96, cases=96, samples=250; * p < 0.1; ** p < 0.05; *** p < 0.01; n.s. = not significant. Effect size f^2 should be more than 0.02 for small effects, more than 0.15 for medium effects and more than 0.35 for large effects (Chin 1998b).

Figure 2: Path Model

In summary, we confirm H1, H2a, H2b, H2c, H3a, H3b, H4b, H5b, H6a, H6b, H7, and partly confirm H8. Hypotheses H4a and H5a cannot be supported, as the analysis does not provide significant results.

Hypothesis 8 aimed at an explorative analysis of the moderating effects of the level of aggression of the partnering NGO. Therefore, we performed a multi-group causal analysis (Henseler/Chin 2010). In doing so, we segmented two groups according to their perceptions of the level of aggression of their partnering NGO. In dividing the sample above and beyond the median of the factor-value given out for the construct, we generated two groups with almost the same sample size (n=49 with a perceived low level of aggression of their partnering NGO, n=47 for those with a high level of aggression). Using the parametric approach of Keil et al. (2000), we compared both groups with each other, using a t-test, incorporating the standard errors generated by a bootstrapping approach, and calculated the t-values for the difference of the path coefficients (Henseler/Ringle/ Sinkovics 2009). The results are displayed in Table 3.

Path Coefficient	Low Level of Aggression of the Partnering-NGO		High Level of Aggression of the Partnering-NGO		t-value (comparison)
	path coeff.	t-values	path coeff.	t-values	
H1:Opportunistic Behaviour → Trust	-0.222	1.3922*	-0.158	1.852**	-0.351 (n.s.)
H2a: Communication → Trust	0.232	1.9669**	0.154	1.666**	0.524 (n.s.)
H2b: Communication → Cooperation	0.201	2.0398**	0.596	7.1031****	-3.0786***
H2c: Communication → Idios. Resources	0.391	3.9161****	0.630	9.1291****	-1.9759*
H3a: Shared Values → Trust	0.290	2.1139**	0.494	4.9511****	-1.2083 (n.s.)
H3b: Shared Values → Commitment	0.307	3.5384****	0.150	1.8829**	1.3449*
H4a: Trust → Cooperation	0.01	0.0142 (n.s.)	-0.131	1.0553 (n.s.)	0.877 (n.s.)
H4b: Trust → Commitment	0.225	2.9870***	0.530	7.8786****	-3.0500***
H5a: Idios. Resources → Comp. Advantage	-0.01	0.0522 (n.s.)	0.03	0.2980 (n.s.)	-0.2343 (n.s.)
H5b: Idios. Resources → Commitment	0.473	6.4020****	0.296	4.5971****	1.8202**
H6a: Commitment → Comp. Advantage	0.321	2.3938***	0.194	1.5183*	0.6923 (n.s.)
H6b: Commitment → Cooperation	0.491	4.6859****	0.255	2.5984***	1.6585**
H7: Cooperation → Comp. Advantage	0.109	0.7657 (n.s.)	0.238	1.658**	-0.6454 (n.s.)
R^2	0.153		0.155		/

Bootstrapping-Procedure Sample 1 (Low Level of Aggression of the Partnering-NGO): n=49, cases=49, samples=250

Bootstrapping-Procedure Sample 2 (High Level of Aggression of the Pertnering-NGO): n=47, cases=47, samples=250

Level of Significance (one-sided): n.s.=not significant, ****$p \leq 0.001$, ***$p \leq 0.01$, **$p \leq 0.05$, *$p \leq 0.1$.

Table 3: Explorative Analysis of Moderating Effects (H8)

With regard to the moderating effect of the level of aggression of the partnering-NGO, we identified significant differences between both groups in Hypotheses 2b, 2c, 3b, 4b, 5b, and 6b.

7. Discussion and Implications

The main purpose of this study was to empirically test whether partnerships between companies and NGOs can be analysed analogously to firm-firm collaborations. Taking the results of our analysis into account, we encourage the suggestion of Teegen/Doh/Vachani (2004) to apply theories of business alliances to the analysis of firm-NGO collaborations as well.

As to the antecedents of the factors leading directly to a competitive advantage for a company, opportunistic behaviour from the cooperating NGO leads to mistrust of the company and should therefore be minimised by NGOs. Communication has a strong and significant influence on the generation of trust, cooperation and on idiosyncratic resources. With respect to its influence on cooperation, as well as on idiosyncratic resources, this effect is significantly stronger in CSR-alliances with radical NGOs, presumably due to the fact that an intensive communication with a respected or even infamous NGO can break the ice for a successful cooperation.

While shared values have a significant and positive influence on the trust of the cooperating company, we cannot identify a significant correlation between trust and cooperation. This is most likely due to the fact that there are several ways, in which companies can cooperate with NGOs that call for trust, which need not be intensive (e.g. stakeholder dialogues). Nevertheless, we did find that trust positively influences the commitment of the cooperating company, a correlation that is especially strong in relationships with highly aggressive NGOs. In contrast, the correlation between shared values and commitment is even stronger in the case of a CSR-alliance with a moderate NGO. When cooperating with radical NGOs, there are other factors that positively influence the commitment of the cooperating company, such as a deep trust in the partnering-NGO.

As to the factors leading directly to a competitive advantage, we found no support for a positive and direct impact of idiosyncratic resources. This may be because CSR-alliances themselves are frequently idiosyncratic in nature, as the resources developed in a firm-NGO-relationship are often very specific and customised with regard to the needs and purposes of both parties. However, we did find a strong and significant effect of idiosyncratic resources on commitment, which indicates that companies develop a strong motivation through the joint development of relationship-specific resources. This holds especially for companies cooperating with moderate NGOs, while firms with an aggressive NGO-partner reveal a minor, but also significant correlation. With regard to the direct influences on competitive advantage, commitment yields the strongest effect, followed by cooperation. Furthermore, commitment has a significant and positive effect on cooperation. This effect is significantly stronger in alliances with moderate NGOs, as the business partner can rely more on the NGO.

The key managerial implication of this paper is that CSR-alliances between companies and NGOs can contribute to a competitive advantage of the companies. Retail companies, consumer goods manufacturers as well as service companies can benefit from such relationships. Nevertheless, the choice of a partner with regard to radicalness has a clear impact on the effects between the factors leading to a competitive advantage, for example commitment and trust. In the course of a partner-selection process, managers should carefully weigh up the opportunities and risks with regard to shared values or potential opportunistic behaviour before deciding with whom to cooperate. If it comes to the choice of a commonly aggressive partnering-NGO, intensive communication can pave the way for a successful collaboration.

For NGOs, the following implications can be deduced: CSR-alliances enable NGOs to raise their concerns in a constructive manner, rather than polarising or airing grievances without contributing to their resolution. A reduction in opportunistic behaviour positively influences the level of trust on the part of the cooperating company, which is conductive to a prospering relationship. Radical NGOs should try to foster cooperation through intensive communication, as well as by proactively building up trust. Moderate NGOs, on the other hand, should enhance the creation of idiosyncratic resources as well as the communication of shared values, as both positively influence commitment and hence the intensity of cooperation on the part of the cooperating company.

8. Conclusion and Limitations

The paper shows that the success of CSR-alliances can indeed be analysed with lenses commonly used for analysing alliance success in firm-firm co-operations. Such factors as intensive cooperation, commitment, trust, shared values or the absence of opportunistic behaviour contribute to the evolution of a mutually prosperous relationship. Furthermore, depending on the level of aggression of the partnering NGO, a suitable scale for considering the different degrees of radicalness of NGOs can be generated.

Although our study contributes to the understanding of CSR-alliances, several limitations ought to be stated. For example, we focused on retail companies, consumer goods manufacturers and service companies in German-speaking Europe. A future survey could have a more international focus, including the analysis of cultural or country-specific differences evolving over the course of a firm-NGO relationship. Furthermore, a more specific analysis, for instance focusing explicitly on retail companies, or a comparative analysis focusing on commonalities and differences in CSR-alliances between retail companies and consumer goods manufacturers, could provide further insights into industry-specific characteristics. Finally, an extension of the model with further elements explaining the competitive advantage of companies generated by CSR-alliances could contribute to our understanding of such relationships.

References

ACHROL, R. (1991): Evolution of the Marketing Organization: New Forms for Turbulent Environments., in: Journal of Marketing, Vol. 55, No. 4, pp. 77-93.

ANDERSON, E.; LODISH, L.M.; WEITZ, B.A. (1987): Resource Allocation Behaviour in Conventional Channels, in: Journal of Marketing Research, Vol. 24, No. 1, pp. 85-97.

ANDERSON, J.C.; NARUS, J.A. (1990): A Model of Distributor Firm and Manufacturer Firm Working Partnerships, in: Journal of Marketing, Vol. 54, No. 1, pp. 42-58.

ANDERSON, E.; WEITZ, B. (1990): Determinants of Continuity in Conventional Industrial Channel Dyads, in: Marketing Science, Vol. 8, No. 4, pp. 310-323.

ANDREASEN, A. (1996): Profits for Non-Profits: Find a Corporate Partner, in: Harvard Business Review, Vol. 74, No. 6, pp. 47-59.

ARGENTI, P.A. (2004): Collaborating with Activists: How Starbucks Works with NGOs, in: California Management Review, Vol. 47, No. 1, pp. 91-116.

ARTS, B. (2002): "Green Alliances" of Business and NGOs. New Styles of Self-Regulation or "Dead-End Roads"?, in: Corporate Social Responsibility and Environmental Management, Vol. 9, No. 1, pp. 26-36.

AUSTIN, J.E. (2000): Strategic Collaboration Between Non-Profits and Businesses, in: Nonprofit and Voluntary Sector Quarterly, Vol. 29, No. 1, pp. 69-97.

BARNEY, J.B. (1991): Firm Resources and Sustained Competitive Advantage, in: Journal of Management, Vol. 17, No. 1, pp. 99-120.

BENDELL, J. (2000): Terms for Endearment: Business, NGOs and Sustainable Development, Sheffield.

BERGER, I.E.; CUNNINGHAM, P.H.; DRUMWRIGHT, M.E. (2004): Social Alliances:Company/Nonprofit Collaboration, in: California Management Review, Vol. 47, No. 1, pp. 58-90.

BERRY, L.L.; PARASURAMAN, A. (1991): Marketing Services, New York.

BRUMLEY, K.M. (2010): Understanding Mexican NGOs: Goals, Strategies, and the Local Context, in: Qual Sociol, Vol. 33, No. 3, pp. 389-414.

CHATMAN, J.A. (1991): Matching People and Organizations: Selection and Socialization in Public Accounting Firms, in: Administrative Science Quarterly, Vol. 36, No. 3, pp. 459-484.

CHEN, I.J.; PAULRAJ, A. (2004): Understanding Supply Chain Management: Critical Research and a Theoretical Framework, in: International Journal of Production Research, Vol. 42, No. 1, pp. 131-163.

CHIN, W.W. (1998a): Issues and Opinion on Structural Equation Modeling, in: MIS Quarterly, Vol. 22, No. 1, pp. vii–xvi.

CHIN, W.W. (1998b): The Partial Least Squares Approach for Structural Equation Modeling, in: MARCOULIDES, G.A. (Ed.): Modern Methods for Business Research, Mahwah, pp. 295-336.

CORLETTE, J.A. (1989): The "Modified Vendetta Sanction" as Method of Corporate Collective Punishment, in: Journal of Business Ethics, Vol. 8, No. 12, pp. 937-942.

DAS, T.K.; TENG B. (1998): Between Trust and Control: Developing Confidence in Partner Cooperation in Alliances, in: Academy of Management Review, Vol. 23, No. 3, pp. 491-512.

DOH, J.P.; GUAY, T. (2006): Corporate Social Responsibility, Public Policy, and NGO Activism in Europe and the United States: An Institutional-Stakeholder Perspective, in: Journal of Management Studies, Vol. 43, No. 1, pp. 47-73.

DOH, J.P.; TEEGEN, H. (2002): Nongovernmental Organizations as Institutional Actors in International Business: Theory and Implications, in: International Business Review, Vol. 11, No. 6, pp. 665-684.

DUSCHEK, S. (2004): Inter-Firm Resources and Sustained Competitive Advantage, in: Management Revue, Vol. 15, No. 1, pp. 53-73.

DWYER, F.R.; SCHURR, P.H.; OH, S. (1987): Developing Buyer-Seller Relationships, in: Journal of Marketing, Vol. 5, No. 2, pp. 11-27.

DYER, J.; SINGH, H. (1998): The Relational View: Cooperative Strategy and Sources of Interorganisational Competitive Advantage, in: Academy of Mangement Review, Vol. 23, No. 4, pp. 660-679.

ELKINGTON, J.; BELOE, S. (2010): The Twenty-First-Century NGO, in: LYON, T.P. (Ed.): Good Cop/Bad Cop: Environmental NGOs and their Strategies Toward Business, Washington D.C., pp. 17-47.

FORNELL, C.; LARCKER, D.F. (1981): Evaluating Structural Equation Models with Unobservable Variables and Measurement Error, in: Journal of Marketing Research, Vol. 18, No. 1, pp. 39-50.

FREEMAN, R.E. (1984): Strategic Management: A Stakeholder Approach, Marshfield.

FROOMAN, J. (1999): Stakeholder Influence Strategies, in: Academy of Management Review, Vol. 24, No. 2, pp. 191-205.

GLASBERGEN, P.; GROENENBERG, R. (2001): Environmental Partnership in Sustainable Energy, in: European Environment, Vol. 11, No. 1, pp. 1-13.

GRAF, N.F.S.; ROTHLAUF, F. (2012): Firm-NGO Collaborations: A Resource-Based Perspective, in: Zeitschrift für Betriebswirtschaftslehre, Vol. 82, No. 6, pp. 103-125.

HUNT, S.D.; LAMBE, C.J.; WITTMANN, C.M. (2002): A Theory and Model of Business Alliance Success, in: Journal of Relationship Marketing, Vol. 1, No. 1, pp. 17-34.

HENSELER, J.; CHIN, W.W. (2010): A Comparison of Approaches for the Analysis of Interaction Effects Between Latent Variables Using Partial Least Squares Path Modeling, in: Structural Equation Modeling: A Multidisciplinary Journal, Vol. 17, No. 1, pp. 82-109.

HENSELER, J.; RINGLE, C.; SINKOVICS, R. (2009): The Use of Partial Least Squares Path Modeling in International Marketing, in: Advances in International Marketing, Vol. 20, pp. 277-320.

JAMALI, D.; KESHISHIAN, T. (2009): Uneasy Alliances: Lessons Learned from Partnerships Between Businesses and NGOs in the Context of CSR, in: Journal of Business Ethics, Vol. 84, No. 2, pp. 277-295.

JAP, S.D. (1999): Pie-Expansion Efforts: Collaboration Processes in Buyer-Seller Relationships, in: Journal of Marketing Research, Vol. 36, No. 4, pp. 461-475.

JAP, S.D. (2001): Perspectives on Joint Competitive Advantages in Buyer-Supplier-Relationships, in: International Journal of Research in Marketing, Vol. 18, No. 1–2, pp. 19-35.

JOHN, G. (1984): An Empirical Investigation of Some Antecedents of Opportunism in a Marketing Channel, in: Journal of Marketing Research, Vol. 21, No. 3, pp. 278-289.

JOUTSENVIRTA, M. (2011): Setting Boundaries for Corporate Social Responsibility: Firm-NGO Relationship as Discursive Legitimation Struggle, in: Journal of Business Ethics, Vol. 102, No. 1, pp. 57-75.

KEIL, M.; TAN, B.C.Y.; WIE, K.K.; SAARINEN, T.; TUUAINEN, V.; WASSE-NAAR, A. (2000): A Cross-Cultural Study on Escalation of Commitment Behaviour in Software Projects, in: MIS Quarterly, Vol. 24, No. 2, pp. 299-325.

KONG, N.; SALZMANN, O.; STEGER, U.; IONESCU-SOMERS, A. (2002): Moving Business/Industry Towards Sustainable Consumption: The Role of NGOs, in: European Management Journal, Vol. 20, No. 2, pp. 109-127.

KUMAR, N.; SCHEER, L.; STEENKAMP, J. (1995): The Effects of Perceived Interdependence on Dealer Attitudes, in: Journal of Marketing Research, Vol. 32, No. 3, pp. 348-356.

LAMBE, C.J.; SPEKMAN, R.E.; HUNT., S.D. (2002): Alliance Competence, Resources, and Alliance Success: Conceptualization, Measurement, and Initial Test, in: Journal of the Academy of Marketing Science, Vol. 30, No. 2, pp. 141-158.

LAMBELL, R.; RAMIA, G.; NYLAND, C.; MICHELOTTI, M. (2008): NGOs and International Business Research: Progress, Prospects and Problems, in: International Journal of Management Reviews, Vol. 10, No. 1, pp. 75-97.

LIU, C.L.E. (2012): An Investigation of Relationship Learning in Cross-Border Buyer-Supplier Relationships: The Role of Trust, in: International Business Review, Vol. 21, No. 3, pp. 311-327.

LUCEA, R. (2010): How We See Them versus How They See Themselves: A Cognitive Perspective of Firm-NGO Relationships, in: Business & Society, Vol. 49, No. 1, pp. 116-139.

MACMILLAN, K.; MONEY, K.; MONEY, A.; DOWNING, S. (2005): Relationship Marketing in the Not-For-Profit Sector: An Extension and Application of the Commitment-Trust Theory, in: Journal of Business Research, Vol. 58, No. 6, pp. 806-818.

MACNEIL, I.R. (1980): An Inquiry into Modern Contractual Relations, New Haven.

MORGAN, R.M.; HUNT, S.D. (1994): The Commitment-Trust-Theory of Relationship Marketing, in: Journal of Marketing, Vol. 58, No. 3, pp. 20-38.

NEVIN, J.R. (1995): Relationship Marketing and Distribution Channels: Exploring Fundamental Issues, in: Journal of the Academy of Marketing Science, Vol. 23, No. 4, pp. 327-334.

NIJSSEN, E.J.; DOUGLAS, S.P. (2008): Consumer World-Mindedness, Social-Mindedness, and Store Image, in: Journal of International Marketing, Vol. 16, No. 3, pp. 84-107.

NUNNALLY, J.C. (1967): Psychometric Theory, New York.

PHILLIPPS, R.R.E.; FREEMAN, A.; WICKS, A.C. (2003): What Stakeholder Theory is Not, in: Business Ethics Quarterly, Vol. 13, No. 4, pp. 479-502.

RIVARD, S.; HUFF, S.L. (1988): Factors of Success for End-User Computing, in: Communications of the ACM, Vol. 31, No. 5, pp. 552-561.

RONDINELLI, D.A.; LONDON, T. (2003): How Corporations and Environmental Groups Cooperate: Assessing Cross-Sector Alliances and Collaborations, in: Academy of Management Executive, Vol. 17, No. 1, pp. 61-76.

SEITANIDI, M.; CRANE, A. (2009): Implementing CSR through Partnerships: Understanding the Selection, Design and Institutionalisation of Nonprofit-Business Partnerships, in: Journal of Business Ethics, Vol. 85, No. 2, pp. 413-429.

SIMONIN, B.L. (2004): An Empirical Investigation of the Process of Knowledge Transfer in International Strategic Alliances, in: Journal of International Business Studies, Vol. 35, No. 5, pp. 407-427.

STAFFORD, E.R.; HARTMAN, C.L. (1996): Green Alliances: Strategic Relations Between Businesses and Environmental Groups, in: Business Horizons, Vol. 39, No. 2, pp. 55-59.

STANKO, M.; BONNER, J.; CALATONE, R. (2007): Building Commitment in Buyer-Seller Relationships: A Tie Strength Perspective, in: Industrial Marketing Management, Vol. 36, No. 8, pp. 1094-1103.

TEEGEN, H. (2003): International NGOs as Global Institutions: Using Social Capital to Impact Multinational Enterprises and Governments, in: Journal of International Management, Vol. 9, No. 3, pp. 271-285.

TEEGEN, H.; DOH, J.P.; VACHANI, S. (2004): The Importance of Nongovernmental Organizations (NGOs) in Global Governance and Value Creation: An International Business Research Agenda, in: Journal of International Business Studies, Vol. 35, No. 6, pp. 463-483.

TSANG, E. (2002): Acquiring Knowledge by Foreign Partners from International Joint Ventures in a Transition Economy: Learning-by-Doing and Learning Myopia, in: Strategic Management Journal, Vol. 23, No. 9, pp. 835-854.

VAKIL, A.C. (1997): Confronting the Classification Problem: Towards a Taxonomy of NGOs, in: World Development, Vol. 25, No. 12, pp. 2057-2070.

VALOR, C.; DIEGO, A.M. (2009): Relationship of Business and NGOs: An Empirical Analysis of Strategies and Mediators of Their Private Relationship, in: Business Ethics: A European Review, Vol. 18, No. 2, pp. 110-126.

VÁZQUEZ, R.; IGLESIAS, V.; ÁLVAREZ-GONZÁLEZ, L.I. (2005): Distribution Channel Relationships: The Conditions and Strategic Outcomes of Cooperation Between Manufacturer and Distributor, in: International Review of Retail, Distribution and Consumer Research, Vol. 15, No. 2, pp. 125-150.

WILLIAMSON, O.E. (1975): Markets and Hierarchies: Analysis and Antitrust Implications, New York.

WYMER, W.W.J.; SAMU, S. (2003): Dimensions of Business and Nonprofit Collaborative Relationships, in: Journal of Nonprofit & Public Sector Marketing, Vol. 11, No. 1, pp. 3-22.

Part 4:
Functional and Sectoral Perspectives

Sustainability in Collaborative Supply Chains

Dirk Morschett and Valentin Wepfer

Overview

1. Introduction

While the responsibility of business for the broader society has been mentioned in literature and discussions for a very long time, it has been mainly since the beginning of the new millennium that it has developed from a side issue to a main stream topic for businesses around the world.

The reasons are manifold: An increasing globalisation of value chains which creates a link between the buyer of consumer goods and production facilities in countries with very low labour standards; the discussion on climate change and other environmental issues that create a sense of urgency for all actors; the increasing value that consumers put on sustainable products; the pressure from governments for self-regulation of business; the pressure from NGOs; the enhanced transparency on production conditions and value chains due to the Internet; faster spreading of negative information via social media but also more attention on these issues from traditional media. This list of reasons is by far not exhaustive but overall, they result in the absolute need for companies to commit themselves to more sustainability.

The consumer goods sector is strongly involved in this issue (GS1 Germany 2012, p. 6): Consumer products are produced and delivered in complex networks and they are in touch with consumers very immediately. At the same time, production, logistics and distribution have a strong influence on economic, ecological and social aspects. This illustrates a major characteristic of the consumer goods sector: The value is created not by single companies but by complex value networks: From raw material producers, often located in less-developed countries, over final goods manufacturers, located either close to the resources or close to the dispersed markets, via networks of logistics service providers in different modalities, down to the wholesale and retail companies that distribute the goods (see e.g., Morschett/Schramm-Klein/Zentes 2010, pp. 323-337). Even though some companies have long been engaged in improving the sustainability of their activities, this shows that effects on sustainability can only to a small part be influenced by each single company in but that it needs a *holistic perspective* on the overall value network and a collaborative approach. Major industry associations, e.g. ECR, The Consumer Goods Forum, and GS1, that combine retailers and consumer goods manufacturers (as well as logistics services providers), have therefore integrated sustainability initiatives in their portfolio of activities and as overarching organisational focus.

2. Dimensions of Sustainability

One of the most often used definitions of *sustainability* is based on the Brundtland commission of the United Nations, officially named the World Commission on Environment and Development (WCED), which discussed it in its report "Our Common Future" in 1987. There, the general understanding and challenge is characterised broadly and a kind of definition is given:

"Humanity has the ability to make development sustainable to ensure that it meets the needs of the present without compromising the ability of future generations to meet their own needs" (WCED 1987, p. 7).

In current academic and practitioners' literature, other terms for related issues are being used, e.g. "Corporate Social Responsibility" (CSR), "Business Ethics", "Corporate Citizenship". Most of these concepts have a strong common core, namely the requirement for companies to generate value and benefit to society, to respond to conflicting stakeholder interests in a balanced manner and to be responsible to an audience with reward or sanction power. Highly important aspects are the *creation of value*, the *long-term perspective* and the *responsible use of resources* to protect the interest of future generations and the *stakeholder perspective*, i.e. the understanding that multiple stakeholders are influenced by the actions of a company and have the legitimate interest to have their perspectives considered (Schwartz/Carroll 2008). While the different concepts may put different focuses on these aspects, the distinction has become blurry in the last years and, broadly speaking, the four terms are used interchangeably today (for a discussion on the differences and commonalities, see Schwartz/Carroll 2008 and Gimenez/Sierra 2013).

The domains of sustainability or CSR differ with authors. For example, some authors classify CSR into four domains: *community support*, *employee relations*, *environmental support* and socially responsible and sustainable *product and business practices*, the latter one also covering ethical sourcing (McGuire/Dow/Archgeyd 2003; see also the article by Schramm-Klein/Steinmann in this book). Others propose more detailed frameworks, including six different domains, e.g. *community support*, *diversity*, *employee support*, *environment*, *non-domestic operations* and *product* (Bhattacharya/Sen 2004, p. 13). Comparing and discussing the different frameworks would go too far in this article, but it can be argued that more detailed frameworks are more practical to develop managerial implications. On the other hand, to get a broad understanding of the concept and make initiatives better comparable, the simple and broadly accepted three-dimensional framework that is shown in Figure 1 is sufficient. It is discussed with the name "Triple Bottom Line" (Elkington 1997), 3-P (Profit, People, Planet), and others (Mellahi/Frynas/Finlay 2005, p. 19). Sometimes, those three perspectives are labelled as *pillars of sustainability* but the pillar illustration neglects their interdependence. While the framework is likely to be known to the reader, it should still be displayed to further penetrate the understanding of a necessary holistic view on the three dimensions.

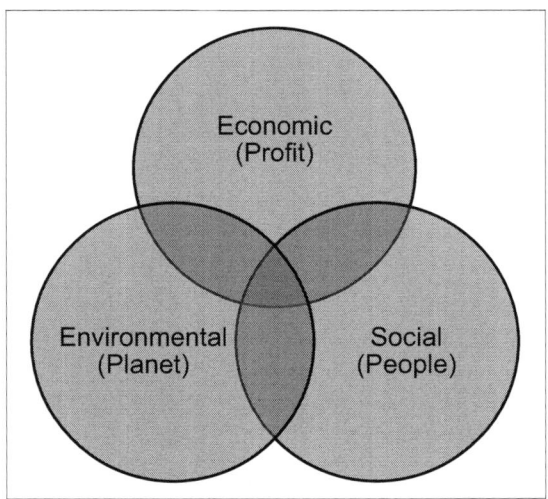

Figure 1: The Three Dimensions of Sustainability

There is an extensive discussion on the relationship between the three dimensions. While some authors argue that a strong emphasis on environmental and social aspects of the business activities may deteriorate the profits of a company, others argue that sustainable business activities will benefit the profits of a company for several reasons, e.g. because resources are economised, dependence on critical inputs is reduced, corporate culture and employee motivation is strengthened, etc. (for an overview on the discussion, see Morschett/Schramm-Klein/Zentes 2010, pp. 227-229).

With regard to the supply chain, a positive relationship has long been assumed. Best practice supply chains focus on establishing reliable and high logistics quality with the lowest possible resource use, e.g. transport kilometres. A study in 1998 already demonstrated that an integrated perspective of quality management (in the supply chain) and environmental management is helpful for both perspectives (Baumgarten et al. 1998). On top of the traditional end-of-pipe strategy, more and more optimisation strategies like efficiency, consistency and sufficiency are in operation or in development (GS1 Switzerland 2013).

3. Collaborative Supply Chains and Institutions to Stimulate Collaboration

The *supply chain* in the consumer goods sector includes all parties directly or indirectly involved in receiving and fulfilling customer demand, e.g. manufacturers, raw material suppliers, packaging suppliers, wholesalers, retailers, third party service providers (e.g. transporters, warehouse operators, information providers), and customers (Chopra/Meindl 2004, p. 4). These actors are closely interrelated. *Supply Chain Management* (SCM) is the planning and management of all business activities involved in fulfilling customer demand, such as procurement, operations, marketing and logistics management. It has long been emphasised that SCM does not only focus on processes or functions within one particular company, but also includes the coordination and collaboration with other parties in the supply chain (Stank/Davis/Fugate 2005; Zentes/Schramm-Klein/Morschett 2011, p. 364).

A strong interdependence between the processes of different actors has long been recognised, e.g. in the well-known *bull-whip effect* (Zentes/Schramm-Klein/Morschett 2011, pp. 364-366). In the consumer goods industry, it was the mid-1990s when collaborative initiatives between consumer goods manufacturers and retail companies, later including logistics service providers, emerged. Under the "Efficient Consumer Response" (ECR) movement, industry associations emerged that focused on developing and highlighting best practice processes in the collaboration and on overcoming barriers between the different companies. The focus in those days was clearly on efficiency gains (e.g. reduced transport kilometres, reduced products in stock, enhanced shelf-life of products by shorter supply chain durations etc.) but in the consequence, these initiatives also helped to reduce the negative environmental impact of consumer goods supply chains.

Today, there are a number of important *industry associations* that focus on the improvement of all aspects of the supply chain in a collaborative manner. In most cases, sustainability has been strongly integrated in the associations' objectives (descriptions of associations are mainly taken from their websites and internal documents):

- *ECR Europe and national ECR initiatives*: As a joint initiative of trade and industry, ECR Europe is an umbrella organisation of National ECR initiatives and leading companies across Europe. ECR Europe shapes and adapts collaborative best practice processes (concerning the demand side and the supply side of consumer goods value chains) on a European level, in projects which affect several European countries or direct company members. National ECR initiatives shape collaborative best practices in their respective countries and promote their implementation. The vision of ECR Europe explicitly states the relevance of sustainability: "Our vision is that companies along the entire value chain are working together to fulfil consumer wishes better, faster and at less cost in a sustainable way."
- *The Consumer Goods Forum (CGF)*: The globally oriented CGF brings together the senior management of over 400 retailers, manufacturers, service providers and other stakeholders across 70 countries. The Forum's vision is "Better lives through better business". To fulfil this, its members have given the Forum a mandate to develop common positions on key strategic and operational issues affecting the consumer goods business. Key players in the sector together develop and lead the implementation of best practices along the value chain. To this end, the CGF has identified five strategic priorities. Sustainability is one of these priorities.
- *GS1 in Europe*: GS1 organisations that exist in most countries around the world are intending to improve collaboration and efficiency in the value chain by providing standards. The focuses of GS1 organisations are data standards and EDI/e-Commerce for supply and demand chain management that make it faster, cheaper and safer for companies to serve their customers. With regard to sustainability, there are multiple impacts: First, using the same data standards is important to create transparency and allow reliable product identification in the supply chain. Furthermore, data standards are necessary for an efficient supply chain (e.g. GDSN - Global Data Synchronisation Network). Which information is needed in, e.g., master data, is jointly decided and includes more and more often aspects of sustainability. Also, in some countries, GS1 organisations take charge of the national ECR initia-

tive. Some national GS1 organisations have provided guidelines or reflections on collaborative measures to improve the sustainability in the supply chain, e.g. GS1 Germany (2012) and GS1 Switzerland (2013).

From the perspective of the authors, these associations already have and will continue to have a major impact on the sustainable business practices because in these platforms, the main actors in the supply chain can jointly identify the main issues, they can develop and test collaborative best practice processes for those issues and stimulate the broad implementation of these processes.

4. Principles and Methods to Improve Sustainability in Collaborative Supply Chains

4.1 Overview

Eventually, concrete steps to improve sustainability in the supply chain must be taken in specific activities, e.g. waste, greenhouse gas emissions, food safety, etc. However, the principles than can be applied to achieve improvements are usually the same. Most methods are rooted in the same few principles which will be highlighted on the next pages. Such overviews are always selective and to a certain degree subjective but the authors assume that those principles are the most relevant.

4.2 Collaboration

As has been pointed out in the section on collaborative supply chains, the performance in supply chains is highly interdependent. Optimal order quantities, joint forecasting, vendor-managed inventories, joint inventory optimisation, etc. can help to improve the supply chain but frequently, benefits are not occurring at the same stage where the necessary investments have to be undertaken. Isolated measures may just shift the burden to another actor in the supply chain as the ECR initiatives have comprehensively highlighted. Thus, real improvements can nowadays mainly be achieved in collaborative measures where manufacturers, retailers and logistics service providers act together to improve the overall situation. Many aspects of the supply chain involve trade-offs: More packaging may protect the goods better but create more waste; less inventory buffers at the retail stage may reduce cost there (and maybe also food waste stemming from short-dated products) but this may come at the expense of more inventory at the producer stage and more transports. Just a *holistic view* on the supply chain which evaluates all these aspects, which considers how to create win-win-situations for all involved partners and which integrates the economic, social and environmental perspective can achieve sustainable improvements.

Collaboration includes, the development of suppliers to stimulate the consideration of sustainability but also the selection of the right suppliers with the right corporate conduct. This has been an important topic in the academic literature and research has long focused on supplier evaluation (Gimenez/Sierra 2008). Over time, the criteria for supplier selection started to include environmental and social criteria.

From an empirical perspective, instruments to select and to incentive the suppliers to consider sustainability criteria are likely to be intensively used by retailers in the coming years. Figure 2 highlights those instruments that retailers in a recent survey stated they would plan to use in the year 2015.

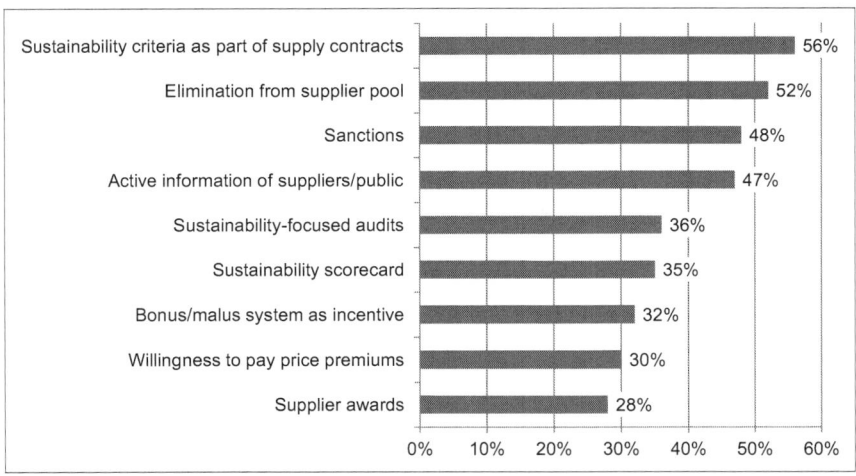

Figure 2: Percentage of Companies That Expect to Use the Respective Instrument for a More Sustainable Procurement in the Year 2015
(Source: Study of BME/Roland Berger; cited from GS1 Germany 2012, p. 19).

It becomes evident that sustainability criteria are likely to become a usual part in supply contracts. Furthermore, compliance with sustainability criteria will be monitored more intensively and sanctions in general, up to the elimination of a supplier from the supplier pool, will be used.

4.3 Transparency and Traceability

Another basic principle to improve sustainability is the transparency of the product and production processes and the traceability. Transparency is important on all levels of the supply chain, i.e. for the involved companies as well as for the consumer. Companies rate transparency very high in very different fields: Raw materials, production locations, production processes, transport routes, ingredients, environmental impact, certificates and social impact are all considered important (GS1 Switzerland 2009, p. 14).

From the consumer perspective, safety is one of the most crucial aspects for the food supply chain (IGD 2013c). Most recently, horsemeat adulteration drastically hurt trust in the food industry. Such scandals result in the industry increasingly coming under pressure from NGOs, the media and government. Supply chain transparency, showing the product origin and the supply chain path from origin to the retailer is a measure than can help to regain consumer trust. Some retailers and suppliers in the food sector have already started to be transparent, using modern technology. Online platforms have emerged to guarantee transparency. For example, after the recent horsemeat scandal, Tesco announced to introduce a new website so the consumer can see what happens within the supply chain. Eventually, the website will allow consumers to view the farms and factories so they can see where the product comes from and how it is produced. Asda has already introduced video cameras at some of its factories that the internet users can view. Nestlé has – after criticism in social media – added QR codes to the KitKat bars so consumers can have information about the nutritional profile but also about the environmental and social impact of the product (IGD 2013c). Coop in Switzerland allows consumers to trace back its organic fruits and vegetables to the producer by means of a product ID and a web solutions as well as a mobile solution. Seafood processors such as Frosta and Iglo display intensive information about the origin of their fish on packages via QR codes, in most cases far exceeding the legal requirements. Thus, transparency (along the full value chain) is a crucial measure to create trust in the safety of products – and this is a major aspect of sustainability for the consumer as stakeholder. According to The Institute of Grocery Distribution (IGD 2013c), the "drive for more transparency will also bring the whole supply chain closer together. As recent events have shown, no one part of that chain operates in isolation. Working more closely together would create a more secure and resilient supply chain, helping protect companies against sourcing issues and crucially providing better quality, better service and more transparency for shoppers."

The challenge of this consumer information is to provide the relevant information and to help the consumers to evaluate and interpret it. However, the dilemma that companies face is that different target groups search for different information. More and more information is probably not the answer but to focus on relevant sustainability information and help with the interpretation. GS1 Germany (2012, p. 31) gives a plausible example: For tomatoes from Spain, the efficient, resource-saving water utilisation or the social standards for seasonal workers for the harvest may have to be focused. But for tomatoes from Holland, grown in greenhouses, the efficient and resource-saving heating supply may be the most relevant sustainability aspect. To interpret – in an objective and neutral manner – which aspects of sustainability are crucial, is another requirement.

With regard to labels that intend to increase transparency for consumers, consumers are nowadays confronted with a multitude of labels, certificates, etc. which include very different levels of information and are based on very different criteria (GS1 Germany 2012, p. 22). So the industry most likely has to question itself whether this multitude is indeed helping the consumer or creates confusion. It would be another collaborative task to unify and converge the labels into a more systematic and informative set.

But transparency does not only signal the current sustainability of a product to the consumer, it does more. An extensive discussion between manufacturers and retailers in Germany showed that product transparency is, indeed, the main driver for more sustainability in the supply chain. It is not only a means in itself, to respond to consumer demand for more information, but it is also the *prerequisite for improvement*. If unwanted social or ecological impacts of products are visible to everybody, a joint initiative to remove or at least reduce those impacts is possible and the consumer is enabled to consider these impacts in their buying behaviour (GS1 Germany 2012, p. 6).

Furthermore, to reduce greenhouse gas emissions, a reliable and uniform *measurement* method to capture product-specific climate impact data is required. Such a product carbon footprint is necessary to get a better understanding of the full life cycle emissions of a product and of the effect of specific processes. A product carbon footprint measures the greenhouse gas emissions at each stage of the product's life, i.e. from extraction, production and transportation of raw materials to the manufacturing of the final goods, right through to its use and final reuse, recycling or disposal (IGD 2013a). For example, IGD (2013a, p. 6) demonstrates that for milk, 73% of greenhouse gas emissions are caused at the raw material production stage, while for detergents, the main part (65.5%) is caused during the consumer usage stage. Obviously, such a measurement is necessary to focus sustainability measures at the right stage of the product life cycle and to identify the "hot spots" that require action. The *Product Life Cycle Accounting and Reporting Standard* is a measure to achieve this objective which has been developed with the help of actors along the supply chain (Greenhouse Gas Protocol 2011).

4.4 Bundling

To reduce transports, a bundling of transports can be beneficial. Large retailers have achieved this bundling by using central or regional warehouses from which fully loaded trucks can supply their stores. But for many other retailers, reducing transports and using transport capacity optimally, has not yet been achieved. Logically, such a bundling function can be provided by logistics service providers who can transport products from different manufacturers and/or from different retail companies (see, e.g., Zentes/Morschett 2003 and the cited literature). Bundling transports also allows using different transport modalities with a better ecological balance, e.g. railroads.

Bundling may become even more crucial in the future with the increasing trend towards online-business (with short response times, same-day delivery, etc.) and with further increasing congestion of roads, in particular towards city centres where a large part of retailing is done. *City logistics* concepts have been unsuccessfully tested in the past; however, the need for such concepts has not disappeared.

4.5 Operational Excellence

Supply chain benchmarking has consistently shown that – obviously based on existing practices – the best performers and the worst performers show enormous differences in all performance criteria, including those that are relevant for the economic performance (e.g. logistics costs), the environmental performance (e.g. transport kilometres) and social performance (e.g. number of accidents in warehouses). Thus, a great achievement for the sustainability of the consumer goods sector in total could already be reached if more companies would catch up with the best-in-class.

Again, industry associations stimulate the spreading of operational excellence. For example, ECR Europe sees this as a mission. The organisation defines, develops and accredits best practice processes that help to optimally operate consumer goods value chains with a holistic, integrated perspective. ECR Europe also drives implementation of the best practices. At the same time, as a part of its mission, ECR Europe is dedicated to develop and disseminate solutions that enhance the sustainability of the value chain as requested by the members. These words from the organisation's internal mission statement clearly demonstrate the relevance of operational excellence but also the readiness of the best companies to share a lot of their knowledge with others for the benefit of sustainability.

5. Key Sustainability Issues in Collaborative Supply

5.1 Overview

The principles and methods described above can be applied to a broad array of sustainability issues in the supply chain, including resource utilisation, transport optimisation, waste reduction and many more. A few of these sustainability issues are discussed in this paragraph.

5.2 Resource Utilisation

An overarching issue in the sustainability discussion is the responsible use of resources. The consumer goods industry is heavily using resources around the world. Whether fish or trees, water or land resources, the consumer goods sector (and, eventually, the consumer) is a major user of these resources, either for the products directly or for packaging. Some of these aspects will be discussed in more detail in the following paragraphs.

Closely linked to the climate debate is the use of the resource "forests". Deforestation accounts for 20% of all greenhouse gas emissions. The reasons for deforestation are manifold but from the perspective of the consumer goods sector, it is acknowledged that the biggest drivers are the cultivation of soya and oil palm, logging for the production of paper and board and the rearing of cattle (CGF 2013). The board of the Consumer Goods Forum, which combines most of the largest consumer goods manufacturers and retailers of the world, has agreed in 2010 to help achieve zero net deforestation by 2020. The companies intend to achieve this both by individual company initiatives and by working collectively.

Obviously, closing the loop to reuse raw materials and products after the product lifecycle is the best strategy to increase sustainability (GS1 Germany, p. 14). But also, shifting procurement to products and inputs which are less endangered (e.g. specific fish species) and/or which are produced in a sustainable manner (e.g. wood, paper, water) is reducing the negative impacts. Far beyond the legal requirements, it is specific NGOs (e.g. Greenpeace in the case of sustainable ocean management) that demand high information standards, specific protection etc. These NGOs are also active in shaping the consumer demand into this direction.

5.3 Packaging

In the UK alone, every year around 10 million tonnes of packaging is used of which 70% is accounted for by the food and grocery sector. So packaging has an obvious influence on sustainability but the functions of packaging are manifold. There are different main categories of packaging which are, in each case, linking different actors in the supply chain (IGD 2013a). *Primary packaging* is packaging which forms a sales unit (the packaging the shopper takes home) for the end user; *secondary packaging* is that which contains a number of sales units (the packaging that houses the final packaged product); *tertiary' packaging* is packaging that is used to group secondary packaging together to aid handling and transportation and prevent damage to the products. Approximately half of the packaging is primary packaging and disposed of by households (IGD 2013c).

Beyond the legal requirements that have become much more intense in the last years, voluntary actions are taken by the industry to improve sustainability. This starts with *collecting schemes* in different countries (often at least co-financed by the industry) but basically, the aim of the initiatives is "to minimise the environmental impact of packaging over its whole life cycle, without compromising its ability to protect the product" (IGD 2013a, p. 34). This focuses on a reduction of packaging but also on the use of materials that are easier to reuse or recycle.

However, the total impact of packaging on sustainability is complex to evaluate. ECR Europe, together with The European Organisation for Packaging and the Environment has released a report on packaging in 2009 in which the overall impact is discussed and the many approaches and tools to calculate the life cycle impact of a product are explored, emphasising the importance of taking a variety of sustainability indicators into account (ECR Europe/EUROPEN 2009).

One insight from this which is often overlooked in the public discussion is that there is not only overpackaging but also the risk of underpackaging: It is the main purpose of packaging to protect the product and the right package can strongly increase the shelf-life of products and reduce damages which, in turn, reduces the waste of products. Given how much resources are incorporated in a final product, reducing the waste of that is a highly sustainable measure which may be linked to more packaging and packaging waste (IGD 2013a; ECR Europe/EUROPEN 2009, p. 5). This, again, shows the relevance to have a holistic account of all environmental (and economic) impacts.

5.4 Waste

Reducing the use of resources is closely connected to active waste management. Over the last years, this issue has become more and more sophisticated. From a pure perspective on waste disposal and, later, the consideration of recycling, the methods have become more complex but also more resource preserving. Figure 3 depicts the hierarchy of preferred options in the supply chain to reduce waste in the most sustainable manner.

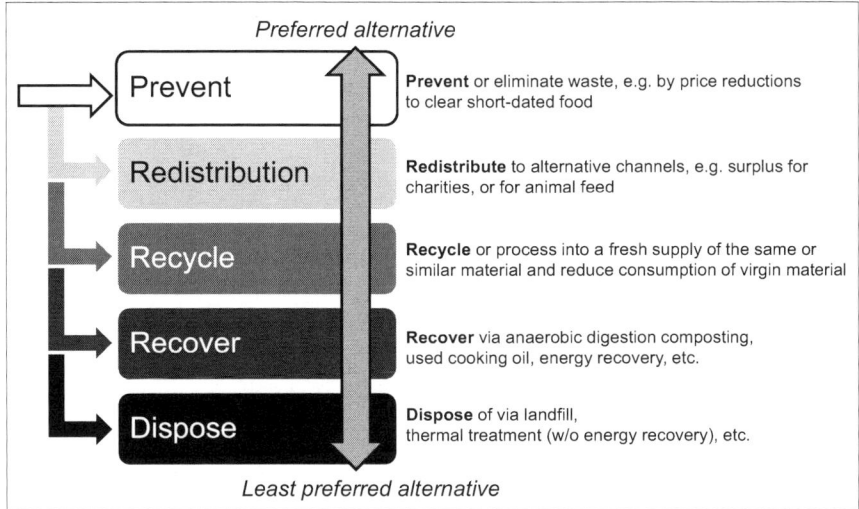

*Figure 3: The Waste Management and Waste Reduction Hierarchy
(Source: IGD 2013b)*

From this, it becomes obvious that waste management is – in almost every alternative – a collaborative activity. Preventing waste is linked to more effective supply chains, e.g. a better management of shelf-life of products, less damages, etc. Redistribution links the company to alternative channels, often upstream. For example, food waste can be redistributed to farmers as animal feed. Recycle and recover involves the collection of waste. Collection schemes for packaging has already been mentioned but collaborative efforts to collect final products (e.g. refrigerators, computers, clothing, paper, etc.) at the end of their usage and bring them back into the cycle are also worth mentioning.

5.5 Climate Protection and Greenhouse Gases

Worldwide, CO_2-emissions that are caused by consumer goods sum up to 8 tons per person annually. The objective of the World Resources Institute and the Intergovernmental Panel on Climate Change IPCC is to reduce this to 2 tons per person. This challenging objective shows that the methods of production and the consumption behaviour will have to be changed drastically in the next years (GS1 Germany, p. 16). As in other fields, collaborative measures and pressure are used to improve the situation. As an example of a horizontally and vertically collaborative approach, the climate protection initiative "Carbon Performance Improvement Initiative" (CIP2) can be mentioned. Main participants in this initiative are German retail companies (e.g. Otto Group, Tchibo, Ernsting's family) and they stimulate their suppliers to reduce energy consumption in their factories. By means of trainings for the suppliers and an online-tool that helps suppliers to identify the weaknesses of their production, the initiative plans to reduce the CO_2-emissions in import goods by several million tons annually. The retailers report that there is not strong resistance of the suppliers because the rising energy costs in most production countries raise the awareness of energy consumption and suppliers appreciate the support (N.N. 2013b, p. 36).

A major impact on greenhouse gas emission is the *transport* sector. ECR Europe points out that 30% of energy consumption in Europe is for transports and that the consumer goods sector has a high share in that (ECR Europe 2009). While efficiency of supply chains has always been a focus of ECR, the current focus on sustainability caused it to look into those measures that improve the environmental impact. The organisation launched a self-assessment tool for manufacturers and retailers that allows identifying – by comparing different activities and functions against benchmarks – the weaknesses in the current supply chain. Considered aspects for the benchmarking include efficient load fills, efficient deliveries but also information sharing with business partners. Measures proposed are often collaborative. In particular in transports, a lot of emissions are not directly done by manufacturers or retailers but by logistics service providers. Up to 50% of CO_2-emissions in food supply chains are caused by third party logistics companies. Thus, the transport sector will get more into the focus of retail company initiatives to reduce emissions (Gogolin/ Klaas-Wissing 2013, p. 52).

Overall, it becomes again obvious that a strong improvement in the transport field can only be achieved along the supply chain. A few measures can be directly implemented by single companies, e.g. use of different fuels (electric or LPG or even waste cooking oil) or use of best vehicle technologies but most measures can only be implemented jointly (IGD 2013a, p. 13):

- reducing the absolute amount of transport required – better loading patterns, route planning, redesigning products and packaging to enhance the load factor.
- reducing "empty running" of trucks.
- collaborating with other transport users and operators to share transport, i.e. bundling.

IGD points out that the consumer goods industry in the UK has drastically saved heavy truck transport kilometres in the last five years and that the sharing of trucks, even among competitors, has strongly contributed to that achievement.

Overall, a reliable measurement tool is required. It is likely that their customers (manufacturers and retailers) will demand logistics companies in the future to provide CO_2-emission data (Gogolin/Klaas-Wissing 2013, p. 52).

Another supply chain aspect that reduces greenhouse gas emissions is *regional procurement and change of transport modality*. Studies show that consumers value regional products and have a higher level of trust in them. At the same time, this obviously reduces transports and is a main aspect perceived by customers. Coop in Switzerland increases local procurement but also greatly reduced transports by air and used – where sourcing is intercontinental – ships. Where this is not possible, the products are signalled with a sticker "by air" so consumers can take a well-informed decision. Also, Coop compensates for the CO_2-emissions of this transport modality.

5.6 Food Safety

For the consumer, a crucial issue in sustainability is the safety of their food. As a basic principle, it has been described above that transparency is a major step to increase consumer trust. But transparency alone does not yet improve the situation, it is just the prerequisite. As an immediate reaction after the last food scandals, many retail companies and producers have shortened their supply chains. For example, Rewe announced after the horsemeat scandal to start using only German beef in their private label products; Coop in Switzerland, Tesco in the UK, and Carrefour and Intermarché in France declared similar plans and to further increase the domestic procurement of meat.

5.7 Social Responsibility in (Global) Procurement

Most of the previous sustainability issues were focussing on the environmental impact of supply chains. Sustainability aims, however, also at the social impact. In the context of global procurement, more and more frequently labour-intensive production stages are carried out in low-cost countries. A number of scandals in the last decade have drawn the attention of the consumers (and government institutions as well as NGOs) to the sometimes inacceptable conditions under which production of consumer goods is carried out. Starting from scandals of IKEA or Nike, in the last years Apple has become under heavy criticism due to the working conditions in the factories of its contract manufacturer Foxconn in China. In 2013, the collapse of a production building in Bangladesh in which more than 1,000 workers have been killed demonstrated that the previous sustainability measures have not been sufficient.

Different measures are being taken by companies (retailers and manufacturers) mainly from Western countries to influence their suppliers' conduct in Asian or South-American production countries. Many companies have developed their own code of conduct and include criteria for supplier selection and supplier conduct in their supply contracts (as has been pointed out in the section on collaboration). But monitoring and implementation is more efficient in standardised systems or broader associations. A first step has been the *United Nations Global Compact* that is concluded between companies and the United Nations Organisation to reduce negative social and ecological consequences of globalisation.

On the level of supply chains, a number of initiatives have emerged. A code of conduct that focuses more explicitly on labour rights is the Social Accountability SA8000, based, among other standards, on the international workplace norms of the *International Labour Organisation* ILO (see Morschett/Schramm-Klein/Zentes 2010, pp. 226-227, for more details). As another example with a stronger supply chain perspective, the *Business Social Compliance Initiative BSCI* was established in 2003 by the European Foreign Trade association "in order to create consistency and harmonisation for companies wanting to improve their social compliance in the global supply chain. BSCI aims to establish a common platform for the various European companies Codes of Conducts and monitoring systems, it also lays the groundwork for a common monitoring system for social compliance" (BSCI 2013). The practical implementation of the code is monitored by independent and accredited auditing organisations. BSCI further strives to develop suppliers towards better social performance and encourages them to apply for SA8000 certification (Morschett/Schramm-Klein/Zentes 2010, pp. 225-226).

But recent scandals have shown that more activity is needed. Still, the basic direction of the measures (collaboration between companies that import and setting of standards for the suppliers) is maintained. For example, in mid-2013, a group of 34 large companies, mainly clothing importers, have signed a binding agreement, under the lead of two global union umbrella organisations to improve the building and fire protection situation. Standards and a more intensive compliance monitoring are some of the measures of the initiative (N.N. 2013a).

6. Conclusion

The triple bottom line approach, i.e. the attempt to consider and to measure not only the economic performance of a company but also how socially responsible and how environmentally responsible a company has been (Elkington 1997), has created major challenges for companies but it is nowadays widely accepted in the consumer goods sector that this approach is right.

Measuring each supply chain issue in itself (e.g. packaging, transports, waste, social impact) is already a challenge for the coming years. But since the impact on social and environmental consequences does not stem from isolated activities but from their overall effect, the task becomes even more complex. Saving packaging may reduce packaging waste but result in more product waste with an even more severe ecological impact. Shorter supply chains may reduce transport costs and CO_2-emissions but the labour cost may go up. Furthermore, shifting production away from emerging countries may make it easier to prevent labour conditions scandals in the short run but may have adverse influences on the development of the respective countries. Attempts to avoid waste in stores may lead to out-of-stocks. These are just a few examples but they highlight the strong level of interdependence between the different activities in the supply chain. Such supply chain interdependence has long been acknowledged in supply chain management but lead to complexity even when only considering the economic perspective. Having the interdependence in all functions and between the three dimensions of sustainability makes it even tougher.

Facing today's challenges, the number of measures that could be undertaken is shear endless. Within the holistic perspective on sustainability, a *feasibility perspective*, also from the economic standpoint, is necessary. It is, thus, reasonable to focus on the most relevant activities that have the strongest sustainability impact. Several organisations, e.g. within GS1, ECR but also the Consumer Goods Forum, have started to identify so called "hot spots" within the specific value chains as the most crucial sustainability challenges. It seems reasonable to identify those hot spots jointly within industry associations that follow a collaborative approach because a joint understanding of the most decisive challenges is a requirement for finding joint solutions, joint actions and joint measuring.

References

BAUMGARTEN, H.; STABENAU, H.-P.; STEGER, U.; ZENTES, J. (1998): Qualitäts- und Umweltmanagement logistischer Prozessketten, Bern et al.

BHATTACHARYI, C.B.; SEN, S. (2004): Doing Better at Doing Good: When, Why and How Consumers Respond to Corporate Social Initiatives, in: California Management Review, Vol. 47, No. 1, pp. 9-24.

BSCI (2013): Business Social Compliance Initiative, www.bsci-intl.org, accessed on September 27, 2013.

CGF (2013): Sustainability Pillar, http://www.theconsumergoodsforum.com/sustainability.aspx, accessed on September 20, 2013.

CHOPRA, S.; MEINDL, P. (2004): Supply Chain Management, 2nd ed., Upper Saddle River.

ECR EUROPE (2009): Sustainable Transport Roadmap, Brussels.

ECR EUROPE; EUROPEN (THE EUROPEAN ORGANIZATION FOR PACKAGING AND THE ENVIRONMENT) (2009): Packaging in the Sustainability Agenda: A Guide for Corporate Decision Makers, Brussels.

ELKINGTON J. (1997): Cannibals with Forks: The Triple Bottom Line of 21st Century Business, Oxford.

GIMENEZ, C.; SIERRA, V. (2008): Sustainable Supply Chains: Governance Mechanisms to Greening Suppliers, in: Journal of Business Ethics, Vol. 116, No. 1, pp. 189-203.

GOGOLIN, M.; KLAAS-WISSING, T. (2013): Handel will genaue Schadstoffwerte, in: Lebensmittelzeitung, No. 22, p. 52.

GREENHOUSE GAS PROTOCOL (2011): Product Life Cycle Accounting and Reporting Standard, Washington et al.

GS1 GERMANY (2012): Nachhaltigkeit in der deutschen Konsumgüterwirtschaft, Köln.

GS1 SWITZERLAND (2009): GS1 Report 2009: Nachhaltigkeit schafft Sicherheit, Bern.

GS1 SWITZERLAND (2013): White Paper Nachhaltigkeit, Bern (*forthcoming*).

IGD (2013a): Environmental Sustainability Matrix: Understand sustainability issues across the supply chain, Watford.

IGD (2013b): Supply Chain Waste Prevention Guide 2013: From Factory in-gate to Till, www.igd.com/our-expertise/Supply-chain/Sustainable-supply-chains/2661, accessed on September 26, 2013.

IGD (2013c): Trust, Transparency and Technology, www.igd.com/our-expertise/ Sustainability/Distribution/13366/Trust-Transparency-and-Technology, accessed on September 29, 2013.

MCGUIRE, J.B.; DOW, S.; ARCHGEYD, K. (2003): CEO Incentives and Corporate Social Responsibility; in: Journal of Business Ethics, Vol. 45, No. 4, pp. 341-359.

MELLAHI, K.; FRYNAS, J.; FINLAY, P. (2005): Global Strategic Management, Oxford.

MORSCHETT, D.; SCHRAMM-KLEIN, H.; ZENTES, J. (2010): Strategic International Management, 2nd ed., Wiesbaden.

N.N. (2013a): Die Branche stellt sich ihrer Verantwortung, in: Textilwirtschaft, No. 21, p. 28.

N.N. (2013b): Klimaschutz ist Unternehmenssache, in: Textilwirtschaft, No. 13, p. 36.

SCHÄDLICH, S. (2012): Lidl lohnt sich nicht für jeden, TAZ (Tageszeitung), accessed on March 21, 2012.

SCHWARTZ, M.S.; CARROLL, A.B. (2008): Integrating and Unifying Competing and Complementary Frameworks, in: Business & Society, Vol. 47, No. 2, pp. 148-186.

STANK, T.P.; DAVIS, B.R.; FUGATE, B.S. (2005): A Strategic Framework for Supply Chain Oriented Logistics, in: Journal of Business Logistics, Vol. 26, No. 2, pp. 27-45.

WCED (1987): Our Common Future, New York.

ZENTES, J.; MORSCHETT, D. (2003): Die Servicebausteine in der Logistik, in: MERKEL, H.; BJELICIC, B. (Eds.): Logistik und Verkehrswirtschaft im Wandel, Unternehmensübergreifende Versorgungsnetzwerke verändern die Wirtschaft, München, pp. 419-436.

ZENTES, J.; MORSCHETT, D.; SCHRAMM-KLEIN, H. (2011): Strategic Retail Management, 2nd ed., Wiesbaden.

How IT Can Enable Sustainability Throughout Supply Chains

Christian Berg, Stefan Hack and Constantin Blome

Overview

1. Introduction

Sustainability is critical for supply chain management and supply chain management is critical for the realisation of more sustainability – this has been proven both by several studies as well as practical examples from business throughout the past few years. Whereas most large corporations have implemented management systems for quality, environment, occupational health and safety or others for their own operational excellence and could thereby improve quality, efficiency, environmental footprint or incident rates and occupational diseases, the situation looks quite different in the respective supply chains. Many multinational corporations (MNC) have realised that the biggest lever for, for example, reducing the environmental footprint of their products lies in their supply chain. Global brands of different industries have calculated their environmental footprint and communicated that up to 90% of their footprint stems from their supply chain, for example documented by the following case of Puma.

From the practitioner side Puma set a benchmark in 2011 by issueing their first environmental profit & loss account (Puma 2011). Puma calculated their environmental footprint and estimated the contributions of the different tiers of their suppliers, amounting to a total of 145 m€. Not surprisingly, the vast majority of this negative impact stems from the supply chain: Puma's own operations account only for 6% of that sum, tier 1 suppliers for 9%. tier 2 for 10%, tier 3 for 19%, and tier 4 is with 57% the largest contributor. This example illuminates that it is crucial for firms to focus on sustainability beyond the firm boundaries.

One could even argue that most incidents of non-compliance or non-sustainable behavior which make it to the public are related to issues in the supply chains of large global brands. Protests because of poor working conditions or labour standards in China's high tech industry, toxic toys, exploding batteries, numerous food scandals, or irresponsible issues of occupational health and safety in textile factories in Bangladesh – they all have contributed to a rising awareness that sustainable consumption won't be possible without a sustainable supply chain. In an increasingly interconnected world, in which competition is becoming less "firm vs. firm" and more "supply chain vs. supply chain", with rising expectations regarding transparency, with information spreading around the globe within seconds, supply chain management can no longer ignore sustainability issues. Whereas unsustainable supply chains can be disastrous for the firm, a sustainable one can become an important differentiator in competition (Reuter et al. 2010).

Transparency and information in supply chains thus play a critical role in enabling sustainability along the supply chain which has been also widely acknowledged in practice and research. For example, firms like Ferrero and Nestlé try hard to uncover their full supply chains, which is difficult particularly in commodities as sustainable and unsustainable products could be mixed at each stage of the supply chain (Roberts 2003). Furthermore, sub-tier suppliers are often not disclosed by intermediaries due to the fear of being cut out of the supply chain. Thus establishing the "chain of custody" that allows to document the full supply chain is a great challenge to focal firms which can be only addressed with suitable Information Technology (IT).

However, although there seems to be consensus that information exchange and collaboration along the value chain is critical, there is relatively little attention on concrete tools and measures how to gain this. In particular, the role of IT for more sustainable supply chains has only rarely been studied – partly, of course, because the lacking inter-operability of the respective IT systems did not allow for a smoothly integrated information exchange along the entire value chain.

After a review on the background of our manuscript and an overview on recent studies on the topic, we will provide showcases which demonstrate the great potential IT has for achieving more sustainable supply chains.

2. Background

2.1 Status Quo on Sustainable SCM (SSCM)

Sustainability in supply chains recently developed into one of the major streams of research on supply chain management as such, attracting researchers from various areas. Despite extended research until now "no coherent set of practices in sustainable supply chain management has emerged", as Pagell/Wu (2009, p. 37) conclude. The research on SSCM can be classified into three important streams. Most predominant is the research on greening supply chains considering mainly the environmental dimension as Seuring/Müller (2008) explain in their literature review. Major contributions comprise research on reverse logistics (Carter/Ellram 1998), upstream and downstream integration (Vachon/Klassen 2006), early and late adopters of SSCM (Zhu/Sarkis 2004) or driver and barriers to SSCM (Walker/Di Sisto/McBain 2008).

Another stream of research rather discusses the social dimension of sustainability, stemming more from the domain of business ethics research (Maloni/Brown 2006, Roberts 2003). Nevertheless, recently the social dimension raises more interest also in the classical supply chain domain (Andersen/Skjoett-Larsen 2009). Among the first Carter/Jennings (2002) discussed social responsibility in supply chains. An important concern in this field of research is the role of supplier code of conducts and how they might be implemented effectively (e.g. Jiang 2009).

The most recent trend in empirical SSCM research is to focus the tripartite of the pillars of the triple-bottom line, so that environmental and social dimensions are integrated with the financial dimension of the supply chain. For example, Reuter et al. (2010) have focused on how environmental and social dimensions are related in global supplier management. Hollos/Blome/Foerstl (2012) examine the performance impact of supplier collaboration on the triple-bottom line. In early works Carter (2005) as well as Carter/Jennings (2004) developed the concept of purchasing social responsibility reflecting all dimensions of sustainability. They also have investigated antecedents for achieving purchasing social responsibility. Wu/Pagell (2011) investigated how decision-makers trade-off the different sustainability dimensions in their decisions. Gimenez/Sierra/Rodon (2012) provide a comprehensive overview on this research stream.

Overall, this literature acknowledges the importance of antecedents which need to be in place in order to enable successful SSCM. These pre-conditions are nicely summarised by Seuring/Müller (2008) in the form of a Delphi study, inquiring "which major issues and problems experts report regarding sustainable supply chain management". The following topics were rated highest[1]:

- identifying and measuring economical, social and environmental impacts and performances, in short: sustainability performance measurement
- supply chain-wide cooperation and communication (cross-border information management)
- pressure from stakeholders and need for transparency

All of these topics directly relate to and demand up-to-date business information systems:

- measuring environmental and social impacts and performances might still be difficult conceptually, but it is obvious that this cannot be achieved without a state-of-the-art information management system. The multidimensional relations of causes and effects, the need for aggregation of data across all organisational units in MNCs, and the tracking of the respective impact cannot be done manually.
- similarly, communication across the entire supply chain, even across just one or two tiers, is impossible without IT. Due to the use of mod-

ern communication and information technology it is possible to reorganise entire supply chains and foster intelligent logistics and distribution, which improves flexibility as well as efficiency and reduces resource consumption within distribution systems. Product declarations, for instance, in high tech industry, have become so comprehensive that even manual IT-based processes do not meet today's requirements for legal compliance, safety, and speed of processing.

- finally, the rising consumer awareness in the global knowledge society has increased the importance of transparency on products' genealogy throughout.

In sum, the top issues in sustainable supply chain management have all a direct linkage to business information systems, which thus guide our argumentation in the remainder of the manuscript.

2.2 IT as Enabler for SSCM

Berkhout/Hertin (2001) in their report to the OECD provide a well-structured analysis of the potential impacts of information and communication technologies (ICT) on environmental sustainability. They distinguish three different orders of effects ICT have. First order effects result directly from the production and use of ICT themselves. Second order effects result from changes in procedures due to the use of ICT (e.g. dematerialisation), whereas third order effects would come from respective feedback mechanisms (e.g. rebound effects). ICT are changing the way products and services are designed, produced, and distributed and contribute to a structural change away from tangible assets that are material-, energy- and labor-intensive towards intangible information-intensive activities. The report concludes that impacts can be both positive (largely the case with second order effects) and negative (e.g. first order effects of IT production). As validated in later studies (Erdmann/Hilty 2010, Erdmann et al. 2004) ICT have great potential to foster sustainable development, where the positive effects outweigh the negative effects (e.g. electricity consumption, electronic waste). The recent Global e-Sustainability Initiative (GeSI) analysis concludes that the overall potential of the role of IT would be positive: "the estimated ICT-abatement potential of 9.1 $GtCO_2e$ ... is seven times the size of the sector's direct emissions" (GeSI 2012, p. 11).

Whereas these studies take a macroeconomic perspective, Hack/Berg (2013) investigated the "potential of IT for Corporate Sustainability". By drawing on previous works of Luftman/Koeller (2003), Melville/Kraemer/Gurbaxani (2004), and Dao/Langella/Carbo (2011) they propose a conceptual model for the sustainability value of IT and illustrate how these IT capabilities "can be utilised for improved sustainability performance in a corporate setting". However, they leave out the value chain perspective through IT, although they admit that "a value chain perspective needs to be added to the enterprise view to achieve true global optima instead of just local ones".

Building on Schein (1989) and Cash et al. (1994), Chen/Boudreau/Watson (2008) developed a model that advocates that information systems by automating, informating (up and down) and transforming organisations can promote ecological sustainability. These three roles of information technology deem relevant also when considering the major topics identified as core issues in sustainable supply chain management in the Delphi study by Seuring/Müller (2008). Dao/Langella/Carbo (2011) following a resource-based view developed a framework which claims that the "integration of human, supply chain and IT resources enable firms develop sustainability capabilities" which in turn can lead to sustained competitive advantage. Also other researchers investigated the importance of IT solutions for sustainability within the firm, but only some – like Rai/Patnayakuni/Seth (2006) – found proof that firm performance is increased by IT enabled supply chain integration. Further research will have to be performed to fully understand the impact of information technology on sustainable supply chain management.

As we know not only since the disovery of the Bullwhip effect that sharing of information along the supply chain will result in higher overall supply chain performance (Zhou/Benton 2007, Lee/Padmanabhan/Whang 1997), we argue that the sharing of information will also help in increasing sustainability along the supply chain. This will further be documented practically by the following showcases.

3. Showcases

3.1 Overview

If you consider the environmental and social impact of corporations, you can either take a corporate view or a product life cycle view. The corporate view looks at all functions and lines of business of a corporation and sums up the respective contributions to the environmental and social impact. The advantage of this view is that you have the (ideally) complete view on the impact of a given company and that the respective data are comparatively easy to calculate, since it is only necessary to consider processes within the corporate boundaries. However, the more complex value chains get, the less meaningful such an analysis is. The product life cycle view takes a different view, the product perspective. It follows the product throughout all its life cycle phases, from its conception ("cradle") via development, production, logistics, use phase until the end-of-life phase ("grave"). The benefit of this view is, of course, to get meaningful information about a product's impact. The downside, on the other hand, is that the data are much more difficult to get.

Ultimately, the entire impact of all corporations worldwide would equal the sum of all corporate impacts, which, in turn, would be the entire impact of all goods and services produced.

In both cases it is critical to get information about the early phases of the value chains, which are often taking place in emerging or developing economies. The sourcing of natural resources and the production of consumer goods is to a large extent taking place in these economies, whereas many of the global brands are located in industrialised countries. The corporate impact of companies in the industrialised world is, on average, relatively low compared to those in developing and emerging economies. Often it is only the final value chain phases which are added in industrialised countries. Moreover, environmental and social standards in developing and emerging economies are often considerably lower than in industrialised countries.

This illustrates the paramount importance which a product life cycle perspective has for sustainability. Sustainable supply chain management is therefore a critical lever for corporate sustainability.

The following showcases highlight the potential of IT for sustainable supply chain management. They answer three critical questions around the sustainability of products:

1. Is this product or pre-product safe? Does it only contain substances which are appropriate for the specific use case? Is it fully compliant with all regulatory requirements? These questions are particularly relevant in industries with a high degree of hazardous and toxic substances, like High Tech.
2. Which genealogy does a certain batch or product have? Despite increasing regulation (for instance on environmental and product safety issues), recall incidents are also on the rise. Food scandals, fake drugs, toxic toys or broken brakes necessitate product recalls. Recalls require, however, insight into exactly which batches are affected and where they were shipped to.
3. What is the impact of this product along its life cycle with regards to social and environmental aspects? How much energy was consumed during the production or how much greenhouse gas emissions are related to it?

3.2 IT Solutions for Product Stewardship Networks

Product safety has become a strictly regulated domain. The European Restriction of Hazardous Substances Directive (RoHS) as well as the Waste Electrical and Electronic Equipment Directive (WEEE) Directive, which have been in force for almost a decade now, are just two examples of such compliance regulations. Vendors need to issue compliance declarations when they sell their products. Information and communication along the value chain is thus becoming critical for product safety (see Hack/Berg 2013). The professional buyer needs to know the composition of the semi-manufactured products as criterion for this the decision-making process. According to the current practice, however, every supplier has to provide such information to every customer – or every manufacturer has to request that information from the suppliers. As there is no single standard format for these requests, many companies have a significant administrative burden to monitor their product safety data along the value chain – both upstream and downstream. Why could not every supplier enter their data just once and share them with as many business customers as possible, while the customer has access to the assessment results and benchmarks data from his mainstream sourcing and procurement systems?

This is the background for the network solution for product stewardship SAP has launched recently. The SAP Product Stewardship Network (PSN) "is an online collaboration community for product manufacturers and their supply chains to efficiently collect and manage product sustainability data" (SAP 2013). As these compliance declarations are requested by many business buyers, a network that links suppliers with customers is increasing efficiency as information about the product needs to be edited only once. The user can then decide whether the information will be published to the entire network (i.e. all users of the network) or just a selected group of clients. An underlying authorisation concept ensures that information is only shared based on a conscious decision by the participants of the network. The SAP Product Stewardship Network leverages the power of a cloud solution: it gets stronger with every company using it, a true network effect.

Supplier updates on product declarations will automatically be forwarded to all consumers of that information. The network supports the exchange of Material Safety Data Sheets and provides latest regulatory content on REACH SVHC and RoHS declarations.

This network, conceived for product stewardship transparency, could easily be expanded to other sustainability relevant information. The amount of greenhouse gas emissions related to a certain life cycle phase, for instance, could in just the same mannor be fed into the network as indicators for water consumption, investments in social communities, initiatives of corporate volunteering etc., since the basic idea remains the same: every one who contributes to a certain life cycle phase provides product related information that downstream consumers might be interested to have. Such a solution could effectively support optimisation and planning across the supply chain between business partners. It could support a business community centered around common business needs like mitigating product risk and brand protection. Furthermore, such a network could provide transparency regarding product attributes and regulatory compliance and thereby supports the optimisation of resource usage. Instead of establishing and managing cumbersome one-to-one relationships between supplier and customer the network offers efficiency and scale by actively managing many-to-many relationships based on commonly agreed standards.

Out of the three most critical issues for sustainable supply chain management mentioned above, i.e. impact and performance measurement, communication across the supply chain, and transparency, at least two are addressed by this solution. Both the collaboration along the value chain and transparency about sustainability relevant product information can be greatly enhanced. The impact and performance measurement is not directly addressed by PSN, partly because common standards and metrics for such an impact analysis are still missing.

3.3 IT Solutions for Global Product and Batch Traceability

Despite increasing and strict regulation on product safety, product recalls have been on the rise lately, due to meat scandals, hazardous substances in toys or broken car brakes. Such product recalls require the tracking of products through complex and distributed supply chains, which constitutes a true challenge in densely woven value chain networks. In case of such product recalls companies need to be able to very quickly and effectively take action. They need to have insight into the genealogy of a given batch or product and advise business customers or consumers.

SAP developed a solution which can link finished goods with raw materials or serialised components as well as assets and services used in production (SAP 2012). SAP Global Batch Traceability's tracking features provide insight into the distribution of the respective product or batch to business partners and customers. Intended to help to ensure consumer safety, brand protection, and mitigate risk the tool is able to investigate the product genealogy up-stream as well as down-stream along the supply chain. It can create a complete record of procured batch quantities, specific batches used in production and subsequent manufacturing steps. The application also monitors the distribution of finished goods to customers and can identify who may have received products containing specific raw materials. It is also possible to quickly generate distribution list data and complete where-used lists for multiple batches (SAP 2012). With this information it is possible to quickly respond to potential recall situations, conduct targeted recalls, and take action to reduce potential liability.

Here the two aspects of supply chain wide transparency and information provisioning are most dominant and can both be strongly improved by this business information system.

3.4 IT Solutions for Measuring Product Footprints

When determining the sustainability performance of a company both the direct impacts from on-site processes as well as indirect impacts embodied in the supply chains of a company have to be taken into account (Wied-mann/Lenzen/Barrett 2009). For this purpose the environmental impact of a company's products and services are calculated with the help of so-called Life Cycle Assessments (LCAs).[2]

Expert software vendors provide solutions to perform LCAs (e.g. ifu with a software called Umberto, PE International with GaBi, PRé offers the LCA software SimaPro). These applications help product engineers to understand the environmental impacts of potential product designs and can simulate the effects when innovating to create more sustainable products by replacing materials, changing processes or reducing packaging. Thus, LCA software can support in identifying hotspots in companies' value chains and engaging with suppliers to create products with lower environmental impacts (see Hack/Berg 2013).

However, the current LCA approach and the related product-level carbon auditing of supply chains has a number of problems and limitations as decribed by McKinnon (2010) amongst which are the system boundaries to be identified, the accuracy of data (see Lenzen 2001), the variability of supply chains that subject to frequent change as well as the scaleability, i.e. the ability to extend from a few selected products to the entire product portfolio. For example, the accuracy is limited due to the use of statistical data, e.g. emission factors reflecting industry averages. Using data from databases with industry average data hides differences between suppliers (see Schaltegger 1997).

Hack/Berg (2013) describe the approach that SAP follows and which has been implemented at Danone, French producer of food products. Danone is measuring the carbon footprint of about 35,000 products on a regular basis based on primary data and actual resource consumption in procurement, production, transportation, and distribution. The solution is able to account for differences between suppliers of the same material. Although only the calculation of carbon emissions is currently performed, the solution has been designed to also cover water and other emission types (e.g. waste), along the entire value chain. According to Danone, it provides the company and its decision makers with monthly reports needed to support its ambitious goals of driving down its carbon footprint, namely 30% in the four years between 2008 and 2012 (Danone 2012).

Whereas the activities inside the focal enterprise can be tracked with the help of modern ERP systems, external data from suppliers still represents a challenge and an obstacle to data accuracy. However, through the emergence of electronic platforms recursive balancing systems as described by Schmidt (2009) can be realised, where suppliers exchange foot-print-relevant data directly with their customers. The Sustainability Con-sortium (TSC) has recently evaluated IT-based collaborative platforms to perform sustainability assessments where suppliers (e.g. consumer product companies) can provide their respective environmental data to many re-tailers at the same time.

4. Discussion and Future Developments

4.1 Overview

The most critical issues in creating more sustainable supply chains were, as mentioned above, identifying and measuring the sustainability impact and performance, a supply chain-wide collaboration and communication, and the pressure of stakeholders for greater transparency. The existing showcases demonstrate that business information systems have the poten-tial to address at least two of these issues and improve the sustainability of the supply chain in important aspects already today.

4.2 Communication and Collaboration

Since value chains are densely woven networks spanning the globe, any meaningful and effective way of communication for such entities has to consider and leverage the characteristics of networks as well. Typical characteristics of networks are many-to-many-relations, open communica-tion, mutual benefits and multiple-win-situations.[3]

Traditionally, communication between adjacent partners in the value chain was either one-to-one, or at best, one-to-many. An example for a one-to-many communication would be, if a large retailer sends out a noti-fication on specific requirements to all tier 1 suppliers. The more impor-tant the life-cycle-perspective of products gets (vs. a corporate view), the more important it will be that information flows across the full supply chain, not only to adjacent members in the value chain or in one direction, but across several tiers in the value chain, upstream and downstream. This is exactly what a cloud platform could provide, in which companies can share information about products, but also about their own operations, in a deliberate manner with either just one, several, or all other members of the network. As with any other network, the potential and benefit of the network increases with every new member. This has a huge efficiency potential for the communication and collaboration across value chains, since one supplier doesn't need to communicate one-to-one to all its customers, nor does a given customer needs to communicate one-to-many to all its direct suppliers. Instead of 100 direct communication events a supplier has to organise with its 100 customers, just one channel can achieve the same. It thus creates multiple wins: both sides (supplier and customer) win, since they can greatly improve the efficiency of their communication.

Moreover, the power of network effects in communication and collaboration are visible in the adoption of social media and networks like Facebook or Twitter. Further analogies can also be drawn between social or business networks: for instance regarding peer respectively market pressure which can trigger a "domino-effect" to participate in such networks and hence encourage mass adoption in favor of better exchange of relevant information which often leads to a more efficient use of resources.

4.3 Transparency

Such platforms have the potential to enhance transparency on sustainability data along the value chains considerably. All showcases mentioned above feed into such transparency: be it product safety, batch traceability, or product footprint information. Of course, technology can only provide the framework for such transparency. It will have to be used to increase transparency also for consumers. Furthermore, so far only certain aspects of sustainability criteria are addressed in the solutions mentioned. They are concentrating on product safety for high tech industry as well as on batch traceability for pharma, consumer products, or manufacturing industries. Furthermore, the footprint calculation is *de facto* often still limited to carbon emissions, sometimes including other emission types or water consumption as well – but hardly used for a comprehensive environmental (or even social) product footprint.[4]

Finally, any business information system can only be as good as the data fed into it. The largest issues for the overall footprint of most products can hardly be addressed because they are caused "early" in the supply chain. This can only be improved if those early contributors get a clear guidance on how to meet the requested standards and assistance in the operational execution. Pressure from downstream customers will be necessary but not sufficient for this. Complementary measures (e.g. educational programs) will be needed. However, unless there is the technological possibility to have full transparency along the entire value chain on all criteria needed or deemed important, any such measure won't be successful in the long-run, simply because their success cannot be tracked.

4.4 Sustainability Impact and Performance

The final critical issue of more sustainable supply chains mentioned here is the hardest one: measuring the impact of products and their genealogy regarding environmental, social and economic aspects.

In the past few years much has been done to establish common standards for measuring the environmental footprint. ISO has, for instance, developed several standards, for example, for Environmental Labeling and Declaration (ISO 14025 and ISO14020 series), for Life Cycle Assessments (ISO 14040/14044), and for the Carbon Footprint of Products (ISO 14067). The related assessments, however, can be quite troublesome and tedious. Furthermore, in most cases the respective calculations can only be done based on statistical data, and they only include environmental aspects. Other actors, like The Sustainability Consortium (TSC), a multi-stakeholder consortium, directly address the supply chain and aim at a more sustainable consumption "to advance science to drive a new generation of innovative products and supply networks that address environmental, social, and economic imperatives" (The Sustainability Consortium 2013).

However, despite such initiaitives and significant improvements, the sustainability impact assessment remains to be the most difficult challenges, simply due to the nature of the concept of sustainability. How would you assess a product which has less toxic substances but consumes more energy than a competitive product? How would you compare a product which is energy efficient and environmentally-friendly but which is produced under suboptimal labour conditions to one which has a larger environmental footprint but a better social one? Finally, how would you rate two products with identical environmental footprints, but one creating jobs in country A, the other in country B? Who wants to decide which product leads to a more sustainable development?

Progress in sustainability impact and performance will therefore not be possible based on technological developments alone. Nevertheless, technology will be as necessary as in any other cases of performance measurement in today's corporations.

5. Conclusion

While international standards for sustainable consumption are still being developed and have not been widely adopted, there are both risks and opportunities for companies as well as for software vendors. No firm can be sure that IT solutions they implement really pay off in the long-run. At the same time, this field also provides the chance to differentiate oneself from other firms. As everybody is aware that sustainability implementation, particularly along supply chains, requires an immense amount of time and effort, sustainable supply chains can be an important source of competitive advantage. Imagining the case that one firm can document sustainability compliance along its supply chains whereas the other firm cannot, for example, be sure that child labour is a non-issue will tremendously help in case a supply chain risk materialises.

Traceability and transparency as well as the measurement of sustainability performance are key drivers to compare and benchmark performance which is the driver for fair competition. Today, firms can still claim to be sustainable, even though they not necessarily act so, due to intransparency, missing measures etc., but we see that IT systems are available that allow to make supply chains more easily traceable, transparent, and measurable. Even though it is not yet clear which standards will eventually be enacted, first movers might benefit from these developments as it can be foreseen that sustainability requirements as well as transparency and traceability requirements will grow in the future.

Again, technology will not resolve these issues alone. Conceptual work is needed and ultimately also business judgement. However, technology in general, and business information systems in particular, can provide the infrastructure which is necessary in order to calculate footprints, track batches, and increase transparency for more sustainable supply chains.

Notes

1   Seuring/Müller (2008) actually name four issues in sustainable supply chain management. Their first issue, however, is "(1) pressures and in-

centives for sustainable supply chain", a kind of meta-issue. It is addressed in the current paper throughout and therefore left out in this list. We concentrate on the other three topics Seuring/Müller highlight.
2 This section is illustrating a showcase which two of us have recently described elsewhere (see Hack/Berg (2013)).
3 For more details on the characteristics of networks, see Berg (2005).
4 This is partly due to the fact that standards and metrics for such calculations are still under development, see next paragraph.

References

ANDERSEN, M.; SKJOETT-LARSEN, T. (2009): Corporate Social Responsibility in Global Supply Chains, in: Supply Chain Management: An International Journal, Vol. 14, No. 2, pp. 75-86.

BERG, C. (2005): Vernetzung als Syndrom: Risiken und Chancen von Vernetzungsprozessen für eine nachhaltige Entwicklung, Frankfurt.

BERKHOUT, F.; HERTIN, J. (2001): Impacts of Information and Communication Technologies on Environmental Sustainability: Speculations and Evidence, Report, University of Sussex.

CARTER, C.R. (2005): Purchasing Social Responsibility and Firm Performance: The Key Mediating Roles of Organizational Learning and Supplier Performance, in: International Journal of Physical Distribution & Logistics Management, Vol. 35, No. 3, pp. 177-194.

CARTER, C.R.; ELLRAM, L.M. (1998): Reverse Logistics: A Review of the Literature and Framework for Future Investigation, in: Journal of Business Logistics, Vol. 19, No. 1, pp. 85-102.

CARTER, C.R., JENNINGS, M.M. (2002): Social Responsibility and Supply Chain Relationships, in: Transportation Research Part E: Logistics and Transportation Review, Vol. 38, No. 1, pp. 37-52.

CARTER, C.R.; JENNINGS, M.M. (2004): The Role of Purchasing in Corporate Social Responsibility: A Structural Equation Analysis, in: Journal of Business Logistics, Vol. 25, No. 1, pp. 145-186.

CASH, J.I.; ECCLES, R.G.; NOHRIA, N.; NOLAN, R.L. (1994): Building the Information-Age Organization: Structure Control and Information Technologies, Boston.

CHEN, A.J.W.; BOUDREAU, M.-C.; WATSON, R.T. (2008): Information Systems and Ecological Sustainability, in: Journal of Systems and Information Technology, Vol. 10, No. 3, pp. 186-201.

DANONE (2012): Danone 2011 Sustainability Report, http://www.danone.com/images/pdf/sustainable_report_2011.pdf, accessed on May 21, 2013.

DAO, V.; LANGELLA, I.; CARBO, J. (2011): From Green to Sustainability: Information Technology and an Integrated Sustainability Framework, in: Journal of Strategic Information Systems, Vol. 20, No. 1, pp. 63-79.

ERDMANN, L.; HILTY, L.M. (2010): Scenario analysis: Exploring the Macroeconomic Impacts of Information and Communication Technologies on Greenhouse Gas Emissions, in: Journal of Industrial Ecology, Vol. 14, No. 5, pp. 824-841.

ERDMANN, L.; LORENZ, H.; GOODMAN, J.; ARNFALK, P. (2004): The Future Impact of ICTs on Environmental Sustainability, Report, European Commission Joint Research Centre.

GLOBAL E-SUSTAINABILITY INITIAVE (GeSI) (2012): GeSI SMARTer 2020: The Role of ICT in Driving a Sustainable Future, Brussels.

GIMENEZ, C.; SIERRA, V.; RODON, J. (2012): Sustainable Operations: Their Impact on the Triple Bottom Line, in: International Journal of Production Economics, Vol. 140, No. 1, pp. 149-159.

HACK, S.; BERG, C. (2013): The Potential of IT for Corporate Sustainability: Conceptual Model for the Sustainbiltiy Value of IT, accepted for publication in: Sustainability.

HOLLOS, D.; BLOME, C.; FOERSTL, K. (2012): Does Sustainable Supplier Co-operation Affect Performance? Examining Implications for the Triple Bottom Line, in: International Journal of Production Research, Vol. 50, No. 11, pp. 2968-2986.

JIANG, B. (2009): Implementing Supplier Codes of Conduct in Global Supply Chains: Process Explanations from Theoretic and Empirical Perspectives, in: Journal of Business Ethics, Vol. 85, No. 1, pp. 77-92.

LEE, H.L.; PADMANABHAN, V.; WHANG, S. (1997): Information Distortion in a Supply Chain: The Bullwhip Effect, in: Management Science, Vol. 43, No. 4, pp. 546-558.

LENZEN, M. (2001): Errors in Conventional and Input-Output-Based Life-Cycle Inventories, in: Journal of Industrial Ecology, Vol. 4, No. 4, pp. 127-148.

LUFTMAN, J.N.; KOELLER, C.T. (2003): Assessing the Value of IT, in: LUFTMAN, J.N. (Ed.): Competing in the Information Age, 2nd ed., New Jersey, pp. 77-105.

MALONI, M.J.; BROWN, M.E. (2006): Corporate Social Responsibility in the Supply Chain: An Application in the Food Industry, in: Journal of Business Ethics, Vol. 68, No. 1, pp. 35-52.

MCKINNON, A.C. (2010): Product-Level Carbon Auditing of Supply Chains: Environmental Imperative or Wasteful Distraction?, in: International Journal of Physical Distribution & Logistics Management, Vol. 40, No. 1/2, pp. 42-60.

MELVILLE, N.P.; KRAEMER, K.; GURBAXANI, V. (2004): Review: Information Technology and Organizational Performance: An Integrative Model of IT Business Value, in: MIS Quarterly, Vol. 28, No. 2, pp. 283-322.

PAGELL, M.; WU, Z. (2009): Building a More Complete Theory of Sustainable Supply Chain Management Using Case Studies of 10 Exemplars, in: Journal of Supply Chain Management, Vol. 45, No. 2, pp. 37-56.

PUMA (2011): PUMA Completes First Environmental Profit and Loss Account which values Impacts at € 145 million, http://about.puma.com/puma-completes-first-envir onmental-profit-and-loss-account-which-values-impacts-at-e-145-million/, accessed on August 22, 2013.

RAI, A.; PATNAYAKUNI, R.; SETH, N. (2006): Firm Performance Impacts of Digitally Enabled Supply Chain Integration Capabilities, in: MIS Quarterly, Vol. 30, No. 2, pp. 225-246.

REUTER, C.; FOERSTL, K.; HARTMANN, E.; BLOME, C. (2010): Sustainable Global Supplier Management: The Role of Dynamic Capabilities in Achieving Competitive Advantage, in: Journal of Supply Chain Management, Vol. 46, No. 2, pp. 45-63.

ROBERTS, S. (2003): Supply Chain Specific? Understanding the Patchy Success of Ethical Sourcing Initiatives, in: Journal of Business Ethics, Vol. 44, No. 2-3, pp. 159-170.

SAP (2012): Drive Product Traceability Throughout Your Supply Network, Walldorf.

SAP (2013): Overview, https://www54.sap.com/pc/tech/cloud/software/product-stewardship-network/overview/index.html, accessed on August 29, 2013.

SCHALTEGGER, S. (1997): Economics of Life Cycle Assessment: Inefficiency of the Present Approach, in: Business Strategy and the Environment, Vol. 6, No. 1, pp. 1-8.

SCHEIN, E.H. (1989): The Role of the CEO in the Management of Change: The Case of Information Technology, Working Paper, Massachusetts Institute of Technology (MIT).

SCHMIDT, M. (2009): Carbon Accounting and Carbon Footprint, in: International Journal of Climate Change Strategies and Management, Vol. 1, No. 1, pp. 19-30.

SEURING, S.; MÜLLER, M. (2008): From a Literature Review to a Conceptual Framework for Sustainable Supply Chain Management, in: Journal of Cleaner Production, Vol. 16, No. 15, pp. 1699-1710.

THE SUSTAINABILITY CONSORTIUM (2013), About the Consortium, http://www.sustainabilityconsortium.org/who-we-are/, accessed on August 22, 2013.

VACHON, S.; KLASSEN, R.D. (2006): Extending Green Practices Across the Supply Chain: The Impact of Upstream and Downstream Integration, in: International Journal of Operations & Production Management, Vol. 26, No. 7, pp. 795-821.

WALKER, H.; DI SISTO, L.; MCBAIN, D. (2008): Drivers and Barriers to Environmental Supply Chain Management Practices: Lessons from the Public and Private Sectors, in: Journal of Purchasing and Supply Management, Vol. 14, No. 1, pp. 69-85.

WIEDMANN, T.O.; LENZEN, M.; BARRETT, J.R. (2009): Companies on the Scale: Comparing and Benchmarking the Sustainability Performance of Business, in: Journal of Industrial Ecology, Vol. 13, No. 3, pp. 361-383.

WU, Z.; PAGELL, M. (2011): Balancing Priorities: Decision-Making in Sustainable Supply Chain Management, in: Journal of Operations Management, Vol. 29, No. 6, pp. 577-590.

ZHOU, H.; BENTON JR.,W.C. (2007): Supply Chain Practice and Information Sharing, in: Journal of Operations Management, Vol. 25, No. 6, pp. 1348-1365.

ZHU, Q.; SARKIS, J. (2004): Relationships Between Operational Practices and Performance Among Early Adopters of Green Supply Chain Management Practices in Chinese Manufacturing Enterprises, in: Journal of Operations Management, Vol. 22, No. 3, pp. 265-289.

Financial Reporting and Sustainability

Christopher Hossfeld and Alain Mikol

Overview

1. Introduction

At the end of the 1980s and the beginning of the 1990s one could observe the general awakening of a worldwide consciousness of the necessity to protect the environment. Soon after, a moral dimension is added to the economic activities of companies: it is the social responsibility that leads companies progressively to think about the social and environmental impacts of its investments and activities.

The first environmental reports have been published at the end of the 1980s in the US, primarily to respond to expectations from the government (Burh/Freedman 2001). At that time, these reports were destined to explain a company's policy regarding the environment and in particular how the company wanted to reduce the pollution related to its activities (Antheaume/Marcenac 1999).

Towards the end of the 1990s companies started to publish wider reports allowing them to describe their economic, social, and environmental performances (Antheaume 2003). The sustainable report or report on sustainable development was born, deriving its name from the principle of sustainable development. The latter dates back to the UN conference of 1974 in Cocoyoc (Mexico) but it was made popular in 1987 when the UN's Brundtland Commission published its report "Our Common Future".

The purpose of financial reporting – a legal requirement in most countries – is to produce financial information that is disclosed to stakeholders of companies such as investors or creditors. This information helps them to make decisions regarding their investment in a company. The focus of financial reporting is on the economic or financial situation and performance of an individual company and not on the social, societal or environmental impacts of the activities of this company. As a consequence, those impacts do in general not influence financial reporting numbers since their cost is not individually attributable to the company. However, there are few exceptions (see Chapter 2).

In case the financial reporting information does not include the environmental and other impacts, it is possible that the activity of a company, although financially beneficial, generates for the society as a whole a negative "return" because the unreported negative impacts exceed the financial profits (Tanski 2013, p. 41). With the growing public awareness regarding sustainability there is increased pressure on companies (and regulators) to close this information gap. Also, there is a behavioral component in reporting on sustainability: once companies start to report these impacts, a change in their behavior will take place easier.

When companies started to publish social and environmental information on a voluntary basis they used frameworks recommended by private, non-governmental institutions. While we use the term "sustainable reporting", these reports have also been referred to as corporate social reporting, corporate social responsibility reporting, triple bottom line reporting, environmental reporting, social audit etc. (Ditlev-Simonsen 2010; Rankin et al.

2012, p. 317). The most commonly pursued goals of sustainable reporting are to gain a competitive advantage by differentiating and to satisfy the social responsibility of the company stakeholders, both goals going very often hand in hand (e.g. von Ahsen 2001, pp. 121ff.; KPMG 2011, p. 19)

The diversity of terms and contents of these reports leads to the problem of comparability of sustainable information. Also, since it is mostly voluntary information there is not necessarily an external audit of a third, independent party. As we will show in Chapter 4 France is one of the few countries in the world that passed two laws in 2001 and 2010 making sustainable reports and their external verification mandatory.

The rest of the paper is organised as follows. The next chapter explains how sustainability issues are currently considered by financial reporting principles. Chapter 3 presents international initiatives of sustainable reporting. Chapter 4 shows as country examples how Germany and France treat this topic. Chapter 5 discusses the more recent development of integrated reporting and Chapter 6 concludes.

2. How Does Current Financial Reporting Consider Sustainability?

2.1 Overview

The scope of financial reporting is the individual company and the financial reporting process leads to financial statements to be published. Financial statements are composed of the balance sheet – presenting assets (rights), liabilities (obligations), and equity of the company -, the income statement which shows revenues and expenses, and the notes disclosing additional information. Depending on the regulation in a given country other elements may be added, such as a cash flow statement and/or a statement of changes in shareholders' equity.

Currently, there is no specific regulation how to incorporate sustainability-questions into financial statements. However, aspects of sustainability may be captured by Generally Accepted Accounting Principles (GAAP) and, therefore, included in the financial statements. The most common forms of this integration are provisions in the balance sheet and information in the notes. Less frequent but also possible is the appearance of sustainability related expenses as intangible assets: for example, a purchased license to pollute or qualifying[1] development expenses.

2.2 Provisions

If we take the definition of International Accounting Standard 37, Provisions, Contingent Liabilities and Contingent Assets, as an example[2], a provision has to be recognised when a company has a present obligation as a result of a past event requiring an outflow of resources to settle the obligation and the amount of the obligation can be estimated with reliability.

For example, an obligation to decontaminate a production site once the license for using it expires (nuclear power plant, chemical industry etc.) will be shown on the balance sheet as a provision and the corresponding expenses will reduce accounting profits.

The principal accounting problems that arise here are in which accounting period to recognise the provision and the related expenses (over several periods or in just one period, being the one where the contamination takes place or where the decontamination becomes necessary), and, of course, what amount to recognise as provision.

In the case of the abovementioned decontamination obligation, the present value of the estimated obligation is recognised in the period when the production, and hence the pollution, starts.

A possible list of sustainability related provisions that can be commonly found in financial statements – if the definition is met - includes:

- provisions for decontamination, decommissioning, and restoration
- provisions for fines and penalties relating to environmental damages
- provisions for termination benefits when laying off employees (compensating the harm for employees)
- provisions for the management of electrical and electronic equipment waste (see International Financial Reporting Interpretation Committee Interpretation 6)
- provisions for end-of-life vehicle recycling
- provisions for managing radioactive waste
- provisions for the purchase of emission rights in a cap-and-trade system.

It is noteworthy from a sustainability point of view that the accounting treatment of these issues in the form of provisions is not necessarily helpful to promote a sustainable economic development (Deegan 2013; Spence/Chabrak/Pucci 2013)[3]. First, a provision has to be accounted for only in (the limited) cases where the company has an obligation; otherwise, a provision cannot be recognised. Second, the accounting rules apply in cases where the company has to repair (environmental) damages or to pay fines for pollution or non-respect of regulation. Hence, these rules do not give an incentive to avoid damages in the first place. Third, International Accounting Standard 37 states that "where the effect of the time value of money is material, the amount of a provision shall be the present value of the expenditures expected". Most sustainability related provisions are long-term and, therefore, the time value effect is material which leads to a systematic discounting of the future cost. Economically, discounting is correct. But this results in low provision amounts today, making the (repair, clean-up etc.) obligation eventually look insignificant and drawing less attention by stakeholders which benefits the current generation and burdens future generations with the real cost.

2.3 The Notes

According to International Accounting Standard 1, Presentation of Financial Statements, "notes provide narrative descriptions or disaggregation of items presented in the balance sheet or the income statement and information about items that do not qualify for recognition in those statements". The same purpose can be found in national accounting regulations, for example explicitly in section L. 123-13 of the French Commercial Code or implicitly in the German Commercial Code.

As part of information about items not recognised in the balance sheet companies are allowed to provide sustainability related information in the notes. However, in order to avoid information-overload in the financial statements in general and the notes in particular, only material information should be presented. Immaterial information can be omitted. The same is true for the German accounting regulation whereas French accounting is even stricter. The latter allows only material information in the notes and, hence, prohibits immaterial information.

According to French accounting information is material if:

- its importance could influence valuations and decisions that financial statement users make ; this same definition can be found in International Accounting Standards and in the German accounting regulation,
- its non-disclosure is susceptible to modify the judgment of shareholders,
- it includes the necessary explanations for a better understanding,

- it is relevant and useful and does not clearly appear in the balance sheet or income statement.

Studies show that companies include rarely their sustainable reporting in the notes (Institut für ökologische Wirtschaftsforschung und future e.V. – verantwortung unternehmen 2012, pp. 13ff.; KPMG 2011, p. 25). It is more common to include them in a document completely separate from the financial statements (stand-alone sustainability report) or to provide them in the management report which, together with the financial statements, forms the annual report. However, most companies use multiple reporting formats (reports, web-site etc.) in parallel.

As we discussed in this section, sustainable information is not explicitly regulated by accounting standards. Hence, the question arises what guidelines companies use to define the content and structure of their sustainability reporting.

3. An Abundance of Rules and Recommendations - International Initiatives of Sustainable Reporting

3.1 Overview

The disclosure of sustainable information has been accompanied by a growing number of rules and recommendations that help companies to publish their reports, the names and contents of which having changed over the years. Most of this regulation is not mandatory. However, there are a few countries with some sort of mandatory sustainability reporting requirements, such as Australia, Canada, Denmark, and the USA (Rankin et al. 2012, p. 324). In Chapter 4 we will present in detail the requirements of France as an example.

The different normative, but not mandatory, texts based on which companies currently disclose information in their sustainable reports can be grouped in two categories[4].

3.2 Management Frameworks

- The UN Global Compact (www.unglobalcompact.org in English, German, French and other languages) initiative for companies that engage in aligning their operations and strategies with principles in the areas of human rights, labor, environment and anti-corruption. Companies which joined the initiative have to make an annual progress report.

- ISO standards (www.iso.org in English and French) 14000s on Environmental Management and ISO 26000 on Social Responsibility. The ISO 14000 family proposes practical tools for companies looking to identify and control their environmental impact and constantly improve their environmental performance. Some of them include reporting related guidance, in particular ISO 14063 on environmental communication. ISO 26000 contains guidance on how companies can operate in an ethical and transparent way that contributes to the health and welfare of society. It includes a communication requirement on social responsibility.

- The OECD (www.oecd.org in English and French) Guidelines for Multinational Companies (version of 2011) contain recommendations for a responsible business conduct in a global context. A list of very broad information (enterprise objectives, issues regarding workers etc.) that should be disclosed is provided.

3.3 Reporting Frameworks

- The most widely recognised reporting guidelines are the Sustainability Reporting Guidelines issued by the Global Reporting Initiative (GRI; www.globalreporting.org in English, German, French and other languages). GRI was established in 1997 and is a not-for-profit organisation in the form of a network of over 600 organisations from more than 60 countries. The objective of GRI is to work towards a sustainable economy by providing sustainability reporting guidance. The latest version of these guidelines (G4: Reporting Principles and Standard Disclosures), complemented by an Implementation Guidance, were issued in 2013.

  There are Principles for Defining Report Content describing the process to be applied when identifying the report content (Stakeholder Inclusiveness, Sustainability Context, Materiality, and Completeness) and Principles for Defining Report Quality (Balance, Comparability, Accuracy, Timeliness, Clarity, and Reliability).

  The disclosures are grouped in three categories: economic, environmental, and social, the social category being divided in the four subcategories labor practice and decent work, human rights, society, and product responsibility. There are Core Disclosure items and additional Comprehensive Disclosure items; a total of 150 items although not all of them are applicable in all circumstances.

- on a European level, guidelines have been published by DVFA Society of Investment Professionals in Germany in conjunction with EFFAS, the European Federation of Financial Analysts Societies. The latest version 3.0 of Key Performance Indicators for Environmental, Social & Governance Issues was issued in 2010 (www.effas-esg.com). The purpose of this document is to propose the basis for the integration of environmental, social, and governance data into corporate performance reporting. Therefore, it sets out guidelines for the preparation and presentation of sustainability reports, and minimum requirements regarding topics and information to be disclosed. 114 industrial subsectors are distinguished.

In April 2013, the EU Commission proposed an amendment to existing accounting regulation in order to improve the transparency on environmental and social matters. Once adopted, certain large companies will have to disclose information on policies, risks and results as regards environmental matters, social and employee-related aspects, respect for human rights, anti-corruption and bribery issues, and diversity on the boards of directors.

Many countries in the world[5] have national regulation regarding sustainability reporting, primarily on a voluntary basis. However, most countries do not define their own framework but relate to one of the above, in particular GRI. In the following section we will study two country examples from the EU: Germany as the biggest economy in the EU and France having the oldest (2001, last updated in 2012) and strictest regulation in the EU, including a verification requirement for sustainable reporting.

4. Sustainable Reporting in Germany and France

4.1 Sustainability Reporting in Germany

Germany has currently no legislation requiring sustainability reporting by companies and the Federal Government does not plan to introduce one (Federal Government of Germany 2012, p. 127). However, in 2011 (updated in 2012) the German Council for Sustainable Development (www.nachhaltigkeitsrat.de in English and German), a body appointed by the Federal Government with the mission to make proposals in order to advance Germany's sustainability strategy[6], adopted the German Sustainability Code as a recommendation.

The scope of the code is not limited to companies but includes also other organisations, such as NGOs, trade unions or universities. External verification of the sustainability report is not required by the code; nevertheless the conformity declaration is established by means of an attestation issued by a third independent party (concept of limited assurance).

The code requires information in four areas: Strategy, Process Management, Environment, and Society. Process Management is split in the subcategories: rules and processes, incentive schemes, stakeholder engagement, as well as innovation and product management. Concerning Society subcategories are: employee rights and diversity, human rights, corporate citizenship, political influence, and corruption.

Although the code contains its own information requirements that are rather general, it does not define specific indicators in the different areas or subcategories. Instead, it refers to specific key performance indicators included in the highest reporting standards of GRI or DVFA/EFFAS. Compliance with one of those standards means automatically compliance with the code.

As of August 2013 (only) 52 companies submitted a declaration of conformity with the German Sustainability Code. This does not mean that they are the only German companies to disclose information in this area. In 2007 there were 100 companies publishing a sustainable report in Germany (Bundesministerium für Umwelt, Naturschutz und Reaktorsicherheit 2007, p. 5). In the absence of current statistical data and given the trend to increased sustainability reporting it can be estimated that now far more than 100 companies publish regularly some form of sustainable information. However, in international comparison German companies are lagging their foreign peers (Bundesministerium für Umwelt, Naturschutz und Reaktorsicherheit 2007, p. 6; KPMG 2011, p. 4).

4.2 Sustainability Reporting in France

France was one of the few countries in the world to early introduce mandatory sustainable reporting including required external assurance. It was the law on New Economic Regulations of 2001, introducing section L. 225-102-1 to the Commercial Code, that required listed companies to explain in their management report how they considered the social and environmental consequences of their activities. In 2002, a decree was published listing the items to be disclosed (Delbard 2008)[7].

This regulation was fundamental insofar as the management report has to be published together with the financial statements and it has to be controlled. Indeed, the certified public accountant who audits the financial statements has also to verify that the information disclosed in the management report is faithful and coherent with the financial statements (section L. 823-10 Commercial Code). It is interesting to note that the main part of the New Economic Regulations law was not the social and environmental part but regulation on transparency for financial transactions and against money laundering.

The sustainability reporting requirement of the New Economic Regulations remained unchanged until 2010. As part of broader environmental regulation (known as the "Grenelle 2" laws[8]) three changes were made. First, the scope of the sustainability reporting requirement was extended from only listed companies to large unlisted companies. Starting in 2014, unlisted companies with total assets or sales of 100 million € and with more than 500 employees will fall under the requirement. Second, in the wake of "Grenelle 2" a decree updated in 2012 the list of disclosure items (see Figure 1). These items are to be provided in addition to the still applicable requirement to explain in general how companies considered the social and environmental consequences of their activities.

1° Social Information

a) Employment
  - the number of employees and the distribution of employees by gender, age and geographical zone
  - hires and dismissals
  - compensation and its evolution
b) Organisation of the work
  - organisation of working hours
  - only for listed companies: absenteeism
c) Social relations
  - organisation of the social dialog, in particular the information and consultation procedures with employees and negotiation with them
  - the results of collective bargaining agreements

d) Health and safety
- the health and safety conditions in the workplace
- the results of agreements signed with unions or employee representatives regarding the health and safety conditions in the workplace
- only for listed companies: workplace accidents, in particular their frequency and gravity, as well as occupational diseases

e) Training
- the training policies put in place
- the total number of training hours

f) Equality of treatment
- the measures taken in favor of equality of women and men
- the measures taken in favor of employment and integration of the disabled
- the policy to fight discriminations

g) Only for listed companies: promotion and respect of the stipulations of the labor standards of the International Labor Organisation regarding
- the freedom of association and the right to collective bargaining
- the elimination of employment and professional discriminations
- the elimination of forced labor
- the effective elimination of child labor

2° Environmental Information

a) General environmental policy
- the organisation of the company to consider environmental issues and, eventually, the measures in terms of the evaluation or assurance regarding the environment
- the actions taken in terms of training and information of the employees regarding the protection of the environment
- the means dedicated to the prevention of environmental hazards and pollution
- only for listed companies: the amount of provisions and guaranties regarding environmental risks, if this information does not cause a serious prejudice to the company in an ongoing litigation

b) Pollution and waste management
- the measures for the prevention, reduction or reparation of releases in the air, water or soil affecting heavily the environment
- the measures for the prevention, recycling and disposal of waste
- the consideration of acoustic nuisances and all other types of pollution specific to an activity

c) Sustainable use of resources
- the water consumption and procurement of water depending on the local constraints
- the consumption of raw materials and the measures taken to improve the efficiency of their use
- the consumption of energy, the measures taken to improve energy efficiency, and the use of renewable energies
- only for listed companies: the use of soil

d) Climate change
- the greenhouse gas emissions
- only for listed companies: the adaption to the consequences of climate change

e) Protection of the biodiversity
- the measures taken to preserve or to develop biodiversity

3° Information Regarding the Societal Commitment of the Entity in Favor of Sustainable Development

a) Territorial, economic, and social impact of the activity of the company
- in terms of regional employment and development
- on the neighboring and local population

b) Relations maintained with persons or organisations interested by the activity of the company, in particular associations of assistance to people in difficulty, educational institutions, associations for the protection of the environment, consumer associations, and the neighboring population
- the conditions of dialogue with these persons or organisations
- the actions in terms of partnerships or sponsorships

c) Outsourcing and suppliers
- the consideration in the supply policy of social and environmental issues
- only for listed companies: the importance of outsourcing and the consideration in the relationship with suppliers and subcontractors of their social and environmental responsibility

d) Only for listed companies: trustworthiness of practices
- actions taken to prevent corruption
- measures taken in favor of the health and safety of consumers
- other actions the company has engaged in favor of human rights

Figure 1: Disclosure Items Required by French Regulation

Third and most importantly, mandatory verification by a third independent party was introduced. This feature was highly controversial when the 2010 law was voted. In its first draft, the text stipulated that the certified public accountant should communicate to the supervisory board his observations regarding the social and environmental information in the management report. "Simple" communication was favored over formal certification in order to start off a debate about sustainable development within the board and, eventually, with shareholders. However, during the legislative procedure it was proposed and voted to replace the above communication requirement with a certification requirement by a third independent organisation. This change was justified by the fact that not all sustainable information is disclosed in the management report (only this report is checked by the auditor) and that certified public accountants are not the most competent to verify this type of information. In order to qualify as a "third independent organisation", the organisation needs accreditation from the French official accreditation committee (www.cofrac.fr) or a European equivalent. Independence requirements are fixed in a decree that contains the usual features (no stake or economic interest in the company etc.). Interestingly, the decree refers to the independence requirements for certified public accountants. In other words: a certified public accountant (with accreditation) can be a "third independent organisation"!

Since the new law was applicable for the first time for the financial year 2012 it is too early to see clear effects on French companies sustainable reporting.

5. Integrated Reporting

A new trend in sustainable reporting has emerged over the past couple of years: integrated reporting. The idea is to integrate more closely financial and sustainable reporting to allow investors and other stakeholders to understand the value creation of a company over time. It highlights the short, medium and long term consequences of decisions and establishes a systematic link between financial and non-financial information.

In 2010, the International Integrated Reporting Committee (IIRC; www.theiirc.org) was formed; among the founding members were the Global Reporting Initiative (GRI) but also the International Federation of Accountants and NGOs. The objective of the IIRC is to bring together all actors of sustainable development and financial reporting and to create an integrated reporting framework. In April 2013, the IIRC published a Consultation Draft of the International Integrated Reporting Framework whose purpose is in particular to establish Guiding Principles and Content Elements of an integrated report.

The draft proposes the following Guiding Principles:

- strategic focus and future orientation: Provide insight into the relationship between the company's strategy and short, medium and long term value creation
- connectivity of information: Show the combination, inter-relatedness and dependencies between the material value-creation components
- stakeholder responsiveness: Provide insight into the relationship with key stakeholders
- materiality and conciseness
- reliability and completeness
- consistency and comparability.

The content elements of the proposed framework are expressed as questions that should be answered in an integrated report. They cover the following areas:

- organisational overview and external environment
- governance
- opportunities and risks
- strategy and resource allocation
- business model
- performance
- future outlook.

The information disclosed within the Integrated Reporting Framework has to be verifiable. Also – and this is an important point – it is destined to providers of financial capital in order to support their financial capital allocation decisions. In this, the Integrated Reporting Framework follows in the footsteps of the International Financial Reporting Standards Conceptual Framework which states that "the objective of general purpose financial reporting is to provide financial information ... that is useful to ... investors ... in making decisions about providing resources to the entity". On the one hand this similarity can have a positive impact since it makes it potentially easier for companies to follow the Integrated Reporting Framework and, ultimately, to consider sustainable issues more broadly in their financial decision making. But on the other hand it can also hinder progress in sustainable decision making because sustainable reporting is too close to financial reporting. Therefore, the former may become subject to the same conceptual limitations as financial reporting, not allowing out-of-the-(accounting)box thinking and innovation in terms of sustainable development (Deegan/Unerman 2006; Gray 2013).

Although many companies disclose already their financial and non-financial (sustainable) information in one document, one cannot yet speak of integrated reporting but of "combined" reporting (KPMG 2011, p. 23). The idea of integrated reporting is to present financial and sustainable information together AND to show systematically how both "worlds" are intertwined rather than providing separate information sets.

6. *Conclusion*

Sustainability reporting exists now for some time and has steadily improved. In particular it tries to overcome the shortcomings of treating sustainability questions only in the (limited) context of financial reporting. Nevertheless, there is still a lot of room for improvement.

Sustainability reporting should become mandatory such as financial reporting. This would provide a consistent and comprehensive information base for stakeholders. The requirement would also force companies (and their stakeholders) to think (even) more about sustainability. France is here a good example as a country that pushed this requirement.

The content (and form) of sustainability reports should be more regulated than today where companies can cherry-pick what (not) to report. Some standardisation would improve comparability, consistency and transparency. By providing better information in this sense to stakeholders trust in sustainability reporting and the company would increase.

For the same reason, some kind of mandatory external verification would be beneficial. We can cite France once again as an example here. However, problems remain regarding the questions who should verify and to what extent (level of detail)?

Notes

[1] See as an example for qualifying criteria International Accounting Standard 38, Intangible Assets.

2   These standards are applied in approximately 120 countries in the world. In addition, national definitions in many countries, for example in France and Germany, are similar.

3   For additional limitations of financial reporting in terms of providing sustainability information see Deegan/Unerman 2006, pp. 353-357.

4   For a more detailed review of the following (and some additional) texts see FEE 2011.

5   For more detailed information on individual countries consult the French web-site http://reportingcsr.org of the Study Center for Corporate Social Responsibility (www.orse.org).

6   The sustainability strategy adopted by the Federal Government in 2002 covers 21 topics, mapped to 35 goals (e.g. energy and resource productivity, maintenance of biodiversity, land use, ecological farming, etc.).

7   Delbard discusses also the shortcomings of the New Economic Regulations.

8   "Grenelle" is the name of a street in Paris where negotiations took place.

References

ANTHEAUME, N. (2003): Le rapport environnement/développement durable, pourquoi publier et que publier?, in: Revue Française de Comptabilité, No. 356, pp. 27-31.

ANTHEAUME, N.; MARCENAC P. (1999): Les rapports environnement, in: Revue Française de Comptabilité, No. 313, pp. 11-22.

BURH, N.; FREEDMAN, M. (2001): Culture, Institutional Factors and Differences in Environmental Disclosure Between Canada and the United States, in: Critical Perspectives on Accounting, Vol. 12, No. 3, pp. 293-322.

BUNDESMINISTERIUM FÜR UMWELT, NATURSCHUTZ UND REAKTOR-SICHERHEIT (2007): Nachhaltigkeitsberichterstattung von Unternehmen: Status Quo Report Deutschland 2007, Berlin.

DEEGAN, C. (2013): The Accountant Will Have a Central Role in Saving the Planet ... Really? A Reflection on"Green Accounting and Green Eyeshades: Twenty Years Later", in: Critical Perspectives on Accounting, Vol. 24, No. 6, pp. 448-458.

DEEGAN, C.; UNERMAN, J. (2006): Financial Accounting Theory, Berkshire.

DELBARD, O. (2008): CSR Legislation in France and the European Regulatory Paradox: An Analysis of EU CSR Policy and Sustainability Reporting Practice, in: Corporate Governance, Vol. 8, No. 4, pp. 397-405.

DITLEV-SIMONSEN, C.D. (2010): Historical Account of Key Words in Non-Financial Report Titles, in: Issues in Social and Environmental Accounting, Vol. 4, No. 2, pp. 136-148.

FEDERAL GOVERNMENT OF GERMANY (2012): National Sustainable Development Strategy: 2012 Progress Report, Berlin.

FEE (FEDERATION OF EUROPEAN ACCOUNTANTS) (2011): Environmental, Social and Governance (ESG) in Annual Reports: An Introduction to Current Frameworks, Brussels.

GRAY, R. (2013): Back to Basics: What Do We Mean by Environmental (and Social) Accounting and What is it for? A Reaction to Thornton, in: Critical Perspectives on Accounting, Vol. 24, No. 6, pp. 459-468.

INSTITUT FÜR ÖKOLOGISCHE WIRTSCHAFTSFORSCHUNG UND FUTURE E.V. – VERANTWORTUNG UNTERNEHMEN (Ed.) (2012): Das IÖW/future-Ranking der Nachhaltigkeitsberichte 2011: Ergebnisse und Trends, Berlin et al.

KPMG (2011): KPMG International Survey of Corporate Responsibility Reporting 2011.

RANKIN, M.; STANTON, P.; MCGOWAN, S.; FERLAUTO, K.; TILLING, M. (2012): Contemporary Issues in Accounting, Milton.

SPENCE, C.; CHABRAK, N.; PUCCI, R. (2013): Doxic Sunglasses: A Response to "Green Accounting and Green Eyeshades: Twenty Years Later", in: Critical Perspectives on Accounting, Vol. 24, No. 6, pp. 459-468.

TANSKI, J.S. (2013): Rechnungslegung und Bilanztheorie, München.

VON AHLSEN, A. (2001): Empirische Analysen der Berichtspraxis in Umwelterklärungen, in: Zeitschrift für Betriebswirtschaft, Vol. 72, No. 2, pp. 121-141.

Sustainable Electronic Human Resources Management: Why Information Technology Matters in Sustainable Human Resources Management

Stefan Strohmeier

Overview

1. Introduction – Is Information Technology Irrelevant for Sustainable Human Resource Management?

Sustainability constitutes an idea with inherent potentials and problems so significant that it is difficult to imagine a concept with greater internal tensions. No less is expected from sustainability than the solving of the global economic, ecological, and social problems of mankind, which have become both striking and tenacious in these times. Initially constituting a political concept of the (supra-) national level, sustainability is habitually defined as "... *meet the needs of the present without compromising the ability of future generations to meet their own needs*" (World Commission on Environment and Development 1987). Given that private organisations

220

have strong economic, social, and ecological impacts, the sustainability concept has transferred to the organisational level whereby the resulting concept of corporate sustainability can analogously be defined as meeting the current needs of all organisational stakeholders without compromising the ability to meet the needs of its future stakeholders (e.g., Dyllick/Hockerts 2002). However, despite the ample and long discussions, the concept of corporate sustainability remains diverse, disputed, and developing. As a common agreement, however, it is recognised that sustainability broadly expands the organisational target system by adding *social* and *ecological objectives* on par with the prevalent *economic objectives* of private organisations to assure the organisational as well as the individual and societal long-term basis of existence (for an introduction into corporate sustainability e.g., Dyllick/Hockerts 2002; Elkington 1994; Gladwin/Kennelly/Krause 1995; Hart/Millstein 2003). Implying an extensive change in the underlying orientation, organisations aiming at sustainability need readjust not only their corporate strategies but also their respective corporate functions. Consequently, the reorientation of corporate functions, such as marketing (e.g., Martin/Schouten 2012), supply chain management (e.g., Seuring/Müller 2008), finance (e.g., Soppe 2004), information systems (e.g., Schmidt et al. 2009) or human resource management (e.g., Ehnert 2006), with respect to sustainability are discussed.

Referring to *human resource management* (HRM) as a corporate function, there are crucial links to corporate sustainability. Given that economic, ecological and social outcomes of any organisation are ultimately generated by its employees, HRM is the corporate function that is directly responsible for the organisational key resource for generating sustainability. Moreover, employees constitute a crucial organisational stakeholder group with a broad set of social objectives. Thus, HRM is the corporate function directly responsible for reaching social objectives of this major stakeholder group. Finally, the ongoing performance of HR reflects economic, ecological and social effects that are to be considered in any sustainable organisation. As a consequence, because HRM is seen as a corporate function with key impacts on sustainability, discussions on the topic of "*sustainable HRM*" started approximately a decade ago (Ehnert/Harry/Zink 2014). The extant literature thereby puts high expectations on the field, and quite frequently sustainable HRM is expected to form a new research paradigm that may replace the prolonged research on strategic HRM with a more realistic, more holistic, and thus more prolific approach (e.g., Boudreau 2003; Clarke 2011; Ehnert/Harry/Zink 2014, Jabbour/

Santos 2008; Kramar 2013; Wells 2011). Despite the fact that literature on the topic is quite nascent and heterogeneous, the question of how HRM can contribute to sustainability on different levels constitutes the guiding topic of the field (Ehnert/Harry/Zink 2014).

To discuss this question in the interim, a broad variety of diverse HR aspects is tackled – though *HR information technology (HRIT)* is one systematic exception. While notorious in management research (e.g., Orlikowski/Scott 2008), this systematic exclusion of the technological dimension is perplexing because IT adoption in HRM is significantly advanced, *and* the crucial relevance of IT for sustainability is obvious. Consider recruiting as an example. Research affirms a far advanced adoption of diverse recruiting technologies (e.g., Lang et al. 2011) with multifarious economical (e.g., implementation costs, time savings, and increased application volumes), ecological (e.g., increased energy consumption, paper savings, and reduction of physical transports), and social (e.g., misuse of applicant data, perceived loss of individuality, and digital divide of applicants) implications, which are directly relevant to sustainability (e.g., Lang et al. 2011). However, these effects on *electronic* recruiting have yet to be considered. Abstracting from the recruiting example, this systematic neglecting of HRIT could mean a systematic neglecting of additional effects, which – whether detriments or opportunities – are directly relevant for sustainable HRM. Therefore, the current paper addresses the question, *whether and how HRIT matters in sustainable HRM.* To this end, in a first step, the foundations are laid by briefly discussing the idea of corporate sustainability (Chapter 2). A second step aims to elaborate on a base concept of sustainable HRM (Chapter 3). In a subsequent third step, this base concept is complemented by elaborating on an extended concept of sustainable *electronic* HRM (Chapter 4). The chapter ends with some concluding remarks (Chapter 5).

2. Foundations – Corporate Sustainability

Corporate sustainability constitutes the basic concept to which sustainable (electronic) HRM refers. Understanding corporate sustainability as meeting the current needs of all organisational stakeholders without compromising its ability to meet the needs of its future stakeholders (e.g., Dyllick/ Hockerts 2002), corporate sustainability gives new answers to the questions of the *fundamental purpose* and the *legitimate stakeholders* of private organisations. Adding *ecological objectives* and *social objectives* to the prevalent *economic objectives* of private organisations (e.g., Dyllick/Hockerts 2002; Elkington 1994; Gladwin/Kennelly/Krause 1995; Hart/Millstein 2003) results in the pluralisation of purposes and stakeholders, which constitutes the core of the concept. Accordingly, the proposed tri-section of objectives is habitually called the *"triple bottom line"* (e.g., Elkington 1994) and implies a three dimensional model of corporate sustainability (see Figure 1).

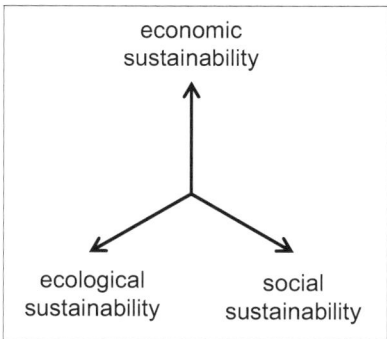

Figure 1: Dimensions of Sustainability
       (Source: adopted from Dyllick/Hockerts 2002)

Economic sustainability refers to the enduring reproduction of financial resources, i.e., the capital invested must persistently yield sufficient re-turns on investment. Ecological sustainability refers to the enduring repro-duction of natural resources, i.e., the consumption and pollution of natural resources must persistently obey the rate of natural reproduction. Social sustainability refers to the enduring reproduction of social resources, i.e., human wealth, health, education, etc. must be persistently enabled. Fol-lowing this tripartite model of sustainability, organisations are sustainable, and thus successful, if they realise these three dimensions (e.g., Dyllick/Hockerts 2002).

While there is basic agreement on this tripartite model, there are differ-ent understandings related to the *reasons*, the *weights* and the *compatibil-ity* of the three objectives.

The *reasons* for the three objectives can be of ethical, rational, econo-mic or legal character or any combination of thereof. *Ethical reasoning* justifies the additional consideration of ecological and social objectives on a normative basis. Pluralisation of objectives and stakeholders is, therefore, a direct consequence of the ethical standard of responsible practise. *Rational reasoning* emphasises that the multifarious ecological and social externalities of economic activity, such as ongoing groundwater intoxication or growing precariousness of larger social groups, in the mid- to long-term constitute severe threats to the success and even existence of the organisation. To access necessary ecological and social resources, such as clean groundwater or a healthy and educated workforce, in the present or in the future, it is rational to add ecological and social objectives to the corporate agenda. *Economic reasoning* focuses on the financial advantages of ecologically and socially responsible behaviour of organisations, such as cost savings due to energy-saving production methods or a loyal customer base due to fair trade procurement policies. Thus, to take advantage of these economic benefits, organisations should also behave in socially and ecologically responsible ways. *Legal reasoning* accepts additional ecological and social objectives due to their definitions according to social (e.g., dismissal protection, working-hour limitations, and minimum wages) and environmental (e.g., pollution control, environmental compatibility control, and energy saving regulations) legislation. Ecologically and socially responsible behaviour then is simply a matter of compliance.

The *weighting* of the three objectives can either be equal or unequal (e.g., Hahn et al. 2010; Norman/McDonald 2004). *Equal weight* means equality of objectives. Accordingly, organisations must adhere equally to economic, ecological, and social objectives. *Unequal weight* ranks the objectives related to their importance or places the objectives into categories such as "very important" and "important". In this case, organisations should adhere to objectives with different emphases based on different weights and, therefore, should prefer, for example, economic objectives over social and ecological objectives.

Finally, the *compatibility* of the three objectives varies based on the positions of convergence *vs.* divergence of the objectives (e.g., Hahn et al. 2010; Norman/McDonald 2004). *Convergence* means that economic, ecological and social objectives are mutually reinforcing. Accordingly, convergent objectives can be met rather easily and therefore constitute a comfortable position for organisations. On the contrary, *divergence* of objectives implies clear conflict between the economic, ecological and social objectives, which requires explicit balancing of trade-offs and compromises and results in a rather uncomfortable position for an organisation aiming at sustainability.

Differing opinions on the actual reasons, weights and compatibilities of the three sustainability dimensions lead to different intensities of corporate sustainability, which can be roughly classified into *weak* and *strong corporate sustainability* (see Neumayer 2003, discusses weak and strong sustainability at the [supra-]national level; see Figure 2).

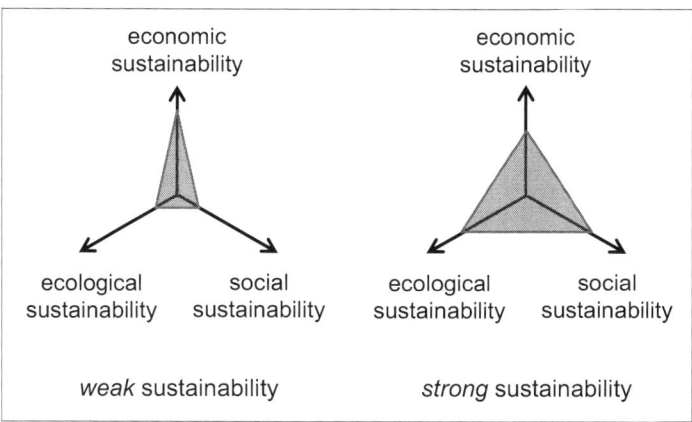

Figure 2: Types of Corporate Sustainability

Weak corporate sustainability is motivated by economic, legal, and, occasionally, by rational reasons. Thus, sustainability is mainly adopted to yield financial benefits, to avoid compliance risks, and to avoid immediate social and ecological threats to the organisation. Correspondingly, as the weighting of sustainability dimensions is unequal, economical sustainability is judged as being more important. While problems with compatibility among the three dimensions may arise, they do not receive a high level of importance given that based on the superiority of economic objectives, emerging conflicts among objectives are solved in favour of economic goals. As a result, social and ecological objectives are considered in the rare cases of converging objectives, while sustainability is taken for a business case (e.g., Elkington 1994). Beyond such business cases, i.e., in the case of divergence, ecological and social objectives are only considered if required by law or to avoid immediate ecological or social threats to the business. It is obvious that weak corporate sustainability is rather undemanding to practise (and evidently *is* broadly practised by many organisations [Norman/McDonald 2004]); however, it is also obvious that it largely misses the potentials of sustainability.

While *strong corporate sustainability* may be motivated by legal and economic reasons, it requires additional anchoring in broad rational argumentation and deep ethical conviction. Accordingly, sustainability is not only a matter of compliance and benefits, but of organisational conviction and culture. Moreover, strong corporate sustainability must consider the objectives equally and, simultaneously, accept persistent divergence. While divergence does not mean that cases of convergence do not exist, it does mean that these cases constitute the exception rather than the rule (Hahn et al. 2010). Strong corporate sustainability, therefore, relentlessly uncovers the demanding complexities and inconsistencies of the sustainable management task and strongly positions the *management of trade-offs* (Hahn et al. 2010) at its core. However, despite the numerous contributions aimed at supporting and realising corporate sustainability in practise, e.g., in the areas of sustainability reporting (e.g., Gray/Milne 2002) and sustainability information systems (e.g., Searcy 2012), workable operationalisations of managing multiple trade-offs as practise still constitute a challenge to research. In this way, actually practising strong corporate sustainability is highly demanding (thus rare), yet mandatory to make full use of the concept's potentials.

Treating weak and strong corporate sustainability as end points of a sustainability continuum, viable practical positions may lie somewhere between the two end points, while strong corporate sustainability should serve, at the least, as a guiding principle.

3. Base Concept – Sustainable Human Resource Management

As the current discussion on sustainable HRM is rather nascent and heterogeneous (e.g., Ehnert/Harry/Zink 2014), it is difficult to grasp and summarise the current state of knowledge. Given this situation, the following section elaborates on a few core tenets of the concept as it emerges.

Sustainable HRM directly refers to the idea of corporate sustainability as previously discussed herein (e.g., Cohen/Taylor/Müller-Camen 2010; de Souza Freitas/Jabbour/Santos 2011; Ehnert 2006). As a corporate function, HRM has crucial links to corporate sustainability. Considering that economic, ecological and social outcomes of any organisation are ultimately generated by its employees, HRM is the corporate function that is directly responsible for the organisation's key resource for generating sustainability. Moreover, as employees constitute a crucial organisational stakeholder group with a broad set of social objectives, HRM is the corporate function directly responsible for achieving the social objectives of this major stakeholder group. Finally, the ongoing performance of the HR function has economic, ecological and social effects, which are to be considered in any sustainable organisation. Given these links, it is common in current literature to assign HRM a *supportive function* for sustainability. Consequently, the major questions underlying current contributions are *what* and *how* can HRM contribute to sustainability (e.g., Boudreau 2003; Colbert/Kurucz 2007; Cohen/Taylor/Müller-Camen 2010; de Souza Freitas/Jabbour/Santos 2011; Ehnert 2006; Ehnert/Harry/Zink 2014; Jabbour/Santos 2008; Kramar 2013; Mariappandar 2014; Pfeffer 2010). Given that HRM, by its basic nature, has always been a supportive corporate function, the innovation of sustainability focuses on *what* HRM should support. According to this general agreement, HRM is regarded as sustainable if it contributes to sustainability at various organisational levels (Ehnert/Harry/Zink 2014). Thus, attempts to explicitly define *sustainable HRM* are clearly based on its supporting function for corporate sustainability (e.g., de Souza Freitas/Jabbour/Santos 2011; Ehnert 2006; Ehnert/Harry/Zink 2014; Kramar 2013). The following definition represents a typical example of such a definition (de Souza Freitas/Jabbour/Santos 2011, p. 226):

"Sustainable human resource management is regarding to achieving organisational sustainability through the development of human resources policies, strategies and practices that support the economic, social and environmental dimensions, at the same time."

While it is undisputed that sustainable HRM is characterised and even defined by its supportive character, the supportive character itself is much less clear, and current contributions offer a rather heterogeneous and incomplete picture. Accordingly, the following is a simple framework of sustainable HRM that clarifies its major supportive effects and allows for a systematic discussion of sustainable HRM (see Figure 3).

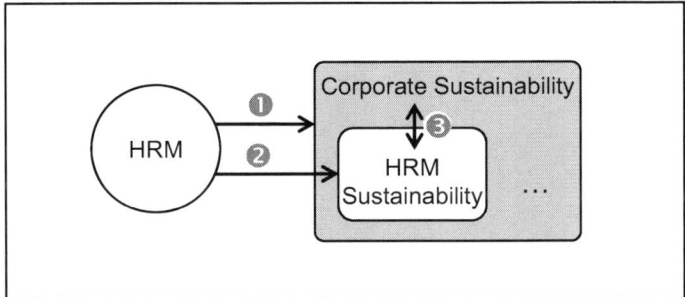

Figure 3: Framework of Sustainable HRM

A first obvious and thus frequently considered and mainly undisputed effect refers to the direct contributions of HRM to corporate sustainability (effect 1). The fact that corporate sustainability ultimately must be produced by the employees throughout the various corporate functions leads to the claim that HRM must create a workforce that is sensitive to and qualified for corporate sustainability and that, as a result, consistently acts in ways that contribute to sustainability (e.g., Ehnert 2014). In this respect, the entire set of established HR functions must be developed and incorporated in such a way that they support a sustainability-enabling workforce. Thus, the recruiting function should attract applicants with the personal characteristics and qualifications necessary for sustainable behaviour, the development function should develop qualifications necessary for sustainable behaviour, the performance management function should set and appraise sustainability objectives, and the compensation function should offer incentives for sustainable work behaviour and reward contributions to sustainability (e.g., Renwick/Redman/Maguire 2013; Jabbour/Santos 2008; Jackson et al. 2011). Given that strategic HRM claims that for more than three decades, that functions and output of HRM must meet corporate strategic requirements (e.g., Lengnick-Hall et al. 2009), this aspect of sustainable HRM very much resembles strategic HRM. However, the qualifications and behaviours required of those employees dealing with the multiple trade-offs of sustainable organisations may show a considerably higher level of inconsistency and complexity, thus placing considerably higher demands on HR functions. The still pending concretisations of these contributions should therefore be the subject of current and future debates on sustainable HRM.

A second supportive effect suggests that HRM itself should be sustainable (Ehnert/Harry/Zink 2014, p. 21), thus implying that the entire set of HR functions should be designed to perform in a sustainable manner (effect 2). As an example, designing the HR development function to perform in a sustainable manner implies simultaneously considering economic objectives (e.g., controlling costs of training measures), ecological objectives (e.g., reducing the physical employee transports to external training centres), and social objectives (e.g., distributing development opportunities fairly among all employees). The same holds for all additional HR functions. Evidently, however, doing so introduces the discussed divergence problem to HRM. As a major consequence, sustainable HRM implies a clear shift towards managing trade-offs, while, again, still pending concretisations (e.g., types of trade-offs, rules of coping with trade-offs in HR, etc.) must be completed by current and future research in sustainable HRM (e.g., Ehnert/Harry/Zink 2014).

Given that, by its very nature, sustainability constitutes a multi-level phenomenon (e.g., Dyllick/Hockerts 2002; Ehnert 2006), it is necessary to consider possible level interaction effects (e.g., Klein/Danserau/Hall 1994); however, thus far, this has not been addressed. Accordingly, the framework adds an interaction effect between HRM sustainability (meso-level sustainability) and corporate sustainability (macro-level sustainability) as the major levels that sustainable HRM should support (effect 3). While at first glance, it appears obvious to assume simple additive relationships between the levels, i.e., meso-level sustainability adds to macro-level sustainability, actual relationships are reciprocal and more complex. The simple example of excessive working hours may illustrate that HRM sustainability not just contributes to corporate sustainability. At the meso-level of HRM, excessive working hours of employees results in multifarious negative social externalities, thereby clearly detracting from (HRM) sustainability. On the other hand, at the macro-level, excessive working hours of employees contribute to excessive output and thus to (corporate) sustainability. Consequently, while contributions of sustainable HRM to different levels of sustainability require careful consideration in practise, the obviously rather complex level interaction effects constitute a third pending task for future research on sustainable HRM. Considering level interaction effects in greater detail may also necessitate a refined framework that decomposes the contribution of HRM to corporate sustainability (effect 1) into multiple effects of HRM on the sustainabilities of further corporate functions at the meso-level (i.e., on marketing sustainability, procurement sustainability, etc.) and conceptualises corporate sustainability as an emergent macro-level result of diverse meso-level sustainabilities.

Facing both, the evident heterogeneity and the evident nascency, the above framework offers a first, albeit rough, understanding of the concept of sustainable HRM. Compared to the currently dominant concept of strategic HRM, sustainable HRM exhibits a supportive character as well. Yet, it extends beyond the prevalent economic objectives and adds ecological and social objectives to the agenda. In other words, sustainable HRM unites existing objective-focussed research streams of economically oriented *strategic* HRM (e.g., Lengnick-Hall et al. 2009), ecologically oriented *green* HRM (e.g., Jackson/Seo 2010), and socially oriented *socially responsible* HRM (e.g., Sharma/Sharma/Devi 2011). From this perspective, sustainable HRM constitutes an extension, rather than a replacement, of strategic HRM (Ehnert/Harry/Zink 2014). The basic pluralisation of objectives constitutes the key potential of the concept as it offers a more holistic, more realistic, and, thus, a more prolific view of HRM. More specifically, with respect to the apparent divergences of economic and social objectives of HRM, a blanked-out conflict with notorious prominence in earlier concepts of managing people is *re*-addressed (e.g., Guest 1987). In this perspective, sustainable HRM may also constitute an overdue adjustment of academic concepts towards the daily practise of HRM that is aimed at balancing the interests of multiple stakeholders and managing trade-offs for decades (Norman/McDonald 2004). However, the pluralisation of objectives also constitutes the key problem of the sustainability concept as it adds considerable complexity and conflict to managing human resources. While the sustainability concept introduces and institutionalises basic societal contradictions in HRM, thus far, they offer few operationalisations or procedures for coping with these contradictions. Thus, both considerable future research efforts and practical experiences are necessary for progress in the field of HRM. Mirroring the situation at the corporate level, weak and strong varieties of sustainability in HRM are conceivable. Weak versions, in fact, may already constitute the reality of numerous HR departments that aim balancing economic and social impacts of their work, while also considering ecological aspects. However, as strong versions are able to realise the full potential of the concept, they should serve at least as the guiding principle for sustainable HRM.

4. Extended Concept – Sustainable Electronic Human Resource Management

4.1 Introduction and Framework

As IT has been used for more than half a century to support HRM (e.g., Bondarouk/Furtmüller 2012; Strohmeier 2007), a rough summary distinguishes three phases of developments. A first and early phase was characterised by mainframe applications of HRIT, which were often operated and applied outside the HR department. Major objectives of support existed in the automation of administrative HR tasks, such as payroll processing and time/attendance recording, thus improving quality, time and costs associated with the processing these tasks. A second phase was initiated by ongoing technological progress, which has led to micro-computer-based applications of HRIT due to the usability increasingly applied within HR departments. In addition to the automation of administrative HR tasks, the support of managerial HRM tasks, such as HR planning, recruiting, development, performance management, and compensation, was also initiated. However, beyond the mere automation advantages, the support of HR decisions and the proactive management of HR already started in this phase. A third phase involves the worldwide web and its ongoing application, thus resulting in the advent of web-based IT-application in HRM. Web-based HRIT applications focus on the networking of distributed actors responsible for HRM, and additionally the support of managerial HRM tasks was continuously expanded. The declared objective of this phase is to support strategic HRM indirectly by liberating HR professionals from administrative burdens and directly by supporting the strategic orientation of HRM functions.

This third phase constitutes the current phase, which is still on-going. Though there were and are varying designations, in the interim, there is growing agreement to label this phase as *electronic HRM*, or more briefly, as *e-HRM* (e.g., Ruël/Bindarouk/Looise 2004; Strohmeier 2007). E-HRM can be understood as the (planning, provision, implementation, operation and) application of information technology for both networking and supporting actors in their shared performing of HRM functions (Strohmeier 2007). In the interim, there is ample evidence of a broad and deep adoption of e-HRM (e.g., Galanaki/Panayotopoulou 2008; Florkowski/Olivas-Luján 2006; Strohmeier/Kabst 2009), which refers to *all* functional areas of HRM. At the outset, IT now, as before, is extensively used to automate and support a broad set of administrative HR tasks (e.g., Isenhour 2009). Moreover, HRIT also covers the entire set of managerial functions, such as recruitment (e.g., Stone/Lukaszewski/Isenhour 2005), development (e.g., MacPherson et al. 2004), compensation (e.g., Dulebohn/Marler 2005), and performance management (e.g., Cardys/Miller 2005). The extant research indicates that IT application in HR functions does not just imply an "electronic blueprint" of the conventional function but that the electronisation of HR functions leads to new phenomena that comprise opportunities as well as threats (overviews on the state of knowledge are, e.g., given by Bondarouk/Furtmüller 2012; Strohmeier 2007; Strohmeier 2012). As a result, it has become commonplace to add *"electronic"* to the respective function, i.e., *e*-recruiting, *e*-compensation, *e*-learning, etc., to indicate that the respective function is IT-supported.

Despite its widespread application and the broad research (e.g., Strohmeier 2014), sustainability aspects of HRIT have yet to be discussed. Nonetheless, there is evidence that HRIT is clearly relevant for sustainable HRM. Initially, the *economic dimension* of sustainability was broadly investigated by research on e-HRM. Given the authority of the strategic HRM paradigm, the discussion diversely addressed the potential of actual relations of e-HRM and strategic HRM (e.g., Bondarouk/Ruël 2013; Marler 2009; Martin/Reddington 2010; Grant/Newell 2013; Schalk/Timmerman/den Heuvel 2013; and the review of Marler/Fisher 2013). Moreover, e-HRM research concurrently provides evidence of the impacts on the *social dimension* when tackling topics such as employee data privacy (e.g., Hubbard/Forcht/Thomas 1998) and digital divide (e.g., Hogler/Henle/Bemus 1998) in e-HRM. On the contrary, the ecological dimension remains mostly unaddressed in current e-HRM literature, though it is obvious that ecological aspects, such as energy consumption of HRIT hardware and substitution of physical transport, are relevant to e-HRM.

Given the obvious relevance of HRIT for sustainability the framework of sustainable HRM previously presented herein is extended by including the effects of HRIT. Effects of HRIT are thereby categorised using an existing and well-established framework of sustainability effects of general IT (Hilty 2008). This framework is based on the two criteria of *immediacy* and *direction of sustainability effects*. Based on the first criterion of immediacy of effects, primary (1st order), secondary (2nd order), and tertiary (3rd order) effects of IT can be distinguished. Primary effects refer to consequences of the physical existence of IT, i.e. the production, application and disposal of IT. Secondary effects refer to the consequences of the application of IT in HRM and the thereby induced changes. Tertiary effects refer to the consequences of general societal changes due to the enduring availability of IT (Hilty 2008). Based on the second criterion of the direction of effects, contributing ("IT as part of the solution") and detracting ("IT as part of the problem") effects can be distinguished (Hilty 2008). Following this categorisation, primary, secondary, and tertiary effects of HRIT are additionally considered in an extended framework of sustainable *electronic* HRM (see Figure 4).

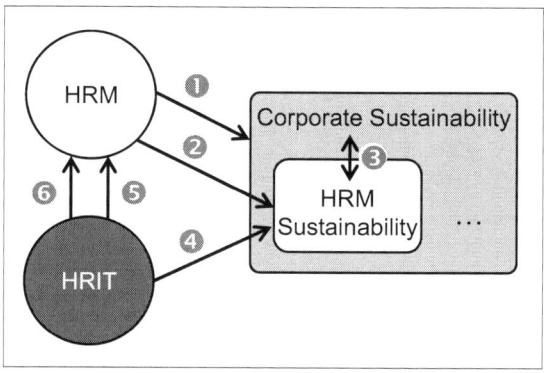

Figure 4: Extended Framework of Sustainable Electronic HRM

In consequence, the framework – now as before – includes the contributions of HRM to macro-level sustainability (effect 1) and meso-level sustainability (effect 2) as well as their interaction effect (effect 3). Additionally, primary (effect 4), secondary (effect 5), and tertiary (effect 6) effects of HRIT are considered. These three additional effects and their consequences for sustainable HRM are therefore discussed herein.

4.2 Primary Sustainability Effects

Primary sustainability effects of HRIT (effect 4) refer to consequences of the physical existence of IT, i.e., the fact that IT is produced, applied and disposed of. To clarify and illustrate such primary effects, the example of HR cloud computing is employed. HR cloud computing stands for the provision of infrastructures (e.g., hardware, networks, memory) and software (diverse HRIS applications) by vendors as a (usually) web-based service, while the vendor assures certain levels of service quality to HRM (e.g.,

Yeh 2012). The fact that, from a user perspective, such services are distant and opaque, i.e., as in "in a cloud", explains the metaphoric denomination of this service model. Because of its specific advantages, cloud computing is increasingly discussed in HRM, increasingly offered by nearly all major vendors of HR software, and likely also increasingly used (e.g., Yeh 2012). Accordingly, HR cloud computing implies diverse primary effects on sustainability (see Table 1).

	economic sustainability	ecological sustainability	social sustainability
contribution	• cost advantages • load scalability • data security • …	• energy efficiency • waste reduction • …	• (data security) • (…)
detraction	• compliance risks • loss of governance • vendor lock-in	• energy for data transfer • infrastructure • …	• (IT job losses) • (…)

Table 1: Primary Sustainability Effects (example HR Cloud Computing)

Initially, there are *primary economic effects* of cloud computing. For instance, based on economies of scale, the centralised provision of infrastructure and software saves costs compared to any in-house provision of infrastructure and services (e.g., Yeh 2012). HR cloud computing thus contributes to economic sustainability. On the other hand, depending on the respective data protection legislation, HR cloud computing may involve compliance risks with costly rescissions, surcharges, etc. (e.g., Yeh 2012), which would clearly detract from economic sustainability. Moreover, there are *primary ecological effects*. For example, the centralisation of computing on fewer centralised servers contributes to energy efficiency compared to computing on numerous decentralised servers. However, using centralised servers mandatorily boosts the volume of data that must be transported and thus requires additional energy, thereby detracting from ecological sustainability (e.g., Gottschalk/Kirn 2013). Whether there are also *primary social effects* of cloud computing may be a subject of discussion given that social effects typically constitute secondary or tertiary effects. A detracting effect may, for example, be evidenced by the dismissals of in-house IT-workforce, a contributing effect of increased data security, which is managed professionally in large organisations. These may, however, be perceived as secondary effects that emerge only when actually applying cloud computing in HR.

While these insights are far from a comprehensive discussion of the sustainability effects of HR cloud computing, not to mention HRIT in general, they are sufficient to substantiate that there actually are *primary sustainability effects* of HRIT. Although rather restricted in intensity, these are additional effects *sui generis* that emerge merely due to the existence of IT.

However, accepting that HRM is not the only corporate function that uses IT, it may be questioned and debated whether the primary effects actually affect HRM sustainability (effect 4) or whether primary effects should instead be conceptualised as affecting IS sustainability (e.g., Schmidt et al. 2009), a further meso-level sustainability not considered in the framework. This once again raises the question regarding framework refinement to include the incorporation of further corporate functions and further meso-level sustainabilities related to sustainable HRM (Kramar 2013).

4.3 Secondary Sustainability Effects

Secondary sustainability effects of HRIT (effect 5) refer to the consequences associated with the application of IT in HRM and the thereby induced effects on sustainability. By definition, secondary effects are *indirect*, i.e., they contribute to meso-level *or* macro-level sustainability indirectly by changing HRM. Such indirect effects can be evidenced in the example of e-recruiting. E-recruiting refers to the technology-based processes of attracting, identifying, and convincing suitable applicants (e.g., Lang et al. 2011; Laumer/Eckhardt/Weitzel 2009). Recent research clear shows that e-recruiting has changed the entire recruiting process (e.g., Holm 2012). While not explicitly researched to date, e-recruiting implies varied secondary effects on sustainability, as indicated in Table 2.

	economic sustainability	ecological sustainability	social sustainability
contribution	• time savings • cost savings • range increase • …	• paper savings • substitution of physical transport • …	• diversity enabling • labour market transparency • □ …
detraction	• proliferation of applications • loss of information sovereignty • …	• energy needs of e-communication • e-communication infrastructure • …	• digital divide • privacy violations • … •

Table 2: Secondary Sustainability Effects (example e-Recruiting)

Initially, there are *secondary economic effects*. As research indicates, for example, there are considerable *time savings* when using IT for recruiting (Laumer/Eckhardt/Weitzel 2009), which constitutes an indirect contribution of HRIT to meso-level sustainability. However, as the mere number of applications considerably increases (Lang et al. 2011), there are detracting effects at the meso-level of economic sustainability as well. Interestingly, this proliferation of applications seems to indicate a typical *rebound effect* (e.g., Hilty 2008) on the applicant side such that electronic applications increase time-efficiency, while at the same time, this increased efficiency results in a substantial increase in the number of applications. Moreover, there are also macro-level effects. HRIT, for instance, increases the spatial range of job advertisements (e.g., Lang et al. 2011), and thus it increases the probability of reaching suitable applicants needed for sustainable organisations. E-recruiting also results in *secondary ecological effects*. An obvious example is the extensive savings of paper that literally millions of conventional applications and their copies required for diverse internal addressees would have produced, and which are now presented as electronic files (e.g., Holm 2012). An effect detracting from the ecological sustainability may be found in the proliferation of electronic communication on different channels and the associated energy consumption. While communication in conventional recruiting was restricted to a few contacts using one channel, e-recruiting tends to multiply electronic contacts as channels (e.g., Holm 2012) and thus increases energy consumption throughout the entire set of network infrastructure. The possibility of real-time application tracking, which allows applicants to access the state of their applications on different devices and at any time, is but one example of increased communication volume. Again, hinting at a rebound effect, increased communication efficiency obviously has led to a substantial increase in communication regarding recruitment. Finally, e-recruiting clearly implies *secondary social effects*. A contribution to social sustainability, for example, is the support of equal employment opportunities by systematic diversity monitoring and corresponding specific target group oriented recruiting campaigns (e.g., Pearce/Tuten 2001). Conversely, as a negative effect, the digital divide refers to the phenomenon of excluding and thus discriminating against certain applicant segments, such as the elderly or the less educated persons, by means of electronic recruiting (Lang et al. 2011).

While this, again, is far from a comprehensive discussion of secondary sustainability effects of IT in recruiting, let alone in HR, it exemplifies secondary effects of HRIT on the meso- and macro-level of sustainability. Again, these are effects *sui generis* that would not have occurred without HRIT. Given that e-functions are not just blueprints of conventional functions, but often imply diverse and deep changes of the function (e.g., Strohmeier 2007; 2009), secondary effects tend to constitute the most important category of sustainability effects.

4.4 Tertiary Sustainability Effects

Tertiary sustainability effects of HRIT (effect 6) refer to long-term and fundamental societal changes due to the ongoing availability of IT. Such fundamental changes may affect HRM and, thus, affect indirectly meso- and macro-level sustainability. An example of such a tertiary effect may be given by the phenomenon of "*e-lancing*" (also known as crowd-sourcing), a phenomenon that may drastically change HRM in the future (Aguinis/Lawal 2013) and thereby provoke indirect meso- und macro-level effects on sustainability. E-lancing is based on web-based marketplaces where organisations offer certain tasks to be performed by interested persons for payment. Based on a bid process, tasks are assigned to interested persons. After an electronic transfer, the respective task is performed and electronically retransmitted to the organisation, which then pays the agreed upon price (Aguinis/Lawal 2013). It is evident that e-lancing is particularly well-suited for mental tasks, while it is less well-suited for manual tasks. E-lancing is quickly spreading on a global scale and may well constitute an important future labour market segment (Aguinis/Lawal 2013). Accordingly, e-lancing shows consequences for sustainability, as suggested in Table 3.

	economic sustainability	**ecological sustainability**	**social sustainability**
contribution	• overcoming labour market shortages • flexibility • cost savings • …	• substitution of physical trans-port • …	• independence in terms of time/space • interesting variety of tasks • …
detraction	• loss of depend-ability • loss of inim-itability • …	• energy needs of global data transfers • …	• social isolation • impoverishment • self exploitation • …

Table 3: Tertiary Sustainability Effects (example e-Lancing)

An exemplary and particularly positive *tertiary economic effect* of e-lancing may be that organisations in developed countries will be able to overcome threatening labour market shortages by contracting a skilled workforce in developing countries (Aguinis/Lawal 2013). On the other hand, an imaginable negative economic effect may be the loss of depend-ability due to the unclear availability of "e-lancers". Increasingly relying on external persons neither contractually nor mentally committed to the organisation may lead to interim workforce shortages accompanied by a delay in production. Additionally, widespread e-lancing will *induce ter-tiary ecological effects*. An obvious contribution effect will be the substi-tution of daily physical transport of employees, and thus the avoidance of energy consumption and pollution caused by public and private transport. However, widespread e-lancing will simultaneously boost global data traf-fic, and thus energy consumption and pollution due to necessary net in-frastructures. Finally, there are also *tertiary social effects* of e-lancing to be expected. On the contributing side, e-lancing may result in the growing independence of e-lancers in terms of time and space, and thus, it may contribute to the reconciling of work and family life. On the negative side, e.g. a growing social isolation of e-lancers and the resulting mental draw-backs (e.g., Bailey/Kurland 2002) are to be expected.

Again, e-lancing is an example of a possible future tertiary effect, and again the sustainability effects of e-lancing are only exemplarily discussed. However, the existence of relevant HRIT tertiary effects *sui generis* can be clearly demonstrated.

5. Conclusions

Sustainability constitutes a global key concept for improving human affairs. Consequently, to contribute to the improvements expected from sustainability, diverse scientific disciplines elaborate on the concept. In particular, management scholars elaborate on the concept of corporate sustainability, as it should guide private organisations in contributing to their own good as well as to the public good. As part of these developments, the concept of sustainable HRM is developed and discussed. While the rather nascent and heterogeneous discussion considers multifarious aspects, it systematically excludes information technology. Information technology, however, constitutes the source of one of the major changes in HRM during the last two decades (e.g., Strohmeier 2012) and, accordingly, is of obvious direct relevance for sustainability. The current chapter therefore aimed at uncovering the relevance of information technology to sustainable HRM. To accomplish this, a simple *framework of sustainable HRM* was presented, and its major effects were discussed. To incorporate additional effects caused by IT, an *extended framework of sustainable electronic HRM* was presented, which added primary, secondary and tertiary effects of HRIT on sustainability. Based on brief examples, these additional effects were substantiated and discussed herein.

In doing so, the *additivity*, *variety*, *relevance*, and *ambivalence* of primary, secondary and tertiary technological effects on sustainability could be determined. Technological effects on sustainability are first *additive* as they occur only due to information technology and therefore in electronic HRM but not in conventional HRM. Technological effects furthermore are *various*. As noted in the exemplary discussion, each of the three effect categories is comprised of a multiplicity of individual effects that currently – due to a clear lack of research – are unknown. Referring to the three dimensions of sustainability, the economic effects have received the most attention from researchers. This is followed by social effects, which are sometimes considered, and ecological effects, which, thus far, have been ignored by research. The technological effects are also *relevant* for sustainability. Evidently, however, the relevance of effects varies greatly, as there are small, negligible effects as well as intense, non-negligible effects. At the categorical level, secondary effects seem to be of the greatest relevance, followed by tertiary and primary effects. There are also intra-categorical differences to be considered in detail. Technological effects are clearly *ambivalent*, as there are individual effects that contribute to sustainability and individual effects that detract from sustainability. In this way, IT is both part of the problem *and* part of the solution (Hilty 2008).

In summary, it can be principally shown *that* and *how* information technology matters in sustainable HRM and that HRIT warrants consideration in future research on sustainable HRM. It is hoped that this chapter constitutes a starting point for and gives an impetus to future research on sustainable *electronic* HRM.

References

AGUINIS, H.; LAWAL, S.O. (2013): eLancing: A Review and Research Agenda for Bridging the Science-Practice Gap, in: Human Resource Management Review, Vol. 23, No. 1, pp. 6-17.

BAILEY, D.E.; KURLAND, N.B. (2002): A Review of Telework Research: Findings, New Directions, and Lessons for the Study of Modern Work, in: Journal of Organizational Behavior, Vol. 23, No. 4, pp. 383-400.

BONDAROUK, T.V.; FURTMUELLER, E. (2012): E-HRM Research: Promises, Hopes, Facts and Path Forward: Reviewing Four Decades of Empirical Evidence, in: TANSLEY, C.; WILLIAMS, H. (Eds.): Proceedings of the Fourth International e-HRM Conference: Innovation, Creativity and e-HRM, Nottingham Trent University, pp. 25-60.

BONDAROUK, T.V.; RUËL, H. (2013): The Strategic Value of e-HRM: Results from an Exploratory Study in a Governmental Organization, in: The International Journal of Human Resource Management, Vol. 24, No. 2, pp. 391-414.

BOUDREAU, J.W. (2003): Sustainability and the Talentship Paradigm: Strategic Human Resource Management Beyond the Bottom Line, CAHRS Working Paper Series, Cornell University ILR School, 40.

CARDYS, R.F.; MILLER, J.S. (2005): e-HR and Performance Management: Consideration of Positive Potential and the Dark Side, in: GUEUTAL, H.; STONE, D.L. (Eds.): The Brave New World of e-HR: Human Resources Management in the Digital Age, San Francisco, pp. 138-165.

CLARKE, M. (2011): Sustainable HRM: A New Approach to People Management, in: CLARKE, M. (Ed.): Readings in HRM and Sustainability, Melbourne, pp. 1-7.

COHEN, E.; TAYLOR, S.; MÜLLER-CAMEN, M. (2010): HR's Role in Corporate Social Responsibility and Sustainability, SHRM Foundation Executive Briefing, Alexandria.

COLBERT, B.A.; KURUCZ, E.C. (2007): Three Conceptions of Triple Bottom Line Business Sustainability and the Role for HRM, in: Human Resource Planning, Vol. 30, No. 1, pp. 21-29.

DE SOUZA FREITAS, W.R.; JABBOUR, C.J.C.; SANTOS, F.C.A. (2011): Continuing the Evolution: Towards Sustainable HRM and Sustainable Organizations, in: Business Strategy Series, Vol. 12, No. 5, pp. 226-234.

DULEBOHN, J.H.; MARLER, J.H. (2005): e-Compensation: The Potential to Transform Practice, in: GUEUTAL, H.; STONE, D.L. (Eds.): The Brave New World of e-HR: Human Resources Management in the Digital Age, San Francisco, pp. 166-189.

DYLLICK, T.; HOCKERTS, K. (2002): Beyond the Business Case for Corporate Sustainability, in: Business Strategy and the Environment, Vol. 11, No. 2, pp. 130-141.

EHNERT, I. (2006): Sustainability Issues in Human Resource Management: Linkages, Theoretical Approaches, and Outlines for an Emerging Field, Proceedings of the 21st EIASM SHRM Workshop, Birmingham.

EHNERT, I.; HARRY, W.; ZINK, K.J. (2014): Sustainability and HRM, in: EHNERT, I.; HARRY, W.; ZINK, K.J. (Eds.): Sustainability and Human Resources: Developing Sustainable Business Organizations, Heidelberg et al., pp. 3-32.

ELKINGTON, J. (1994): Towards the Suitable Corporation: Win-Win-Win Business Strategies for Sustainable Development, in: California Management Review, Vol. 36, No. 2, pp. 90-100.

FLORKOWSKI, G.W.; OLIVAS-LUJÁN, M.R. (2006): The Diffusion of Human-Resource Information-Technology Innovations in US and Non-US Firms, in: Personnel Review, Vol. 35, No. 6, pp. 684-710.

GALANAKI, E.; PANAYOTOPOULOU, L. (2008): Adoption and Success of e-HRM in European Firms, in: TORRES-CORRONAS, T.; ARIAS-OLIVA, M. (Eds.): Encyclopedia of Human Resource Information Systems, Hershey, pp. 24-30.

GLADWIN, T.N.; KENNELLY, J.J.; KRAUSE, T.S. (1995): Shifting Paradigms for Sustainable Development: Implications for Management Theory and Research, in: Academy of Management Review, Vol. 20, No. 4, pp. 874-907.

GOTTSCHALK, I.; KIRN, S. (2013): Cloud Computing as a Tool for Enhancing Ecological Goals?, in: Business & Information Systems Engineering, Vol. 5, No. 5, pp. 299-313.

GRANT, D.; NEWELL, S. (2013): Realizing the Strategic Potential of e-HRM, in: The Journal of Strategic Information Systems, Vol. 22, No. 3, pp. 187-192.

GRAY, R.: MILNE, M. (2002): Sustainability Reporting: Who's Kidding Whom?, in: Chartered Accountants Journal of New Zealand, Vol. 81, No. 6, pp. 66-70.

GUEST, D. E. (1987): Human Resource Management and Industrial Relations, in: Journal of Management Studies, Vol. 24, No. 5, pp. 503-521.

HAHN, T.; FIGGE, F.; PINKSE, J.; PREUSS, L. (2010): Trade-Offs in Corporate Sustainability: You Can't Have Your Cake and Eat it, in: Business Strategy and the Environment, Vol. 19, No. 4, pp. 217-229.

HART, S.L.; MILSTEIN, M.B. (2003): Creating Sustainable Value, in: The Academy of Management Executive, Vol. 17, No. 2, pp. 56-67.

HILTY, L.M. (2008): A Conceptual Framework for ICT Effects on Sustainability, in: HILTY, L.M. (Ed.): Information Technology and Sustainability: Essays on the Relationship Between Information Technology and Sustainable Development, Norderstedt, pp. 145-158.

HOGLER, R.L.; HENLE, C.; BEMUS, C. (1998): Internet Recruiting and Employment Discrimination: A Legal Perspective, in: Human Resource Management Review, Vol. 8, No. 2, pp. 149-164.

HOLM, A.B. (2012): E-recruitment: Towards an Ubiquitous Recruitment Process and Candidate Relationship Management, in: German Journal of Research in Human Resource Management, Vol. 26, No. 3, pp. 241-259.

HUBBARD, J.C.; FORCHT, K.A.; THOMAS, D.S. (1998): Human Resource Information Systems: An Overview of Current Ethical and Legal Issues, in: Journal of Business Ethics, Vol. 17, No. 12, pp. 1319-1323.

ISENHOUR, L.C. (2009): HRIS and HR Administration, in: KAVANAGH, M.J.; THITE, M. (Eds.): Human Resource Information Systems: Basics, Applications, and Future Directions, Thousand Oaks, pp. 211-228.

JABBOUR, C.J.C.; SANTOS, F.C.A. (2008): The Central Role of Human Resource Management in the Search for Sustainable Organizations, in: The International Journal of Human Resource Management, Vol. 19, No. 12, pp. 2133-2154.

JACKSON, S.E.; SEO, J. (2010): The Greening of Strategic HRM Scholarship, in: Organizational Management Journal, Vol. 7, No. 4, pp. 278-290.

JACKSON, S.E.; RENWICK, D.W.; JABBOUR, C.J.; MÜLLER-CAMEN, M. (2011): State-of-the-Art and Future Directions for Green Human Resource Management: Introduction to the Special Issue, in: German Journal of Research in Human Resources, Vol. 25, No. 2, pp. 99-116.

KLEIN, K.J.; DANSEREAU, F.; HALL, R.J. (1994): Levels Issues in Theory Development, Data Collection, and Analysis, in: Academy of Management Review, Vol. 19, No. 2, pp. 195-229.

KRAMAR, R. (2013): Beyond Strategic Human Resource Management: Is Sustainable Human Resource Management the Next Approach?, in: The International Journal of Human Resource Management, forthcoming.

LANG, S.; LAUMER, S.; MAIER, C.; ECKHARDT, A. (2011): Drivers, Challenges and Consequences of E-recruiting: A Literature Review, ACM Proceedings of the 49th SIGMIS Annual Conference on Computer Personnel Research, San Antonio, pp. 26-35.

LAUMER, S.; ECKHARDT, A.; WEITZEL, T. (2009): Status Quo and Trends in e-Recruiting: Results from an Empirical Analysis, Proceedings of the International Conference on Information Resources Management (CONF-IRM).

LENGNICK-HALL, M.L.; LENGNICK-HALL, C.A.; ANDRADE, L.S.; DRAKE, B. (2009): Strategic Human Resource Management: The Evolution of the Field, in: Human Resource Management Review, Vol. 19, No. 2, pp. 64-85.

NEUMAYER, E. (2003): Weak versus Strong Sustainability: Exploring the Limits of Two Opposing Paradigms, Cheltenham.

NORMAN, W.; MACDONALD, C. (2004): Getting to the Bottom of "Triple Bottom Line", in: Business Ethics Quarterly, Vol. 14. No. 2, pp. 243-262.

MACPHERSON, A.; ELLIOT, M.; HARRIS, I.; HOMANN, G. (2004): E-learning: Reflection and Evaluation of Corporate Programs, in: Human Resource Development International, Vol. 7, No. 3, pp. 295-313.

MARIAPPANADAR, S. (2014): The Model of Negative Externality for Sustainable HRM, in: EHNERT, I.; HARRY, W.; ZINK, K.J. (Eds.): Sustainability and Human Resources, Developing Sustainable Business Organizations, Heidelberg et al., pp. 181-203.

MARLER, J.H. (2009): Making Human Resources Strategic by Going to the Net: Reality or Myth?, in: The International Journal of Human Resource Management, Vol. 20, No. 3, pp. 515-527.

MARLER, J.H.; FISHER, S.L. (2013): An Evidence-Based Review of e-HRM and Strategic Human Resource Management, in: Human Resource Management Review, Vol. 23, No. 1, pp. 18-36.

MARTIN, D.; SCHOUTEN, J. (2012): Sustainable Marketing, Upper Saddle River.

MARTIN, G.; REDDINGTON, M. (2010): Theorizing the Links Between e-HR and Strategic HRM: A Model, Case Illustration and Reflections, in: The International Journal of Human Resource Management, Vol. 21, No. 10, pp. 1553-1574.

ORLIKOWSKI, W.J.; SCOTT, S.V. (2008): Sociomateriality: Challenging the Separation of Technology, Work and Organization, in: The Academy of Management Annals, Vol. 2, No. 1, pp. 433-474.

PEARCE, C.G.; TUTEN, T.L. (2001): Internet Recruiting in the Banking Industry, in: Business Communication Quarterly, Vol. 64, No. 1, pp. 9-18.

PFEFFER, J. (2010): Building Sustainable Organizations: The Human Factor, in: The Academy of Management Perspectives, Vol. 24, No. 1, pp. 34-45.

RENWICK, D.W.; REDMAN, T.; MAGUIRE, S. (2013): Green Human Resource Management: A Review and Research Agenda, in: International Journal of Management Reviews, Vol. 15, No. 1, pp. 1-14.

RUËL, H.; BONDAROUK, T.; LOOISE, J.K. (2004): e-HRM: Innovation or Irritation: An Explorative Empirical Study in Five Large Companies on Web-Based HRM, in: Management Revue, Vol. 15, No. 3, pp. 364-380.

SCHALK, R.; TIMMERMAN, V.; DEN HEUVEL, S.V. (2013): How Strategic Considerations Influence Decision Making on e-HRM Applications, in: Human Resource Management Review, Vol. 23, No. 1, pp. 84-92.

SCHMIDT, N.H.; EREK, K.; KOLBE, L.M.; ZARNEKOW, R. (2009): Sustainable Information Systems Management, in: Business & Information Systems Engineering, Vol. 1, No. 5, pp. 400-402.

SEARCY, C. (2012): Corporate Sustainability Performance Measurement Systems: A Review and Research Agenda, in: Journal of Business Ethics, Vol. 107, No. 3, pp. 239-253.

SEURING, S.; MÜLLER, M. (2008): From a Literature Review to a Conceptual Framework for Sustainable Supply Chain Management, in: Journal of Cleaner Production, Vol. 16, No. 15, pp. 1699-1710.

SHARMA, S.; SHARMA, J.; DEVI, A. (2011): Corporate Social Responsibility: The Key Role of Human Resources Management, in: SIMONS, R. (Ed.): Human Resource Management: Issues, Challenges and Opportunities, Oakland, pp. 9-18.

SOPPE, A. (2004): Sustainable Corporate Finance, in: Journal of Business Ethics, Vol. 53, No. 1-2, pp. 213-224.

STONE, D.L.; LUKASZEWSKI, K.M.; ISENHOUR, L. (2005): e-Recruiting: Online Strategies for Attracting Talent, in: GUEUTAL, H.; STONE, D.L. (Eds.): The Brave New World of e-HR: Human Resources Management in the Digital Age, San Francisco, pp. 22-53.

STROHMEIER, S. (2007): Research in e-HRM: Review and Implications, in: Human Resource Management Review, Vol. 17, No. 1, pp. 19-37.

STROHMEIER, S. (2009): Concepts of e-HRM Consequences: A Categorisation, Review and Suggestion, in: The International Journal of Human Resource Management, Vol. 20, No. 3, pp. 528-543.

STROHMEIER, S. (2012): Assembling a Big Mosaic: A Review of Recent Books on Electronic Human Resource Management (e-HRM), in: German Journal of Research in Human Resource Management, Vol. 26, No. 3, pp. 282-294.

STROHMEIER, S. (2014): Research Approaches in e-HRM: Classification and Analysis, in: LOPÉZ-MARTINÉZ, F. (Ed.): e-Business Strategic Management, Berlin et al., forthcoming.

STROHMEIER, S.; KABST, R. (2009): Organizational Adoption of e-HRM in Europe: An Empirical Exploration of Major Adoption Factors, in: Journal of Managerial Psychology, Vol. 24, No. 6, pp. 482-501.

WELLS, S. (2011): HRM for Sustainability: Creating a New Paradigm, in: CLARKE, M. (Ed): Readings in HRM and Sustainability, Melbourne, pp. 133-146.

WORLD COMMISSION ON ENVIRONMENT AND DEVELOPMENT WCED (1987): Our common future, Oxford.

YEH, C.W. (2012): Cloud Computing and Human Resources in the Knowledge Era, in: Human Systems Management, Vol. 31. No. 3, pp. 165-175.

Sustainable Business Models in Health Care

Martin Dietrich, Nadine Molter and Matti Znotka

Overview

1. Introduction

An aging and declining population, an increase of chronic diseases, a mismatch between highly fragmented health care delivery and an increasing need for full cycle health care – these are among the main factors that threaten sustainability in the organisation and financing of modern health care systems. These demographic, epidemiologic and societal changes are going to transform health care needs substantially in the next decades (Gröne/Garcia-Barbeo 2001). For example, according to the "Statistisches Bundesamt der Bundesrepublik Deutschland" (Federal Statistical Office), in 2030, over one-third (37%) of the population in Germany will be 60 years and older (Statistische Ämter des Bundes und der Länder 2011, pp. 8ff.). As a consequence, chronic illnesses are and will continue to be the most frequent causes of death in modern societies, and the treatment of these illnesses absorbs the largest part of health care resources. But what our health care systems deliver is mainly acute medical care that is not capable of adapting to current and future full cycle health care needs. This is why sustainability in health care is at stake.

From a health system perspective, unsustainability of the whole systems can be ascribed to misconceptions of value propositions and revenue models in health care business models in the delivery of health care. In health care delivery, current business models are not health-oriented because revenues are based on diagnoses, diseases and treatments. Current structures of health care business models do not directly allow for earnings derived from preventing medical treatments or maintaining health: "[...] physicians have the incentive to treat rather than to minimise the need for treatment, prevent disease, or, more generally, improve health care value" (Porter/Teisberg 2006, p. 74). Another misconception in the organisation of health care is the highly fragmented delivery of health care. Various providers such as hospitals, general practitioners or specialists, often act isolated from each other and are financed by incompatible reimbursement schemes that do not allow for the provision of integrated health care across sector boundaries. Integrated care models that attempt to cover the full cycle of care require business models that take into account coordinated health delivery rather than isolated treatments of medical conditions.

In this chapter, we address sustainability in health care from a business model perspective. Thereafter we discuss the issue of sustainability in health care and point out that it strongly depends on a market orientation in the design of business models for integrated health care. We then illustrate, from a market based view, which aspects are to be considered in sustainable business models by discussing revenue and market models for population based integrated care programs. In particular, we describe shared savings contracts and propose market segmentation as an effective way to address target populations for prevention. We conclude with a discussion of our results and implications for the sustainability of business models in health care delivery.

2. Conceptual Framework

2.1 Sustainability in Health Care

Broadly speaking, sustainability means the preservation of resources for the current and future needs of societies (World Commission on Environment and Development 1987, p. 43); and includes economic, social and environmental dimensions (Enquete-Kommission 1998). The economic dimension, for example, is related to effective action, responsible handling of resources and long-term implementation of goals such as profits or economic growth. The social dimension is based on general principles for present and future generations such as human dignity, individual freedom, social peace, solidarity and social security. The primary objective of the environmental dimension is to save resources and to protect the environment. To pursue all three dimensions and their simultaneous harmonisation is a necessary condition for sustainability (Scherenberg 2011).

With respect to health care systems, sustainability especially depends on the responsible utilisation of available resources so that an adequate provision of health care would be preserved for succeeding generations across all layers of society. The aim of the economic dimension is to promote long term economic viability in health care so that future pressure on financing health care is compensated by appropriate health care structures for which the foundation has to be set today.

Unfortunately, current conditions of regulated health care markets do not allow for a sufficiently fast adaption of health care business models to meet changing health care needs. Health care regulations and market conditions impede the innovation and diffusion of new forms of health care. Due to third party payer systems, current forms and structures of health care delivery do not depend directly on demand and users' needs, rather, they are set by the statutory agencies and health care organisations. Sustainability therefore requires the development of new business models and the re-invention of health care.

Because of its network character and striven coordination, as well as the cooperation of otherwise separated service providers, integrated health care concepts are promising approaches to regain sustainable health care structures on the delivery level. Nevertheless, the diffusion of such health care delivery structures has not yet met expectations. Although a promising approach, integrated health care models appear to suffer from a lack of market orientation. This lack of market orientation has a direct impact on the failure of many implicitly set business models. It might be assumed that an explicit business model perspective on new forms of health care delivery could help to understand how integrated health care models might become more successful. The success of integrated health care models appears as a necessary condition for health care systems to become more sustainable as a whole.

2.2 Business Models in Health Care

The business model concept has been developed as a viable tool for strategic management (e.g. Baden-Fuller/Morgan 2010) and is beginning to enter strategic thinking in health care management as well. Particularly when developing health oriented structures that encompass full cycle care, the business model approach appears to be suitable to delineate necessary conditions for sustainable health care delivery structures (Hwang/Christensen 2007, pp. 1331ff.; Johnson/Christensen/Kagermann 2008, pp. 3ff.).

Business models in general can be defined as "[...] a description of a value a company offers to one or several segments of customers and the architecture of the firm and its network of partners for creating, marketing and delivering this value and relationship capital [...]" (Osterwalder 2004, p. 15). In other words, the model is a "concise representation of how an interrelated set of decision variables in the areas of venture strategy, architecture and economics are addressed to create sustainable competitive advantage in defined markets" (Morris/Schindehutte/Allen 2005, p. 727).

Several representations and conceptual frameworks, usually consisting of a varying number of interrelated partial models (e.g. Wirtz 2010), that describe the business model approach have been suggested. In the following we suggest a consolidated framework to illustrate our concept of business models in which we use two conceptual dimensions to which we relate five partial models. One dimension differentiates between the organisational and the market side of a business model, the other dimension refers to the operating and the financial level of business models. Two partial models on the organisational side of a business model, namely the resources model and the cost model, describe issues of how different types of resources, such as material and immaterial resources, abilities, processes, activities and other inputs, are organised to physically provide goods and services, as well as to what costs these provisions can be realised. On the market side, the market and revenue models describe, explain and prognosticate the needs of potential users (overt and latent), as well as how revenues can be generated from the utilisation of the organisation's offerings. With respect to the operational level, relating the resource model to the market model elucidates how an organisation's contribution effectively meets users' needs and creates value on the utility level. With respect to the financial level, relating revenues to costs results in economic value. Taken together, the physical value and the economic value combined constitute the fifth partial model that establishes the value proposition as the core of every business model.

In health care, the compatibility of goals at the systems level and the value propositions of organisations at the delivery level constitute a necessary condition of sustainability. In terms of business models, the value propositions as the core of business models of health care organisations are largely not aligned with the overall goals of the health care system. Especially current revenue models, in which health care providers are reimbursed on a fee for service principle, do not allow for full cycle care business models. But on the systems' level, all health care systems define the population health as being their ultimate objective. Threats to health in the beginnings of social security were acute illnesses, so that health care organisations fulfilled system level goals by providing treatments for acute medical diseases. In combination with fee for service reimbursement schemes, incentives were set for health care professionals to treat illnesses, not to prevent disease. When it comes to applying traditional health care business models to the objectives of full cycle health care, the production of health would mean to avoid treatments. Producing health in this sense would mean to undermine the revenues of health service providers. As a result, business model innovations which enable providers to earn revenues by avoiding treatments and cut costs by providing more health are needed. This in turn would contribute to sustainability in health care.

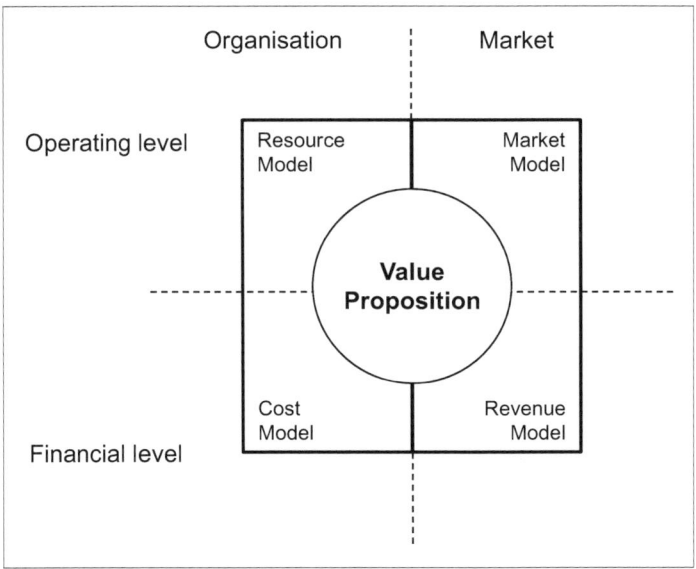

Figure 1: Business Model
(Source: adapted from Dietrich/Molter 2013, p. 211)

2.3 Integrated Health Care

It has been suggested that compatibility between health care provider incentives and the overall objectives of the health system under changing
conditions may be achieved by enforcing population based integrated
health care programs (Hildebrandt et al. 2010). Integrated care is aimed at
integrating the delivery of health care services across different providers
of in- and outpatient health services (Gröne/Garcia-Barbero 2001) in order
to provide full cycle health care.

The value proposition in integrated health care programs is that preventive services and effective coordination of acute care leads to better health
outcomes, avoids medical treatments and is therefore cost containing in
the long run. The comparative advantage to classical care unfolds specifically in vulnerable population groups where the development of chronic
diseases will become a serious issue. Population based integrated care programs are open to all insurants of a sickness fund in a given region. The
target groups for such programs are those individuals that show the highest risk to suffer from chronic diseases. The core value of such a program

is to give insurants the opportunity to participate in coordinated preventive activities that are effective in the prevention of chronic diseases. In addition to the prospects for positive health outcomes in the future, participants might qualify to receive financial compensations for the positive results of their preventive actions, e.g. reduced subscription fees.

Integrated care has been developing as a promising form of sustainable health care that appears to be especially suited to provide preventive health care programs. Nevertheless, the diffusion of these health care models has not met current expectations. We propose that one reason may be the lack of market orientation in designing integrated care business models. We therefore propose that a market based approach to business model design in integrated health care may strengthen the success of these programs. The market based approach to business model management puts revenue and the market models at the center of conceptual considerations. Hence, we will delineate basic aspects of revenue and market models for integrated health care business models and their respective implications in turn.

3. Market Based Sustainability in Integrated Health Care

3.1 Overview

As mentioned above, future demands on health care require appropriate incentives for health care providers not only for the treatment of diseases, but for preventive health services as well. As a result, a necessary condition is to make full health care cycle activities and outcomes reconcilable with incentives for health care providers to provide value concepts that are based on health. To foster positive health outcomes and restrain health care costs in the long run, the basic idea of prevention programs is to take actions that support health maintenance of its participants, especially in respect to cost-intensive chronic diseases. Health maintenance regarding chronic diseases means that the interventions should prevent or postpone the occurrence of illness (Siegel et al. 2012, pp. 148ff.). Due to demographic and epidemiologic changes, programs that will reduce or delay these cost-intensive illnesses become increasingly relevant for sustainable health care.

3.2 Revenue Models and Shared Cost Savings

Although it is widely recognised that prevention will play a central role in full cycle health care delivery, positive financial incentives for health care providers that result from preventive interventions are still not part of current reimbursement schemes. One basic problem is that valid health outcomes as a basis for revenues cannot be modeled directly as a commonly accepted measure for health. For that reason, health outcomes at present cannot serve as the quantity structure of revenues in health care revenue models. Thus, a workaround to financially address health production in revenue models in innovative business models for full cycle health care has to be found. As an alternative to direct health measures, a comparison of costs in a risk-adjusted population of patients that undergo preventive, full cycle care interventions versus patients that do not receive this intervention has been suggested. The basic idea in this comparison-approach is that differences in population based health status can be expressed in differences of population based costs of health care. The assumption is that when full cycle health care is in fact more effective in producing health than highly fragmented, classical acute care, then populations that receive full cycle interventions should be healthier than populations that don't receive these interventions. As a result, a healthier population should produce lower costs than a less healthy population. Consequently, these cost savings have to be translated into revenue streams for health care providers that are part of the integrated care concept. Business model architectures that are built around this approach are known as shared savings contracts and have been tested in promising pilot projects (Hildebrandt et al. 2010).

Prerequisites in the structures of a health care system and in the intervention and control populations that allow for shared saving contracts are manifold. Important prerequisites are (risk adjusted) norm costs by which health insurances are financed per insurant, as well as known actual costs per insurant. When an insurant's actual costs are lower than the risk adjusted norm costs, a health insurance earns a surplus for this insurant. When the population groups of insurants that take part in integrated health care are healthier than other population groups of insurants, the sum of actual costs in this population should be lower than the sum of the risk adjusted norm costs of the comparison (or control) population group. In sum, the production of health should result in a financial surplus for the intervention population. The differences in costs are an economic representation of health produced. The payout of these cost differences to health care providers means a health centered revenue model. Arrangements and contracts between health insurers and health care providers who run integrated care models are necessary. Another prerequisite is a methodological approach in which differences in health care costs between the intervention population and the control population can be causally attributed to the integrated care program. As a method to identify control groups, for example, a propensitiy score (Rosenbaum/Rubin 1983) with the differences-in-differences model has been applied. Further prerequisites are discussed e.g. by Hildebrandt et al. (2010).

3.3 Market Model and Segmentation for Prevention

3.3.1 Prevention in Health Care Systems

The rising number of chronic diseases, such as cardiovascular disease and diabetes, which are accelerated by factors like everyday stress, malnutrition and physical inactivity will exert intense cost pressure on health systems in the future (Bagust et al. 2002; Mai/ Schwarz/Hoffmann 2012). Many chronic diseases are assumed to be correlated with health behavior, so that efforts have been undertaken to better understand the factors that particularly explain preventive health behavior. It has been shown, for example, that the risk of diabetes could be reduced by promoting behavior changes (Tuomilehto et al. 2001). These behavior changes are primarily addressed by prevention programs. Preventive health behavior is any activity that is undertaken by an individual for the purpose of prevention or detection of disease at an early state (Glanz/Rimer/Viswanath 2008; Kasl/ Cobb 1966). A distinction is made between primary, secondary and tertiary prevention. The objective of primary prevention is to avoid the development of new diseases. The progression of a manifest disease is addressed by secondary prevention, for example, with early diagnosis. Due to measures of the tertiary prevention, conditions caused by chronic disease will be minimised or relapses will be avoided (Dekker/Sibai 2001, p. 209). Prevention programs require the effective collaboration of many distinct health care providers so that these health care services are predesignated to be delivered by integrated health care programs.

3.3.2 Segmentation for Effective Prevention

Health behavior research suggests that preventive health behavior is a dynamic process that encompasses several stages. Models of health behavior such as the Transtheoretical Model (TTM), also known as Stages of Change, differentiate between the precontemplation, contemplation, preparation, action and maintenance stage (Prochaska/Redding/Evers 2008). These stages describe the behavioral state of individuals with respect to a specific health behavior. The basic rationale behind defining different behavioral stages is that persons in different stages form homogeneous sub-groups that react differently to promotional activities. For example, individuals that are in the precontemplation stage show other requirements in promoting health behavior than individuals who are in the maintenance stage. These sub-groups are to be addressed differently according to their respective stages in order to effectively promote preventive health behavior changes. A subdivision of markets therefore makes sense as the segments can be addressed more effectively than the population as a whole (Kotler/Keller/Bliemel 2007, pp. 357f.). Based on health behavior models, segmentation in terms of a market based approach in integrated care business models becomes apparent.

A well-known segmentation of consumer behavior research that may be well correlated to preventive health behavior is the Sinus Milieus, by which consumers with similar attitudes to life and lifestyle (psychografic criteria) are divided into specific segments. The milieu-specific settings on health, such as differences in health understanding, appreciation and dealing with their own health (responsibility) are milieu-specific differentiated. In particular, the use of preventive services, such as exercise, depends on the lifestyle. So the Sinus Milieus lends itself as a viable segmentation tool for health behavior approaches in integrated care business models (Sinus Sociovision 2010).

The milieu of the middle and upper social Sinus Milieus constitutes part of the health-conscious society. Thus, health care for the performers represents a valuable asset that secures their future performance in life and career (Merkle/Hecht 2011). Another suited Sinus Milieu is the group of LOHAS (Lifestyles of Health and Sustainability). As the name suggests, it is a holistic lifestyle that promotes the values of health and sustainability and is associated with self-realisation as well as increasing the quality of life in harmony with nature (Ray/Anderson 2000).

However, Sinus Milieus of the lower classes are more similar to vulnerable population groups which are less prone to utilise prevention offers. In particular, socially and health-wise affected disadvantaged people could benefit from quality assured health promotion offerings and prevention services in the future. Therefore, particular attention should be given to the life situations and needs of socially disadvantaged groups when implementing preventive programs. For example, women from socioeconomically disadvantaged backgrounds are less likely to attend cervical cancer screenings (Baker/Middleton 2003; Maxwell et al. 2001; Todorova et al. 2009; McKinnon/Harper/Moore 2010). It has been long known that people with difficult life situations use less preventative offerings than do people from wealthier population groups; furthermore, it is difficult for them to maintain the behavior they have learnt for the long term (Rosenbrock 2007, pp. 714ff.; Rosenbrock 2002). For that reason, the social situation and lifestyle of the population groups should be taken into account with respect to the design and implementation of prevention measures. As a result, social justice is promoted by improving the health chances of disadvantaged groups and, furthermore, costs will be reduced in the long term. In order to be as effective as possible, integrated health care programs need to address population groups for which the effects of preventive health behavior show the strongest effects. Target group-specific approaches for prevention measures will have to be developed, for example, focusing on women with low cervical cancer screening rates, such as those residing in rural areas, US-born ethnic minority women, immigrant women, older women, and the uninsured (Akers/Newmann/Smith 2007, p. 173).

3.3.3 Segmentation Procedures for Communication

Market segmentation involves dividing the market into appropriate submarkets. This process is divided into two stages: the research and the conceptualisation stage. The research stage is used to identify and describe the groups that the marketer may wish to target (see Figure 2). The target marketing stage includes selecting one or more market segments and their positioning and marketing strategies (Andreasen/Kotler 2008).

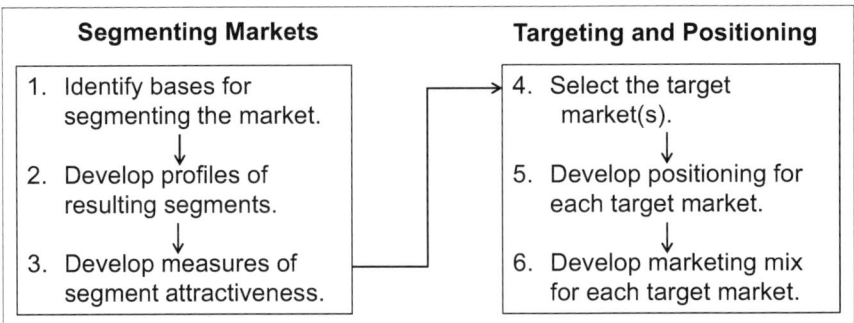

*Figure 2: Steps in market segmentation, targeting and positioning
(Source: Andreasen/Kotler 2008, p. 139)*

In promoting preventive health behavior, communication campaigns play an important role in public health. Communication campaigns for health behavior follow the same principles as communication in health related marketing. In general, »Marketing communications are the means by which firms attempt to inform, persuade and remind customers – directly or indirectly – about the brands they market....They can inform or show customers how and why a market offering is used, by what kind of person, and where and when" (Kotler et al. 2009, p. 690). Communication policies include advertising, sponsorship, exhibition appearance, word-of-mouth communication and explanatory work. In particular, the latter measure has priority in the implementation of preventive measures. Explanatory work and the resulting changes in health behavior are the goal of health related marketing.

Point to what motivates people to behave in a healthier manner and which conditions are needed for changing their behavior. Health psychology, including health behavior models, provides the theoretical framework for this approach (French et al. 2010, p. 3). Motivational models, such as the Health Belief Model, Social-cognitive Model and the Theory of Planned Behavior, make a significant contribution to the explanation of the motives for behavior modification (Clark/Houle 2009). All theories have in common the perception of risk, the outcome expectancies and the self-efficacy ("the conviction that one can successfully execute the behavior required to produce the outcomes", Bandura 1977, p. 193); these components are important to successful behavior modification. Due to the high explanatory power of these components, they should be considered in the design and implementation of health marketing activities. These measures are to be specified with respect to the identified market segments. Hence, prevention measures should demonstrate that the previous lifestyle involves risks and how these risks can be reduced by new behaviors.

Many communication policy measures include only the perception of risk and the outcome expectancy. This is exemplified by fear appeals on cigarette packaging, such as "Smoking can damage your health" or "Stopping smoking reduces the risk of fatal heart and lung diseases". However, the simultaneous response of the outcome expectancy and self-efficacy are more likely to cause a change in behavior than prevention measures that support only one of the components (Schwarzer 2008, p. 7). Even more persuasive findings of research on the design of communication activities, such as message framing, can be used for motivating preventive behavior. For example, it has been shown that gain-framed messages are more effective than loss-framed messages in promoting the adoption of illness prevention behavior (Gallagher/Updegraff 2011).

3.4 Challenges for Sustainability

In terms of sustainability in health care, the long term viability of the cost-comparison based architecture of revenue models will probably pose an issue. The concerns stem from the comparison approach and the need to form a valid control population group. In shared cost savings contracts, revenues are based on cost differences between the integrated and non-integrated care populations ("shared cost savings"). But from the health care system's perspective, the goal is to find sustainable health care structures which, in terms of health outcomes, are more effective than those based on acute and fragmented care alone. Given – as expected – that integrated care programs are successful in achieving this goal, efficient integrated care structures will diffuse into remaining populations. This would mean that risk adjusted cost structures would assimilate as a consequence of integrated care program success. With the same effectiveness of health care structures in whole populations, no population exists that could serve for cost comparisons. Therefore, cost differences as the basis of the revenue models would dissolve. Paradoxically, the success of integrated care concepts that would lead to the adaption as a health care standard in these revenue models would erode the financial basis of the business model in the long run. Although shared costs saving contracts are a promising and necessary first step to overcoming unsustainable and illness based revenue models, true sustainability would not be granted. As a consequence, to further aim at sustainability in health care, performance based revenue models may be developed in which health outcomes directly serve as the quantitative structure of health care business models.

Additionally, market models that address different target groups might result in a selection bias. Since vulnerable population groups would probably benefit most in terms of health gains that are based on prevention programs promoted by integrated health care, effective access to integrated health care programs might not be equally distributed. In terms of social sustainability, equal access to all forms of health care for all population groups might become an issue. The goal of sustainability in health care business models is therefore an ongoing challenge that requires constant attention with respect to all relevant dimensions of sustainability.

4. Conclusions

In this chapter, we discussed how a market oriented business model approach may contribute to more sustainable health care delivery. From a market as well as a revenue model perspective, the topic of preventive systems showed different potentials for improvements.

Sustainability can be fostered by market based business models in which the architecture of health oriented revenue models and segment specific approaches to target population groups may allow for effective and cost containing integrated health care concepts. Shared cost saving contracts, that use cost differences in intervention and comparison population groups as a revenue base, have been discussed as a first step toward more sustainable health care delivery.

A market based business model approach may also be realised by segmenting the market into groups according to their stage of preventive behavior which is mirrored by their observable actions, their social situation and lifestyle. Consumer typologies such as the Sinus Milieus take into consideration not only socio-demographic criteria, but also values, attitudes and lifestyles, and therefore appear as a viable way for specific targeting. A sustainable model in the health care market represents the coordinated provision of preventive measures by disparate health service providers. In order to effectively reach the population groups which will benefit most from preventive measures, these groups should be specifically addressed taking into account different lifestyles and social situations in order to achieve long term health, economic viability and social justice across current and future generations. Target group-specific approaches can be implemented at the operational level by using methods based on marketing communication. Specifically, health behavior models may be used in order to increase the communication campaign effectiveness for prevention measures from a market segmentation perspective. They can be used to develop recommendations for action and to trigger behavioral changes in the various population groups with respect to their health behavior status. In terms of revenue models, those population groups which benefit most from integrated health care concepts with regard to health outcomes would also contribute most substantially to shared cost savings revenues. They would thereby provide a sustainable financial basis for the further development of sustainable health care business models. As has been discussed, further developments beyond shared cost savings and target group specific approaches on the market side of business models in health care models are needed in order to foster true sustainability in modern health care systems.

References

AKERS, A.Y.; NEWMANN, S.J.; SMITH, J.S. (2007): Factors Underlying Disparities in Cervical Cancer Incidence, Screening, and Treatment in the United States, in: Current Problems in Cancer, Vol. 31, No. 3, pp. 157-181.

ANDREASEN, A.R.; KOTLER, P. (2008): Strategic Marketing for Nonprofit Organisations, 7th ed., New Jersey.

BADEN-FULLER, C.; MORGAN, M.S. (2010): Business Models as Models, in: Long Range Planning, Vol. 43, No. 2, pp. 156-171.

BAGUST, A.; HOPKINSON, P.K.; MASLOVE, L.; CURRIE, C.J. (2002): The Projected Health Care Burden of Type 2 Diabetes in the UK from 2000 to 2060, in: Diabetic Medicine, Vol. 19. No. 4, pp. 1-5.

BAKER, D.; MIDDLETON, E. (2003): Cervical Screening, Health Inequality in England in the 1990, in: Journal of Epidemiol & Community Health, Vol. 57, No. 6, pp. 417-423.

BANDURA, A. (1977): Social Learning Theory, Englewood Cliffs.

CLARK, N.M.; HOULE, C.R. (2009): Theoretical Models and Strategies for Improving Disease Management by Patients, in: SHUMAKER, S.A.; OCKENE, J.K.; RIEKERT, K.A. (Eds.): The Handbook of Health Behavior Change, New York, pp. 19-37.

DEKKER G.; SIBAI B.M. (2001): Primary, Secondary, and Tertiary Prevention of Preeclampsia, in: Lancet, Vol. 357, No. 9251, pp. 209-215.

DIETRICH, M.; MOLTER, N. (2013): Kundenmanagement in der Integrierten Versorgung, in: BUSSE, R.; SCHREYÖGG, J.; STARGARDT, T. (Eds.): Management im Gesundheitswesen, 3rd ed., Berlin, pp. 209-223.

ENQUETE-KOMMISSION (1998): Konzept Nachhaltigkeit: Vom Leitbild zur Umsetzung, BT-Drs. 13-11200, http://drucksachen.bundestag.de/drucksachen/index.php, accessed on July 27, 2013.

FRENCH, D.P.; VEDHARA, K.; KAPTEIN, A.A.; WEINMAN, J. (2010): Health Psychology. Introduction to Second Edition, in: FRENCH, D.P.; VEDHARA, K.; KAPTAIN, A.A.; WEINMAN, J. (Eds.): Health Psychology, 2nd ed., New York, pp. 1-10.

GALLAGHER, K.M.; UPDEGRAFF, J.A. (2011): Health Message Framing Effects on Attitudes, Intentions and Behavior: A Meta-Analytic Review, in: Annals of Behavioral Medicine, Vol. 43, No. 1, pp. 101-116.

GLANZ, K.; RIMER, B.K.; VISWANATH, K. (Eds.) (2008): Health Behavior and Health Education: Theory, Research and Practice, 4th ed., San Francisco.

GRÖNE, O.; GARCIA-BARBERO, M. (2001): Integrated Care: A Position Paper of the WHO European Office for Integrated Health Care Services, in: International Journal of Integrated Care, Vol. 1, No. 3, pp. 1-16.

HILDEBRANDT, H.; HERMANN, C.; KNITTEL, R.; RICHTER-REICHHELMM, M.; SIEGEL, A.; WITZENRATH, W. (2010): Gesundes Kinzigtal Integrated Care: Improving Population Health by a Shared Health Gain Approach and a Shared Savings Contract, in: International Journal of Integrated Care, Vol. 10.

HWANG, J.; CHRISTENSEN, C. (2007): Disruptive Innovation in Health Care Delivery: A Framework for Business-Model Innovation, in: Health Affairs, Vol. 27, No. 5, pp. 1329-1335.

JOHNSON M.; CHRISTENSEN, M.; KAGERMANN, H. (2008): Reinventing Your Business Model, in: Harvard Business Review, Vol. 86, No. 12, pp. 50-59.

KASL, S.V.; COBB, S. (1966): Health Behavior, Illness Behavior, and Sick-Role Behavior: I. Health and Illness Behavior, in: Archives of Environmental Health, Vol. 12, No. 2, pp. 246-266.

KOTLER, P.; KELLER, K.V.; BLIEMEL, F. (2007): Marketing-Management: Strategien für wertschaffendes Handeln, 12th ed., München.

KOTLER, P.; KELLER, K.L.; BRADY, M.; GOODMAN, M.; HANSEN, T. (2009): Marketing-Management, Harlow.

MAI, R.; SCHWARZ, U.; HOFFMANN, S. (2012): Gesundheitsmarketing: Schnittstelle von Marketing, Gesundheitsökonomie und Gesundheitspsychologie, in: MAI, R.; SCHWARZ, U.; HOFFMANN, S. (Eds.): Angewandtes Gesundheitsmarketing, Wiesbaden, pp. 3-14.

MAXWELL, C.J.; BANCEJ, C.M.; SNIDER J.; VIK, S.A. (2001): Factors Important in Promoting Cervical Cancer Screening Among Canadian Women: Findings from the 1996–1997 National Population Health Survey (nphs), in: Canadian Journal of Public Health, Vol. 92, No. 2, pp. 127-133.

MCKINNON, B., HARPER, S., MOORE, S. (2010): Decomposing Income-Related Inequality in Cervical Screening in 67 Countries, in: International Journal of Public Health, Vol. 56, No. 2, pp. 139-152.

MERKLE, T.; HECHT, J. (2011): Gesundheit ist das Wichtigste im Leben, in: Pharma Marketing Journal, Vol. 6, pp. 22-24.

MORRIS, M.; SCHINDEHUTTE, M.; ALLEN, J. (2005): The Entrepreneur's Business Model: Toward a Unified Perspective, in: Journal of Business Research, Vol. 58, No. 6, pp. 726-735.

OSTERWALDER, A. (2004): The Business Model Ontology: A Proposition in a Design Science Approach, dissertation, University of Lausanne.

PORTER, M.E.; TEISBERG, E.O. (2006): Redefining Health Care: Creating Value-Based Competition on Results, Boston.

PROCHASKA, J.O.; REDDING, C.A.; EVERS, K.E (2008): The Transtheoretical Model and Stages of Change, in: GLANZ, K.; RIMER, B.K.; VISWANATH, K. (Eds.): Health Behavior and Health Education: Theory, Research and Practice, 4th ed., San Francisco, pp. 97-122.

RAY, P.H.; ANDERSON, S.R. (2000): The Cultural Creatives: How 50 Million People are Changing the World, New York.

ROSENBAUM, P.R.; RUBIN D.B. (1983): The Central Role of the Propensity Score in Observational Studies for Causal Effects, in: Biometrika, Vol. 70, No. 1, pp. 41-55.

ROSENBROCK, R. (2002): Krankenkassen und Primärprävention – Anforderungen und Erwartungen an die Qualität, in: WALTER, U.; DRUPP, M., SCHWARTZ, F.W. (Eds.): Prävention durch Krankenkassen: Zielgruppen, Zugangswege, Wirksamkeit und Wirtschaftlichkeit, Weinheim et al., pp. 40-57.

ROSENBROCK, R. (2007): Primärprävention als Beitrag zu einer zukunftsfähigen Gesundheitspolitik, in: ULRICH, V.; RIED, W. (Eds.): Effizienz, Qualität und Nachhaltigkeit im Gesundheitswesen: Theorie und Politik öffentlichen Handelns, insbesondere in der Krankenversicherung - Festschrift zum 65. Geburtstag von Eberhard Wille, Baden-Baden, pp. 713-734.

SCHERENBERG, V. (2011): Nachhaltigkeit in der Gesundheitsvorsorge, Wiesbaden.

SCHWARZER, R. (2008): Modeling Health Behavior Change: How to Predict and Modify the Adoption and Maintenance of Health Behaviors, in: Applied Psychology, Vol. 57, No. 1, pp. 1-29.

SIEGEL, A.; KÖSTER, I.; SCHUBERT, I.; STÖSSEL, U. (2012): Integrierte Versorgung Gesundes Kinzigtal: Ein Modell für regionale Prävention und Schnittstellenoptimierung, in: KIRCH, W.; HOFFMANN, T.; PFAFF, H. (Eds.): Prävention und Versorgung, Stuttgart, pp. 148-164.

SINUS-SOCIOVISION (2010): Die Sinus-Milieus in Deutschland 2010, http://www.sinus-institut.de/uploads/tx_mppress/Modellwechsel_2010_neue_Charts.pdf, accessed on July 27, 2013.

STATISTISCHE ÄMTER DES BUNDES UND DER LÄNDER (Eds.) (2011): Demographischer Wandel in Deutschland, Heft 1, Wiesbaden.

TODOROVA, I.; BABAN, A.; ALEXANDROVA-KARAMANOVA, A.; BRADLEY, J. (2009): Inequalities in Cervical Cancer Screening in Eastern Europe: Perspectives from Bulgaria and Romania, in: International Journal of Public Health, Vol. 54, No. 4, pp. 222–232.

TUOMILEHTO, J.; LINDSTRÖM, J.; ERIKSSON, J.G. ET AL. (2001): Prevention of Type 2 Diabetes Melitius by Changes in Lifestyle Among Subjects with Impaired Glucose Tolerance, in: New England Journal of Medicine, Vol. 344, No. 18, pp. 1343-1350.

WIRTZ, B. (2010): Business Model Management, Wiesbaden.

WORLD COMMISSION ON ENVIRONMENT AND DEVELOPMENT (WCED) (1987): Our Common Future, New York.

Index of Authors

Univ.-Professor Dr. Heinz-Jürgen Axt held the chair in European Integration and European Politics at University Duisburg-Essen until 2012. He studied Social Science with Political Science, Sociology and Economics at Ruhr University Bochum. He received his doctorate from Philipps-Universität Marburg in 1976 and from 1978 to 1983 he was a research assistant at the TU Berlin. He earned his habilitation at the same university in 1984 and went on to become a freelance consultant in development cooperation and to the European Commission. From 1987 to 1995 he worked as an external collaborator for the SWP, German Institute for International and Security Affairs, Ebenhausen. In 1994 he was appointed Adjunct Professor at the TU Berlin. In 1995 he took up a Professorship at the Gerhard-Mercator University Duisburg, where he was appointed Jean Monnet Professor in 1998 and led the Jean Monnet Research Group. Between 2001 and 2005 he held the post of dean of the Faculty of Social Sciences. He is vice president of the Southeast Europe Association, Munich since the year 2000 and was head of the association's Duisburg branch until 2013. Heinz-Jürgen Axt is a Visiting Professor of the Europa-Institut at Saarland University. He has been on the board of the ZfTI Centre for Studies on Turkey and is a member of the International Advisory Board of the "Cyprus Review", the Advisory Board of the Turkish Institute for Security and Democracy (TISD), Washington D.C., and the Advisory Council of the KFIBS e.V. Cologne Forum for International Relations and Security Policy.

Univ.-Professor Dr. Ansgar Belke is full Professor of Macroeconomics at the University of Duisburg-Essen and Director of the Institute of Business and Economic Studies (IBES), University of Duisburg-Essen. Since 2012 he is (ad personam) Jean Monnet Professor. Moreover, he is member of the Adjunct Faculty Ruhr Graduate School of Economics (RGS Econ) and Visiting Professor of the Europa-Institut at Saarland University and the Hertie School of Governance, Berlin. Additionally, he is member of the "Monetary Experts Panel" of the European Parliament. Formerly, he held Full Professorships for International Economics at the University of Stuttgart-Hohenheim and for Macroeconomics and Applied Econometrics at the Main University of Vienna. He received his PhD in 1995 for scientific work on the theory and empirics of political business cycles and finished his habilitation in 2000 at the Ruhr University of Bochum with a venia legendi for Economics and Econometrics. He was visiting researcher at the CentER Tilburg, CEPS Brussels, IfW Kiel, DIW Berlin and OeNB Vienna. He serves as the editor-in-chief of "Kredit & Kapital", "Konjunkturpolitik – Applied Economics Quarterly" and as a co-editor of "Finance", "Empirica", "International Economics and Economic Policy", "Vierteljahreshefte für Wirtschaftsforschung", "Aestimatio – The International IEB Journal of Finance", "E-conomics" (Kiel Institute of the World Economy) and of the book series "Quantitative Ökonomie", Eul Verlag. He published widely in international refereed journals and other outlets, has regular appearances in the printed press and in national and international TV broadcasts. He spoke at a wide array of conferences, among them in 2010 the "Jeddah Economic Forum", Jeddah/Saudi-Arabia, the "Global Economic Forum", Istanbul/Turkey, and in 2013 the "Greek Government Roundtable" in Athens/Greece. His main areas of interest are in the fields of international macroeconomics, monetary economics, European integration and applied econometrics.

Professor Dr.-Ing. Dr. Christian Berg is Chief Sustainability Architect within SAP Services. He is Honorary Professor of Sustainability and Global Change at Clausthal University of Technology and recurring Visiting Professor of the Europa-Institut at Saarland University for Corporate Sustainability. He also lectured on Sustainability as well as on Global Economics at the University of Design in Schwäbisch-Gmünd. His main fields of interest, in which he published several books and articles, are sustainability, in particular corporate sustainability, technology assessment and ethics of technology. Furthermore, Christian Berg worked as political advisor and led the task force Sustainable Business and Growth in the expert dialogue of German Chancellor Angela Merkel in 2011/12. He holds degrees in physics, philosophy, theology, and engineering and is member of the Board of the German Chapter of the CLUB OF ROME.

Professor Dr. Constantin Blome is GSK Vaccines Chair Professor in Strategic Sourcing and Procurement at the Louvain School of Management, Université catholique de Louvain, Belgium. His expertise is in the field of Supply Chain Management resulting in numerous peer-reviewed articles among others on Sustainable Supply Chain Management which were recognised by awards. Furthermore, Constantin Blome has lectured and provided executive education in this domain at leading universities and for best practice firms around the globe. He is also a regular speaker at scientific and practice conferences being an expert for procurement topics. Finally, he is editorial board member of leading international scientific journals, active in the management of the most prestigious international research associations, and member of the EU-Chapter of the CLUB OF ROME.

Dr. Dermot Breslin is a lecturer in Entrepreneurship at Sheffield University Management School (UK), and a visiting lecturer in Entrepreneurship at Saarland University. Following the completion of his first degree in Mechanical Engineering in 1989 at University College Dublin (Ireland), he spent over 14 years working in the global steel and aluminum industries. He has extensive experience in production management, engineering design and technical sales for a number of companies including VAI Industries (Austria), ILVA (Italy) and Alcan Aluminium. During this time Dermot Breslin also completed an MBA (with distinction) at Warwick University (UK). Since entering academia in 2004 and following the completion of his PhD in 2009, the specific focus of his research has been to use an evolutionary approach to develop a theory-led approach to the study of changing behavior in organisations. To date he has published and reviewed papers in a number of international peer-reviewed journals and conferences, and has been awarded a number of prizes including IJMR "Reviewer of the Year" 2011, and Emerald Literati "Outstanding Paper of the Year" 2013. Dermot Breslin has also acted as guest editor for the International Journal of Organisational Analysis, Journal of Management & Governance, is Associate Editor with the International Journal of Management Reviews, and has co-organised evolutionary tracks at the EURAM annual conference. In his ongoing research, he is working on a variety of approaches including longitudinal ethnographical studies, experimental methods and agent-based simulation modeling techniques.

Univ.-Professor Dr. Martin Dietrich studied business administration and economics from 1994-1999 at Freiburg University, Germany, where he also earned his doctoral degree (2004) and his habilitation (2010). Since 2011, Martin Dietrich is University Professor of Business Administration and Health Care Management at the Faculty of Law and Economics at Saarland University. His research and teaching focuses on understanding the nature and effects of a changing economic environment in health care systems on health care providers' and organisations' behavior and performance. Especially information and workable competition in healthcare markets, the development of managerial economics, behavioral and market oriented approaches as well as market based innovations and business models in healthcare management are on the top of his research and teaching agenda. His research results have been published in Zeitschrift für Betriebswirtschaft/Journal of Business Economics, Zeitschrift für öffentliche und gemeinwirtschaftliche Unternehmen/Journal for Public and Nonprofit Services, Journal of Media Economics, Nonprofit Management and Leadership, Die Betriebswirtschaft, and others. In the faculty Martin Dietrich currently holds the position as the chair of the examination office and serves as the dean's education representative in business administration (equivalent to the dean educ.).

Univ.-Professor Dr. Andrea Gröppel-Klein holds the chair of Marketing, and is director of the Institute of Consumer & Behavioural Research at Saarland University. She studied Business Administration, and received her doctoral degree at the University of Paderborn, Germany, in 1990 (topic: "Emotional Benefits in Retailing"). The habilitation was in 1996 (topic: "Competitive Strategies in Retailing", awarded with the "Büropa-Preis of the Stifterverband der Deutschen Wissenschaft"). From 1996 to 2006 she held the Chair of International Marketing, Consumer Behaviour and Retailing at the European University Viadrina, Frankfurt (Oder), Germany. After having rejected a Professorship at the University of Trier in 2001, she was offered the Chair of Marketing at Saarland University in 2005, she has been holding since 2006. Besides scientific activities such as Visiting Professor at the Universities of Stockholm (Sweden), Innsbruck (Austria), Basel (Switzerland) and Vienna (Austria), she was faculty-member of the EDEN Doctoral Seminar on Consumer Behaviour of the European Institute for Advanced Studies in Management (EIASM) in Brussels as well as faculty member of Doctoral Seminars of the European Marketing Conference. From 2006 to 2007 she was president of the German speaking Scientific Marketing Community of University Marketing Professors in Germany, Austria and Switzerland; from 2009 to 2011 she was editor of Marketing ZFP & Marketing - JRM, member of various editorial boards and reviewer of national and international journals and several conferences. She was also member of the "Beirat für Wissens- und Technologietransfer" of the Land Brandenburg and member of an expert advisory board of the Federal Ministry of Family, Seniors, Women and Youth. Andrea Gröppel-Klein has published more than 160 books and articles.

Dipl. Wi.-Ing. M.B.A. Stefan Hack is Business Senior Manager at SAP and affiliated with the Centre for Sustainability Management (CSM), Leuphana University Lüneburg. He has worked at SAP since 1998 and had previously served as management consultant with McKinsey & Company in Düsseldorf, Germany and KPMG Peat Marwick in Boston, Massachusetts. He studied Industrial Engineering and Management at the University of Karlsruhe, Germany, and was awarded a scholarship to study at the University of Massachusetts, Boston, where he earned an M.B.A. degree. Stefan Hack holds several patents for his work on information systems for SAP and has published in the fields of information technology and sustainability.

Professor Dr. Christopher Hossfeld is Associate Professor at ESCP Europe, Paris, for financial reporting and currently Chair of the Financial Reporting and Audit Department. Christopher Hossfeld is also the academic advisor for the Specialised Master in Management Control and Business Performance. After studying Business Administration at Saarland University he became a research assistant there at the Chair for Banking and received in 1996 his PhD. After spending 5 years at the University of Paris-Sorbonne he joined the Paris campus of ESCP Europe in 2001. He was several times a Visiting Professor at the University of Texas at Austin and has teaching experience in numerous countries. His research covers international financial reporting, in particular comparability of financial statements, and bank regulation. He has published several books and articles in French, German and international journals.

Dipl.-Kfm. Stefan Kolb is Research Assistant at the Chair of Business Administration, especially Foreign Trade and International Management, as well as at the Institute for Commerce & International Marketing (H.I.Ma.) at Saarland University. He has been doing research on the relationship between companies and NGOs for several years and is currently working on his doctoral thesis focusing on the NGO Relationship Management of big and multinational companies.

Professor Dr. Alain Mikol is Professor for financial reporting and audit at ESCP Europe, Paris, where he is in charge of the French CPA track. After graduating from ESCP Europe, Paris, and the Ecole des Hautes Etudes des Sciences Sociales, Paris, he worked for PWC and became a senior manager before joining academics. He received his PhD in 1989 from the University of Paris-Sorbonne and his habilitation à diriger des recherches

(HDR) in 1996 from the University of Paris-Val de Marne. Until 2006, Alain Mikol was a representative of the French "Ordre des experts-comptables" for the "Sustainable development" commission of the Federation of European Accountants. He conducted research seminars in several European and North-African Universities. His research areas are auditing but also green reporting in relationship with the mission of CPAs. He has published 17 books, more than 20 articles in academic journals and over 100 articles in professional journals.

Dipl.-Kffr. Nadine Molter is PhD student and Research Assistant at the Chair of Business Administration and Health Care Management at the Faculty of Law and Economics at Saarland University since 2011. Previously, she studied business administration with focus on Marketing at Saarland University. Her research interests include Marketing, Health Care Marketing and Health Behavior Research.

Univ.-Professor Dr. Dirk Morschett holds the Chair for International Management at the University of Fribourg/Switzerland since 2007 and he is Director of the Centre for European Studies of this university. From 1996 until 2007, he worked as research assistant at the Institute for Commerce and International Marketing (H.I.MA.) at Saarland University. He was and currently is lecturer in different MBA programmes in Switzerland and abroad, where he teaches retail management and internationalisation. Among other locations, he was lecturing in Hong Kong, Dublin, Bangkok, Cluj-Napoca, Santiago de Chile and Lyon.

His focus is on retail and wholesale management, in particular e-commerce, retail formats, collaborative strategies and retail branding, as well as on international management. On these topics, he acts as speaker, facilitator and consultant for retail and wholesale companies, consumer goods manufacturers and IT companies. To name a few examples, Dirk Morschett worked in the mentioned functions for The Conference Group, coop@home, GS1 Switzerland, ECR Europe, Markant, E/D/E, retailsolutions and T-Systems.

Dr. Stefanie Müller was born 1977 in Germany and studied Business Administration at the University of Trier. Since 2004, Stefanie Müller is at the chair of Business Administration, especially Organisation, Human Resource Management and Information Management at Saarland University. In 2011 she received her doctoral degree (doctoral thesis: "Human Capital Ethics"). Her research interests include Human Capital Management, ethical and sustainability issues in Human Resource Management, and divergence and convergence developments within these fields.

Univ.-Professor Dr. Christian Scholz was born 1952 in Austria, studied at the University of Regensburg (Germany) and at the Harvard Business School (USA). Since 1986, Christian Scholz holds the chair of Business Administration, especially Organisation, Human Resource Management and Information Management. He is founding director of the Europa-Institut (MBA School) at Saarland University; from 2010 to 2012 he has been dean of the faculty of law and business. His research interests include organisational behaviour, strategic and international human resource management and changes in the work environment (so called Darwiportunism). He is author of several books (e.g. Human Capital Management 2011 (3rd ed.); Human Resource Management in Europe 2008) and published articles in different reviewed research and practice oriented journals.

Univ.-Professor Dr. Hanna Schramm-Klein holds the Chair in Marketing at Siegen University, Germany. She studied Business Administration and International Business at the University of Gießen. Since 1998 she has been a research assistant at Saarland University (under Univ.-Professor Dr. Dr. h.c. Joachim Zentes). In 2002 she received her doctoral degree (doctoral thesis: "Multi-Channel-Retailing") and in 2008 she habilitated at Saarland University (habilitation thesis: "Location Strategies of Retailing Companies"). Since 2009 she holds the chair in Marketing at Siegen University. She has been lecturer and Visiting Professor at several universities such as University of St. Gallen (Switzerland), University Gabriela Mistral, Santiago de Chile, University of Graz (Austria). Her research fields include retail marketing and management, consumer goods marketing and international management.

Univ.-Professor Dr. Volker Stein is Professor at the University of Siegen, Germany, Chair of Business Administration, especially Human Resource Management and Organisational Behaviour. He is Founding Director of the "Südwestfälische Akademie für den Mittelstand – University Siegen Business School" and Visiting Professor at EM Strasbourg Business School. His current research focuses on HRM especially in mid-sized companies, Human Capital Management, international empirical organisational research, and market-based leadership in organisations. Author of "Emergentes Organisationswachstum" (Emergent Organisational Growth

2000), co-author of "Human Capital Management" 2004, 2011 (3rd ed.)), of "Der Talente-Krieg" (War for Talents 2007), of "Interkulturelle Wettbewerbsstrategien" (Intercultural Competitive Strategies 2013), and co-editor of "Bologna-Schwarzbuch" (Black Book Bologna 2009).

Dr. Sascha Steinmann is Assistant Professor at the Chair of Marketing at the University of Siegen. He studied Business Administration at the University of Bielefeld. Since 2004 he has been a research assistant at the Chair of Marketing at the Georg-August-University Goettingen. In 2010 he received his doctoral degree (doctoral thesis: "Customer Contacts and Customer Contact Sequences in Multi Channel Marketing"). He is a lecturer at Frankfurt School of Finance and Management and has been a Visiting Professor at the University of Koblenz-Landau. His research fields include consumer behaviour, retailing and multi channel marketing.

Univ.-Professor Dr. Stefan Strohmeier holds the chair in Business Administration, in particular Management Information Systems, at Saarland University. His area of research refers to the intersection of Human Resources and Information Systems (e-HRM). The chair aims at a boundary spanner position between technology and management, thus the technological design and the managerial application of innovative Human Resource Information Systems (HRIS) are broadly researched.

M.A. Econ. Florian Verheyen studied Economics at the University of Duisburg-Essen and is currently employed as scientific assistant and PhD student at the Chair for Macroeconomics of Univ.-Professor Dr. Ansgar Belke. Within his PhD thesis which he submitted in June 2013 he focuses on empirical investigations of monetary policy transmission and export demand models. Furthermore, he held numerous presentations at national and international conferences and published in international refereed journals like the International Journal of Money and Finance and Economic Modelling.

Valentin Wepfer works for GS1 Switzerland as Deputy CEO and Director of the Collaborative Supply Chains department. Valentin, half Swiss-half Swedish, was born nearby Zurich in 1966. He is married and has three children. He visited schools in Zurich, Bern and Stockholm where he made his university-entrance diploma. After achieving a diploma in construction engineering and studies in architecture in Biel-Bienne, he was founder and CEO of Perron 8 Management AG (Events & Promotion), Biel. It followed position as CMO & responsible for Sales of Global Village GmbH (Sportsfashion), Heidelberg, communication and retail relations for Promarca (Swiss Association of Branded Goods Manufacturers), Bern, and Founder & CEO of Efficient Consumer Response (ECR) in Switzerland. In 2005, ECR Switzerland merged with the associations EAN and Swiss Logistics Society (SLG) to form GS1 Switzerland. Valentin Wepfer was deputy CEO and Director of Marketing of GS1 Switzerland and since 2012, he is Deputy CEO and Director of the newly formed department Collaborative Supply Chains. Valentin is a member of various Boards and expert groups. He is an initialiser or member of several national and international organisations and initiatives.

Univ.-Professor Dr. Dr. h.c. Joachim Zentes is Professor (International Management, International Marketing) at Saarland University, Director of the Institute for Commerce and International Marketing (H.I.MA.) and Academic Director of the Europa-Institut. He has been Professor (Marketing, Business Administration) at the University of Frankfurt and at the University of Essen and received offers of a chair (Marketing, Management) at the University of Fribourg and at the University of Basel (Switzerland). He is an honorary doctor (Doctor Honoris Causa) of the University of Craiova, Romania. Joachim Zentes is member of various scientific associations and advisory boards.

Dipl.-Volksw. Matti Znotka studied law and economics at Trier University (Germany) and International Business School Budapest (Hungary). Since 2013 he is PhD Student and Research Assistant at the Chair of Business Administration and Health Care Management at the Faculty of Law and Economics at Saarland University. His current fields of research focus on innovative business models in the primary and the secondary health market.